Asphodel P. Long spent her working life as a business press journalist and, on retirement, entered King's College London as a full-time undergraduate, studying theology. Gaining her B.D. (Hons) in Theology at the age of 62, she has continued her fifteen years of research into female aspects of deity, giving workshops and classes throughout the UK and also on the continent of Europe and in the USA. Published widely in the feminist and alternative press, her work has also recently appeared in the Journal of Feminist Studies in Religion and she was a major contributor to *The Absent Mother: Rediscovering the Goddess in Judaism and Christianity*, edited by Alix Pirani.

In a Chariot Drawn by Lions is her first book.

IN A CHARIOT DRAWN BY LIONS

The Search for the Female in Deity

ASPHODEL P. LONG

First published by The Women's Press Ltd 1992
A member of the Namara Group
34, Great Sutton Street, London EC1V ODX

Copyright © Asphodel P. Long

The right of Asphodel P. Long to be identified as the author of this work
has been asserted by her in accordance with the Copyright, Designs and
Patents Act, 1988.

Cataloguing in Publication data is available from the British Library.

ISBN 0 7043 4295 2

Typeset by Contour Typesetters, Southall, London
Printed and bound in Great Britain by
BPCC Hazells Ltd
Member of BPCC Ltd

Contents

Acknowledgements 1

Preface 5

1 Beginning the Journey 11
2 Wisdom Personified in Israel 20
3 The Book of Wisdom of Solomon 37
4 Greek Classical and
  Hellenistic Goddesses and Wisdom 62
5 Wisdom in Egypt 81
6 Wisdom Goddesses
  in the Ancient Near East 101
7 Ancient Hebrew Goddesses 119
8 Wisdom and Christianity 139
9 The Mother of God, God the
  Mother and the Shekinah 165
10 The Decline of Wisdom
   and Decline of Nature 181
11 Wisdom, the Bible and the Present 194

Notes 201
Bibliography 227
Index 259

I would like to thank the following:

Brill of Leiden, Holland for extracts taken from *The Nag Hammadi Library in English*, edited by James M Robinson, 1977.

Carol P Christ for extracts taken from *The Laughter of Aphrodite*, Harper & Row, San Francisco, 1987.

T & T Clark Ltd, Edinburgh, for extracts taken from *Canaanite Myths and Legends*, by G.R. Driver, 1956.

Green Print, an imprint of Merlin Press, for extracts by Rosemary Radford Ruether, Susan Griffin, Ynestra King and Sharon Dubiago, taken from *Healing The Wounds* edited by Judith Plant, 1989.

Harper & Row, San Francisco, for 'Ode 19' from *The Other Bible*, edited by Willis Barnstone, Harper & Row, San Francisco, 1984.

Thorkild Jacobsen for an extract taken from 'The Cosmos as State' in *The Intellectual Adventure of Ancient Man* edited by Frankfort, Frankfort, Wilson, Jacobsen and Irwin, University of Chicago Press, Chicago, 1946.

Oxford University Press, New York, and Oxford University Press, Oxford, for extracts taken from *Hellenistic Religions*, by Luther H. Martin, 1987.

Princeton University Press for extracts taken from *The Ancient Near East, Vol. 1*, edited by James B. Pritchard, 1958.

Rosemary Radford Ruether for extracts taken from 'Misogynism and Virginal Feminism in the Fathers of the Church', in *Religion and Sexism* edited by Rosemary Radford Ruether, Simon & Schuster, New York, 1974.

Mrs Jane Straker for extracts taken from *Science and Politics in the Ancient World*, by Benjamin Farrington, Unwin (University Books), London, 1939, 2nd edition 1965.

A P Watt Ltd Literary Agents on behalf of The Trustees of the Robert Graves Copyright Trust for an extract taken from *The Golden Ass* by Apuleius, translated by Robert Graves.

Zed Books and Kali for Women for extracts taken from *Staying Alive: Women, Ecology and Development*, by Vandana, Shiva, Zed Books, London, 1988.

Acknowledgements

I owe enormous debts of gratitude to the many people who have helped and sustained me over the years it has taken to research and write this book. It is impossible to name them all. I can pick out only some of those whose strength, tolerance and encouragement as well as scholarly discussion has helped me, at last, to complete it.

Diana Scott as my editor with The Women's Press made it possible for me to transform an unwieldy mess of research into a form and structure that could be handled. Her perception, empathy and sheer hard work inspired me to continue during all the difficulties. She made it possible for me to find and keep to Wisdom's trail.

I also thank Loulou Brown for dedication in guiding the typescript through the intricate production stages.

Robin Thodey was a guide and mentor in the early years as she insisted on my getting on with the task. She put the material on a word processor, and discussed knotty problems of theology and feminism with such enthusiasm that I had to continue. Her loving support has never ceased.

To Angela Solstice I owe the fact that I was able to enter a research project formally, and I thank her for that and for all the work she put into reading and commenting on my efforts, supporting me in the task.

Lynn Stagg will remember the many paper table napkins we

covered in café meals discussing and working out the project, while her bibliographic assistance has been invaluable.

Daniel Cohen has given unstinting support of every kind over a very long period, whether chasing elusive classical meanings, discussing textual problems, or taking part, and helping me, in the day-to-day difficulties and excitements of the work. In addition, my thanks to him for putting the bibliography on the word processor, while at the same time helping out with finding books and their references.

My thanks, too, to Robert Kruszinski for helping me with the problem of filling out missing references in the bibliography and taking a large amount of time to do this, since I was unable to visit libraries owing to a complicated leg fracture.

Wendy Hill's editing skills and dedication helped me to make an important decision; she is among many with whom I have discussed the work, and often my problems of staying with it. All have encouraged me to do so, and my loving thanks go to them. They include Amanda Sebestyen, Alex Wildwood, Astra, Blue Moonfire, Cleis Littleowl, Dolores Chaudhury, Lisa Foley, Inge Hyde, Jenny Goodman, Stuart Linke, Jess Michael, Jean Freer, Lindsay River, Lauren Liebling, Lillian Scibberas, Anne Caruana, Liesl Silverstone, Linda Shockey, Judith Todd, Mavis Hill, Marlene Saliba, Ruby Rohrlich, Ruth Green, Serene, Sheena Murray, Laura Sperazi, Nancy Passmore, Wynne Busby, Virginia Noakes, Wren Sidhe, Linda Regan, Micky Jaspan, Alix Pirani, Batya Podos and Shirley Westwood.

Cathy Dagg and Penny Old are among those who have given me special help with specific problems. Myriam Heimlich has sent me cuttings and information from the continent of Europe and the USA. Eahr Joan's loving support as well as her massive work on her own bibliographies which she has shared with me have been a blessing.

I thank William Gray for his scholarly discussions and sharp raising of points in the research project text. Also, grateful acknowledgements to Jan Knappert for encouragement and for helpful guidance.

My thanks to my dear friend Bali Power for all her interest and in particular for translating difficult German theological texts.

Anne Primavesi has opened up new vistas of Christian-Jewish co-operation and sisterhood. Leonore Siegele Wenschkewitz and Marie-Theres Wacker have given me hope and healing as German Christian feminists who are determined that the lessons of the Holocaust will never be forgotten. I am also grateful to Ursula King for encouragement and support.

Magenta Wise has given me strength, healing and inspiration. Rose Cannan's ardent interest and enthusiasm has inspired me. The women in the Brighton Spirituality Group and the partcipants in the workshops and classes in Brighton kept giving me hope, as well as asking questions and initiating discussions and themes. That they took over the classes when my own strength failed healed me enormously. Among them are Alex Sutherland, Anita Silverbirch, Deborah Knowles, Pauline Charles, Georgia Bunting, Karen Hamblett, Yvonne Atkinson and Elizabeth Söderholm. I thank Dorothy Jerrome for her support in encouraging me to give the classes.

The Brighton Older Women's Group has heard of the vicissitudes of the task over an interminable period. My thanks to Pat Aldridge, Diane Harris, Sally Free and Chris Pepper.

My friends at my home in Brighton have helped me in numerous ways. In particular, loving thanks to Anne Alexander for all her book gathering; Joyce Staples for constant help in all the 'small' matters of everyday life that look so large when one is ill; Win Leggett for continuous support as well as fascinating biblical discussions; Jane Berger for feeding and comforting me in emotional as well as practical ways.

I am grateful to Angela Rogers for her care and precision in putting this book on to a word processor, and for raising all sorts of textual points.

My love and thanks to my sons: Tony, for his editing suggestions as well as for long-lasting support of the project, and Joe for always being sure that I could do it, and for his help in translating Greek texts. My grandson David's enthusiasm and questions have helped me greatly, while I have enjoyed his brother Chris' support.

My sister Rosalind I can never thank enough for her warmth and graciousness and generosity in accepting me back after an absence that seemed a lifetime.

Lastly, as ever, I thank my friend Dorothy Swingler, who has been my mentor and inspiration for nearly fifty years, and who introduced me to the ideas of feminism.

Preface

I have often been asked, in the course of my work as a teacher and facilitator of workshops, classes and discussion on the topic of 'Female aspects of deity', which I have been involved with for over fifteen years, why I place so much emphasis on the gender of God. Surely, say many participants, God, if you believe at all, is neither a 'she' nor 'he'? God is all-encompassing, and if 'He' is referred to, in the masculine gender, it is only a matter of convenience, since we have to find a term we can relate to.

There is an emotional reaction, quite out of keeping with this rational view, if I then suggest that we address God not as Lord, Father or King, but as Lady, Mother or Queen. If we try saying, actually speaking out loud, 'Lady', 'Our Goddess', 'Our Mother God', 'Queen Goddess', the situation becomes highly charged. Often women weep, and men become angry and hostile. These reactions come from many who have declared they are not interested in traditional religion and believe it to be oppressive, with little meaning for today's difficulties and problems. They join those who have identified with some form of Christianity or Judaism, nearly all of whom also show some form of terror at pronouncing these words.

Why does addressing God as 'Lady' provoke these reactions? This is the key question I have tried to answer in this book. Beginning the journey, I state in chapter 1, that my search for the female in deity starts with the bible. Despite all the hostility and negative rhetoric about the goddesses contained within it, they continue to be venerated from earliest Hebrew times to a late New Testament period. I describe some of the methods feminist scholars have created to help us counter the bible's androcentric bias, so that we can seek the hidden and overlooked Female Divine.

In chapter 2, I address myself directly to the figure of Divine Wisdom, personified as female, and discuss some of the problems this has created. In particular her presence 'beside God' and her possible identity as creator of the universe and its sustainer and teacher is discussed, as is her position as God's companion and, possibly, his inspiration.

In chapter 3 there is a full-scale laudation of this same Hebrew female Wisdom in the inter-testamental Book of Wisdom of Solomon. Here we are presented with a fully divine female who is the alter ego of God and is also identified with Nature whose secrets she knows and will share with humanity. The praise of Wisdom in this book is inspiring for women for whom she can function as a role model. We also see how attitudes change towards her and how she becomes a possession of greedy men and then disappears.

In chapter 4 we meet goddesses of neighbouring cultures in the Hellenistic world, particularly those associated with Wisdom and with Nature. We also explore attitudes to Nature on the part of Greek philosophers and find an unexpected link between them and the practitioners of magic. We meet the Mother of the Gods who travels 'in a chariot drawn by lions'.

In chapter 5 we turn to Egypt and seek out the ancient goddesses of that land – Isis and Ma'at who represent creation, sustenance and right order in the world, and who, like Wisdom, teach humanity their secrets. There is also the perception of Isis as saviour and the way to immortality. We also examine the Gnostic texts from Egypt of a later period at the entrance to the Christian era, and once more encounter Wisdom-Sophia. Here there is ambivalence: she is both divine and purveyor of all knowledge, but she is also punished for her independence and becomes transformed into a figure of guilt.

In chapter 6 we look back to an earlier period and discover the ancient creation and healing goddesses of Mesopotamia and the Hittites. We see how often they may be discussed in the Hebrew bible.

Chapter 7 explores the descriptions of the Hebrew goddesses and asks whether God was worshipped alongside a consort. We turn to the idea of the Queen of Heaven and the indwelling presence of female divinity within certain places and objects. We link the goddess Asherah with the Garden of Eden stories and the Tree of Life, who is also Wisdom.

Chapter 8, entitled 'Wisdom and Christianity', describes how the New Testament places Wisdom within Jesus Christ and then overviews the effect of the loss of female divinity on the position of women in society. The misogyny later transformed into the witch craze and its settling into an overall sense of inferiority for women is outlined.

In chapter 9 we look at the position of the Virgin Mary and also of the hidden Shekinah – the divine female presence of God in Judaism. We see how women today are at last getting in touch with a sense of female divinity previously denied them. This leads, in chapter 10, to a discussion of the effects of the denial of divine status to nature and to women on the life of the world and of the effects these sustain to the planet. Today's new understanding of ecological needs must have a feminist input and ideas on this subject are discussed.

In conclusion, chapter 11 explores today's relationships between women and men and women and the world, in the light of our understanding of the trajectory of the presence, the decline, and now re-appearance, of a perception of divine female Wisdom.

Above all, we see in this Wisdom an exemplar of women's full potential. It encourages us not only to struggle for social, political, economic and sexual egalitarianism, but also for full acknowledgement and development of our spiritual and intellectual powers.

Because I come from a Jewish background, and was born and brought up in Britain, my parents having emigrated from Poland in the early years of this century, I have confined my searches to the culture which has formed me. I discovered, though, that we do not have to look far afield for the female in deity; she is there to be found the world over. The scope of the search could be so vast, that it was necessary for me to confine myself to the ground that bore me.

In taking as my main resources the Hebrew Bible, the Apocrypha it and the New Testament, with the massive and varied interpretations that they carry, there are two things I have to point out immediately. The first is that I have not been able to spell out the links with Black goddesses of African cultures, which I know to be sources of valuable information and inspiration. I am aware that those who are now engaged in this work provide a necessary corrective to the Eurocentric tradition which has shaped the world I live in. The second is that I am not capable of providing guidelines to the vast rabbinic literature which surrounds my subject. As a younger woman, I was denied access to it, because of my gender; in my older years I have not been able to turn back to it. Both these enormous areas of research will, for those coming after me, elucidate and enhance the material I have been able to present.

I have chosen to concentrate on the female figure of Wisdom – Hochma in Hebrew, Sophia in Greek – since she pervades the background to the bible, and in my view is the hidden female aspect of God in the Western tradition. For a long time she was forgotten, driven deep down into obscurity. Today she is re-emerging in a new landscape.

Finding and celebrating her is not only an academic exercise, although I have used as much scholarly information as I can handle and I have tried to work within the disciplines of scholarship. In fact, I am asking readers either unfamiliar with, or bored with such methods, to bear with me, and to go along with what might at first be thought unnecessary emphasis on the meanings of words or phrases from biblical or classical literature. It is essential to look closely at these since they are the means of elucidating the core problem. And when we do this, we find we change our perceptions and roles in the society we live in.

I am happy to take up the challenge set by Claudia Camp in her major survey on Wisdom and the Feminine in the Book of Proverbs. She writes of the 'obvious difficulty in envisioning personified Wisdom as a Goddess, or at least as a self-existent being beside Yahweh' and states that those who hold such a view have a duty to explain it, 'and this has not been done'.[1] This book is my attempt to do so.

I have used the terms BCE and CE to denote 'before the Christian era' and 'Christian era'. These refer to specific periods of time, and unlike the better known BC and AD do not imply an acceptance of a particular faith. The assumption of 'C' standing for 'common' is incorrect. Many religions do not accept this dating as 'common', as they have their own calendars.

The book makes many references to The bible. Unless otherwise specified I have used the Revised Standard Version (RSV) as the favoured English translation, since this is generally stated by scholars to be nearer the Hebrew of the Hebrew bible and the Greek of the New Testament than the better known King James bible, otherwise known as the Authorised Version (AV). In common with today's thinking, I do not use the term 'Old Testament', since this implies a relationship with the New Testament, which in my opinion is not a valid assumption. The Hebrew bible stands on its own as the bible accepted by people of the Jewish faith. The New Testament, together with the books of the Hebrew bible make up the bible of Protestant Christianity.

Roman Catholics add to these the books of the Apocrypha, otherwise issued in separate form or as a distinct section between the two parts of the bible. The Apocrypha was written in the period between the completion of the Hebrew bible and the start of the New Testament, and there has never been agreement among Christian sects as to whether it should be included within the bible proper.

The term 'Apocrypha' derives from the Greek word 'to hide'. There is some controversy as to whether the Apocrypha books, so termed, are part of the canonical scriptures or not. They do not appear in the Hebrew bible, but are part of the Septuagint (that is, the translation made of the Hebrew biblical literature into Greek about 150 BCE). Consequently, Christians, using the Septuagint, eventually incorporated these books into the canon. They remain today within the Roman Catholic bible. After the Reformation, however, the Protestant bible excluded them. The Apocrypha can be found in the The Revised Standard Version Common Bible and the Oxford Annotated Bible, among others, and is also sold separately as a book in itself.

References are given throughout to the books of the various bibles and the Apocrypha. The texts are laid out, together with the title of the book, for example, The Book of Job, together with chapters and verses. Most bibles have an index of 'books' so that the reference can easily be found.

There are many current translations of the bible. As well as the AV and RSV I have used the Revised Version (RV) the New English Bible (NEB) and the GNB (Good News Bible). In my classes and workshops, with the very basic knowledge that my students and I have of the original languages, we have compared various translations with others. In this way we have been able to discover some of the references to female divinity and have become inspired to explore further.

Throughout the text there are numerous references to other writers and their work. Full details of these are to be found in the comprehensive Bibliography at the end of this book.

1. Beginning the Journey

'Where is Wisdom to be found and where is the place of understanding? . . . It is hid from the eyes of all living.' (Job 28: 12–21)

The biblical prophet's cry is still full of meaning for us. Job's answer was 'The fear of the Lord', but today the search for Wisdom takes us on a new journey. We understand only too keenly that she has been 'hidden from the eyes of the living' for many millenia. I say 'she', because Wisdom – Hochma in Hebrew, Sophia in Greek – comes to us from her biblical setting in the feminine gender. And not only that; she was both understood and addressed as a female. Contradictory biblical texts describe her: she might have been creator of the universe and mentor to God; or she might have been the first of his created beings; his darling child; or she might be a woman men want to marry, or who will be useful to them in their search for power and wealth. She might be the last of a long line of goddesses who represent or who are themselves Nature and who are teachers to human kind and mediators between earth and heaven; or she might be an attribute of God, a female personification of his Wisdom aspect.[1]

She might be – and it is the purpose of this book to suggest that she is – the hidden goddess in the Hebrew religion, the female deity that has for so long been obscured in the patriarchal traditions of Judaism and Christianity; she might have strong links with goddesses in the Ancient, Near Eastern and Hellenistic worlds, and provide a role model for women; she might be creator, sustainer, teacher, healer, repository of all knowledge and an active agent in the ordering of the world, and in herself provide a bridge between the creator and the created; she might be identified with Nature whose ways humans would do well to follow.

We recount her downfall. We lay plans for her renewal.

Goddesses who receive extremely hostile treatment in the bible are not alien to Judaism and Christianity but are an integral part of these religions. Although disguised and banished, and the targets of extreme persecution, they were never defeated. It is our task today to seek out these goddesses and descry the forms they may have had for our foreparents. And all this is not merely of academic interest; it has profound implications for everyday life at both micro and macro levels. Relations between women and men, and the roles they consider appropriate for themselves and each other, have been set for so long in a mode that has oppressed women, whole peoples, and, ultimately, Nature herself.

My theme touches closely on the disastrous changes that came about as Wisdom was banished. Today, reclaiming Wisdom, seeking her, rejoicing in her and understanding her ways, is one way in which changes can be made that must come about if not only relationships in society but also the world itself are to be renwed safely and harmoniously.

I pay tribute to those scholars who have provided academic information, and those seekers who have turned to their own lives, intuitions, and growing insights, as well as to those earlier feminists whose pioneer work uprooted traditional prejudices and created landing stages and runways for today's new understanding. This book seeks to show up facts and interpretations presented throughout the bible and in other biblical literature which demonstrate that the material is, literally, 'double faced'. It is double faced in the usual meaning of the word – it seeks to deceive, and my contention is that its writers meant it to do so. Also, it is double faced given a literal understanding; that what appears to be the case can be taken apart and recreated to indicate something entirely different. It is as if biblical writers and their associates, while wishing to banish the female from divinity and power in society, were not actually able to succeed in destroying the female record. By means of contradictions, negative accounts, hostile epithets and other ways in which the female was denigrated, they present a totally negative picture – but nevertheless the material is still there, to be sought out. In addition, various accounts have been retained which are often called 'perplexing' by traditional commentators. These texts point clearly to the female divine, which have then been reinterpreted to keep them in line with preconceived androcentric religious concepts.

I see the bible as being in the forefront of gender politics, astride two major streams of feminist theological criticism. The first concerns those who want to reinterpret scripture and their own religious tradition in such a way as to keep the form but change much of the content. That is, they seek out a new biblical interpretation of events and narratives that illumine the female both in mundane and sacred space. At the same time they want to keep to the traditional order of festivals and liturgy but actually 'remake' them to include the concept of woman as the image of God in her own right. Both these activities are set within a context that assumes that the 'ur' or 'pristine' religion did indeed contain such material but that this has been weeded out by hierarchy and tradition.

The second stream discards the traditional religions. Whether brought up in them or, as is common today, brought up in a secular background where possibly some form of left-wing thinking replaced religion, seekers, particularly women, demand something that speaks more clearly to their needs. Many look to ancient pagan faiths, perhaps found within the legends and mythology of their own country. But for many women this is not enough. They look to the ancient goddesses and their rituals, sometimes still reflected in the religions of indigenous peoples such as the Native Americans or the South American Indians, or else to those goddesses known to the Western world from classical tradition, or from texts of the ancient world which are becoming more accessible than previously. Many women look deep within themselves and find images and memories which stand alone or blend in with such research.

Part of the urge to explore in this way is to do with the rejection of patriarchal values. The world, run by men and geared to what men want, has been brought to the verge of total disaster. Competition, hierarchy, and an outdated form of 'objective' thinking usually associated with Newton or Descartes are seen to be irrelevant to today's problems. A search for holism must include the female as well as the male in divinity, a sense of the round rather than the linear, of co-operation rather than competition.

When they come across various aspects of 'Goddess spirtuality', women not only protest at their exclusion from the norms of humanity and of divinity; they also assert that a different mode of thought and activity is entirely viable.

Many writers have explored this new and positive area of thought and action. Today it is both possible and acceptable to look again at the goddesses who for so long have been demonised in our traditions. There are two such divinities in particular who are encountered throughout the Hebrew bible, and whose shadows and echoes are to be experienced in the New Testament. These are the goddess figures of Wisdom, and the Lady Asherah, with whom I include Ashteroth and the Lady Anat. I examine the material relating to these female deities in the biblical and extra biblical literature; the effects of their occlusion alongside an attempted deacide, and the enormous importance their re-illumination has for today's struggle for women's spiritual and social autonomy which is of supreme importance in the struggle for an egalitarian world.

The method I have used may be termed a feminist *midrash*. This Hebrew word, whose root conveys study and research, has been used throughout rabbinical tradition to describe, as the *Jewish Encyclopaedia* puts it, 'an exegesis which goes more deeply than the more literal sense. It attempts to penetrate into the spirit of the scriptures, to examine the text from all sides, and thereby to derive interpretations that are not immediately obvious.'[2]

In looking at the texts, we shall not merely be taking them at their face value, or in the way they are normally looked at. We shall examine them from every possible angle and we shall look at their context, and at meanings others have found. In particular, in order to arrive at their meaning, or possible meaning, we shall use every method we know, even if a kind of lese-majeste seems to be involved. We start with the premise that the female is *there*. When we find Her, we proclaim Her.

The *midrash* (plural *midrashim*) has been the tool of Jewish wise men since the religion began. I say 'wise men' advisedly, since although Wisdom calls on all to seek Her and find Her, yet within Judaism only men have had this privilege until the present generation, and it has indeed been the most sacred and elemental duty of men to pursue this path.

In today's new climate, I present a midrash on Hochma and on Asherah – the divine female principles in the Hebrew religion and in later Judaism. It will hope to show that God may be understood as these divinities, or they may be part of God, or in intimate relationships with God; that Wisdom herself may indeed have existed before God, and created the universe, and certainly may be God's mentor and even mother, and the mother of the world and humanity. Further, the midrash will suggest that Wisdom as Nature encompassed the creation and the environment, and possibly was its author, and so is the source of all knowledge, whether in terms of 'scientific' or 'intuitive' understanding and procedures. Because the characteristics of creation, that is, activity related to knowledge and science, have for so long been perceived to be a male province, female Wisdom offers women a new chance to repossess their intellects as well as their souls and bodies.

Asherah will come out from her groves of trees and ancient graves where her dust has been scattered for so long[3] to show that knowledge and wisdom can be, and indeed are, combined with the most sacred of all earthly joys – sexuality. This is associated with the lifegiving process of birth, death and renewal – not only of physical life but of inspiration, creativity and of the spirit.

The female divinities in the hinterland of Judasim and Christianity did not stand alone, isolated from neighbouring and background cultures; we will look at the Hellenistic goddesses of nature and of wisdom and at some of the earlier divinities with whom they have close affinities.

The book's title, *In a Chariot Drawn by Lions*, is taken from an Orphic Hymn to the Mother of the Gods.[4] It was chosen because her description bears so much resemblance to those of the goddesses in the Hebrew bible. The Hymn addresses her as 'Queen of the sky', she is a 'mighty goddess who brings all things to pass', the 'earth is hers' and she gives nourishment to mortals. She rules rivers and seas, and both the gods and humans are her children. She is a giver of prosperity and bestows all manner of good things on humanity. All these attributes also belong to Hochma or to Asherah.

Commonly, in order to preserve the integrity of a fierce monotheism aligned to a deity always addressed in the masculine gender, Jewish commentators have ruled that the personified figure of Wisdom was a poetic method of referring to the Torah – the Books of the Law – where all wisdom was to be found. For some Christians, the female figure of Wisdom became part of the male Jesus and thence the Church, while for many other Christians she became an aspect of the Virgin Mary.

To prise out an alternative picture of Wisdom from the

patriarchal tradition in which she is commonly set is a task of great difficulty. We are facing questions about monotheism, normative Judaism and Christianity, and indeed loosening material into which our acceptance of these has long been fastened. It is encouraging that a number of scholars over a long period of time have brought Wisdom into this focus. While mainline theology has largely ignored or certainly disputed their contributions, yet the work has been done and the material is there. And today we are assisted by the methods originated by feminist scholarship. (See, for example, the works of Elisabeth Schussler Fiorenza, Rosemary Radford Ruether, Carol Christ, Savina Teubal, Bernadette Brooten, Judith Plaskow and Claudia Camp. Some of their major works are listed in the Bibliography at the end of this book.)

Until now, all texts and commentaries, all exegesis, interpretation, homily and simple narrative to do with the bible have been entirely androcentric. Written by men, for men, women's perceptions are absorbed into those of the male, and women's histories – herstories – are entirely forgotten. The feminist method of modern scholarship starts with this assumption in understanding and interpreting the bible and moves on to provide a new and radical perspective of familiar material. Using Elisabeth Schussler Fiorenza's method of bringing women and the female away from the periphery and into the forefront of human reality in biblical material, we find surprising traces of alternative traditions, possibly belonging to an older culture, possibly to part of the cultures described but, for polemic reasons, pushed into obscurity.[5] As we explore these traces they lead us into territory that is new yet at the same time known to us. All is changed, yet the milestones and signposts, the markers, even the architecture and the buildings, are those we have been aware of from childhood, and are part of our language. They are there but they are different. Within what appears to be a totally patriarchal religious history, the female deity of Wisdom has remained hidden. Today as we try to round out our understanding of the world, try to balance better the parts that are played and have been played by women as well as men, we women find we can reclaim that ancient figure who is our heritage.

The work is difficult. The scale is vast. In time, it ranges from the third millenium BCE to the early centuries of the common era. The place comprises the area usually known as the 'Ancient Near East', which also includes Egypt. Within this huge panorama there is no even development, no homogeneous picture; cultures vary, there are wars and conquests, religious beliefs become conflated and altered. But we find numerous themes which occur and recur.

As we seek Wisdom we find that she has to be viewed in the light of the ancient goddesses – the divine female beings throughout Sumerian, Babylonian and Assyrian history, as well as powerful goddesses from Egypt. Numerous scholars have shown that religion which centred on such female deities emanates from very early cultures.

Early goddesses, in many forms, were, in fact, prototypes of Wisdom, or were themselves Wisdom deities. This means the ability to create life. The associated quality is identification with heaven, earth, or even the underworld. In his account of the Great Mother of Phrygia. Vermaseren (1977) points out, 'the earth was worshipped as a goddess . . . the divine authority did not rise in her power to command, but in her mysterious gift of being able continually to create new beings'.[6] He traces the history of the idea of the goddess in Asia Minor, Crete and the early Greek mainland. From being the Great Mother belonging to the earth, she becomes Mother of the gods, then Mother of humans and of beasts. Because what is produced by the earth returns again to the earth, she becomes queen of the underworld, and of the dead, and because she is queen of life and light she is also queen of heaven. 'She holds sway over life and death, the two extremes . . . as queen of Heaven and Light she also becomes queen of the Darkness . . . out of which the light is to spring forth again in an ever rotating cycle'.[7]

Vermaseren calls upon these various aspects to explain her different names and epithets and concludes 'but at all times and everywhere it is recognised that essentially one divine feminine power controls the world as well as the one to come'.[8] Like Plutarch's Isis and the sage's figure of Wisdom in the Book of Wisdom of Soloman, both written between 100 BCE and 100 CE, Vermaseren's goddess moves from sovereignty of the cosmos to that of the world to come.

This picture differs fundamentally from a widely propounded conventional view, that goddess figures denote only fertility principles and are connected solely with the reproduction power of the earth, animals and humans.

In the Hellenistic tradition, we have an alternative picture of 'Nature, mother of all, inventive, untamed (unwedded) guide, eldest of all, self-generative, self-sufficient, presiding over the earth and sea, all wise'. . . The Orphic hymn from which the above lines continue in Nature's praise with such epithets as 'all skilled, architect, accomplisher' calls her 'destiny, necessity and deathless, having everlasting life'.[9]

All these descriptions of Nature were applied to Hebrew Wisdom. The longevity of the Goddess figure associated with Wisdom and the changes that denied her femininity coincided with the changes that produced a revolution in attitudes to nature and to the humans within it.

In seeking Wisdom out, we are not being subjective but are setting the records straight and reintroducing conscious objective perceptions that in the past were intentionally denied us as they were cast in obscurity.

2. Wisdom Personified in Israel

The Lord created me at the beginning of his work, The first of his acts of old.

Ages ago I was set up, at the first, before the beginning of the earth

When there were not depths I was brought forth, when there were not springs abounding with water.

Before the mountains had been shaped, before the hills I was brought forth

Before he had made the earth with its fields, or the first dust of the world.

When he established the heavens I was there, when he drew a circle on the face of the deep.

When he made firm the skies above, when he established the fountains of the deep,

When he assigned to the sea its limits, so that the waters might not transgress his command, when he marked out the foundations of the earth,

Then I was beside him, like a master workman, and I was daily his delight,

Rejoicing before him always, rejoicing in his inhabited world . . . Proverbs 8:22–31. (RSV)

In biblical Israel, Wisdom had a very different character from its present notion as an attribute of God which we take for granted.

Many books in the Hebrew bible contain the figure of Hochma, Wisdom. So various and complex are these texts that they have been understood as a body of material in their own right, and are referred to as the 'Wisdom literature'.[1] From this I see a particular picture emerging which I will isolate, rather as one may pick out one complete continuous strand from a many-layered thread. This picture differs substantially from the conventional view of Wisdom, which is to see instruction on orderly and 'right' modes of living, and to convey truths about the spiritual as well as the mundane journey of the human being in this world who is always addressed in the masculine gender.

In the text I have quoted above, the speaker is Hochma – female Wisdom, and the text is part of the biblical Book of Proverbs, much of which is devoted to different accounts of her. These verses are written in the feminine gender. This passage in Proverbs has always been understood as perplexing, and many suggestions over a very long period of time have been brought forward to try and explain it. It has troubled readers, because it appears to contradict the common knowledge that Judaism is distinguished by its insistence on total monotheism. 'God is one' is the First Commandment given to Moses in the desert; 'Thou shalt worship no other' (Exodus 20:3). Who, then, is this figure, who was 'there', 'at the beginning' who was 'beside' God? Who, indeed, rejoiced in the inhabited world?

Who was there in the beginning?

Female Wisdom is found beside God in the beginning. Much scholarship has been expanded on the question of whether the words can be read to mean that she is the first of God's creations, or whether he encountered her 'there'. It has been pointed out that the Hebrew language in which the scriptures were written uses the masculine as a normative gender, so that if the feminine is used it is not by chance but rather a positive expression of choice. A contrast can thus be seen here with the creation accounts of Genesis, the first book of the bible. The first created being in both stories (Genesis 1 and 2) is Adam, a male.[2] But if we accept Hochma as God's creation, an ancient account of the matter indicates a female as the premier living being.

This passage should be read in conjunction with three other texts to obtain a clearer picture. These are: Proverbs 3:19; Psalm 104:24, and Job 28:27. The first states that the Lord, by (or through) Wisdom, founded the earth; the second sings 'Lord how manifold are thy works, in Wisdom thou has made them all' and the third declares [God] 'saw it [Wisdom] he established and searched it out'.

As we look at these passages, we realise they cannot be shaken off in one way or another as describing Wisdom 'merely' as something that belongs to, or is a characteristic of, God. In fact, Harmut Gese, a distinguished modern scholar, makes a huge leap forward from traditional unquestioning monotheism. He argues (1984)[3] that although at first all these verses seem to indicate the power of the Creator, in fact there is another dimension which needs to be looked at. Wisdom, he writes, is a 'world order, a cosmic law, portrayed almost mathematically . . . it is the prerequisite of the work of creation, and is therefore "perceived" and "ascertained" by God for creation, not physically created'. Wisdom, according to Gese's hypothesis, is a pre-existent, 'cosmic law' uncreated by God, which He must ascertain in order to perform the work of creation. While Gese emphasises that Wisdom is a 'spiritual principle', he also believes strongly that she had the task of mediating God to the world (pp. 207, 209). He declares that 'the very concept of Hochma . . . gives Wisdom precedence over creation'. (p. 207)

In Gese's understanding of Hochma, we see the first of Wisdom's divine attributes: she is a prerequisite of creation, a transcendental force, with an ambivalent relationship to God. Did he create the world through his own Wisdom? Or did he need a pre-existent female Wisdom to guide him in his work? Gese further sums up his view of Wisdom in this period as 'a concept of world order . . . recognised as a transcendental force wherein God unites with the world, and through which percipient man can attain a redeemed existence' (p. 211). As we ponder these immense questions we are faced with a Socratic problem.[4] Does the text tell us that the Lord in his wisdom made the world, or did He create it through the instrumentality of Wisdom already existing? ('When he established the heavens I was there' (Proverbs 8:27).)

We have seen that the biblical text of Proverbs confronts us with a female figure who is 'beside' God from the beginning. This figure, Wisdom, is understood to have arrived 'there' in one of two ways. Either She was created by God, 'the first of his acts' or, following Job, She was 'there' even before He was, since it is through Her instrumentality that He created the world, and indeed it is suggested He needed to search her out. This may indicate that before He did so the world could not be created.

If we take the reading that God created Wisdom (Proverbs 8:22) we also have to look at Proverbs 8:24 'when there were not depths I was brought forth'. Biblical scholars have agonised over this phrase, since the description is that of a female process. (Women 'bring forth' children, from our bodies.) Scholars tell us that the Hebrew word can also mean 'engendered'. What is certain that the word is just as likely to have a female as a male meaning. So we are entitled to imagine not only a female Wisdom, the first created being, but the possibility of a female mother God who brought her forth. Or, taking this a step further, we may look at the other interpretation that it was 'through' Wisdom that God created the world, that he searched out someone who was already 'there' to find out how to do this. In this case, we have what Gese has called a 'cosmic creative figure', and she can be understood as female. We appear to be in a dilemma.

The world of antiquity understood Nature and the cosmos to be a creating mother, who first created herself and then the world. Nature was her own Law and was its personification. I suggest that in the above text some memory of this is entwined within the words. Female Wisdom, Hochma, is the transcendental cosmic order who personifies God who gives birth to Herself.

Architect or little child?

With the notion of a mother creator goddess as a reasonable answer to the puzzle as to who was 'there', we may go on to two other problem statements in the text. The first is in Proverbs 8:30, and deals with a phrase which has caused much difficulty.

The words read: Then I was beside him '*amon*' (Hebrew). The last word is translated variously in the scriptures as:

(a) 'master workman' (for example, RV, RSV, NEB and others);

(b) little child (alternative reading GNB which also suggests 'architect';

(c) as one who was brought up with him (AV).

This is a very wide range of meanings. How can a little child be equated with a master workman? What on earth is the connection?

The Hebrew bible was first translated into Greek in the second century BCE by seventy scholars. This provided its name – the *Septuagint* – from the Latin word of seventy. It is usually referred to by its equivalent in Latin numbers: LXX. When these scholars came to translate the word *amon* in this context, they used the Greek word, *armozouza*. According to Liddell and Scott's Greek–English Lexicon (1929), this means a 'fitting together', as of 'joiners' work'; a second meaning is to marry, take to wife. Yet another meaning is 'setting in order, arranging, governing'.

The first meaning clearly links up with the translation 'master workman', and also connects with the description of Wisdom in Greek as *technites*, which we find in the Book of Wisdom of Solomon. This means an 'artificer', or 'craftsman' or 'architect' –

one who creates and builds things, usually out of material that is already provided. Wisdom as an artificer and architect, one who builds creates and puts things together comes through clearly in many descriptions of her, and indeed it is one of her major characteristics. The 'seven pillars of Wisdom' on which she built her house in Proverbs 9:1, are famous and the attributes of construction and creation are constantly apparent.

Here I turn to the work of a scholar who set himself the task of solving the conundrum, R B Y Scott.[5] He moved through a wide and comprehensive exploration in terms of linguistics, references and disputations, about this one word. He first notes that, whether master craftsman or nurseling, 'Wisdom is pictured as a distinct being and not simply as a personified attribute or function of Jahweh' (p. 214). Looking at the reasons for the translation as child or nurseling, he first finds rabbinic, as well as Christian, evidence for *amon* to be cognate with Hebrew *amun, mun, munim*, which can mean 'faithful ones' – from which we today have the word *amen*, for firm or true.

At the same time, there is, he says, an additional possibility that *amun* may also be 'one cared for, reared as a child', or, as an active participle, one who cares for, or even 'guardian or trustee'. In a discussion on later uses, he refers to a title given to Jesus Christ (Revelation 3:14), in Greek *O Amen* – the true one, and remarks 'it appears to be derived directly from Proverbs 8:30'.

Scott refers to the quite widely held belief that the word *amon* links up with the Babylonian *unmannu*, meaning a wise man, but emphasises that master or skilled craftsman is preferred by most translators. Moving through a wide and comprehensive range of references and discussions about this one word, Scott eventually returns to the suggestion of binding and uniting. He then asks whether this means that Wisdom is united with Jahweh as an associate, or whether it means a binding force in whom all things hold together. (Colossians 1:7), (p. 22). His answer in fact is neither of these. What is 'most likely' is that Wisdom was a link or bond between the creator and his creation. 'The function of Wisdom is twofold. It operated both in the cosmos in creation and in the world of men. This interpretation seems to satisfy all the evidence and contradict none of it' (p. 223).

Finally Scott feels that the 'uniting' or 'binding force' absolves the reader from the need to consider Wisdom as a being independent of God built into either the 'master workman' or the 'cherished child'. 'What we have here', he concludes, 'is simply a poetic personification' (p. 223). After such a conscientious wide-ranging investigation, Scott's last statement, which stands baldly by itself, comes as somewhat of a surprise.

The difficulties inherent in acknowledging Wisdom as a second or other divinity alongside Jahweh have been well observed. At one point in his discussions of 'binding and uniting' Scott brings in the metaphor of a 'doorpost'. In passing, it is worth pointing out that the Hellenistic goddess Cardea, a goddess of the doorpost (*cardo*, a hinge), 'opens what is shut and shuts what is open'. In this she is seen as a solver of puzzles and a divinity who knows the past and the future, in fact, a Wisdom goddess.

Daniel Cohen suggests that the idea of Wisdom as a binding or uniting force may be considered in relationship to Her description as the Tree of Life (Proverbs 3:18).

The Hochma of Proverbs 8:22–31 and other Wisdom texts raises fundamental issues. We see that Hochma has been described in contradictory terms. Wisdom is an uncreated law, a cosmic order perceived and ascertained by God for creation, not physically created. She is:

1 A divine female figure, independent of the traditional concept of God.
2 An architect of creation, master craftsman, etc.
3 A darling child of God, first-born of creation.

4 One who, as a female, gives birth to herself.

5 A guardian or trustee.

6 A binding link.

7 The first of Yahweh's creative acts.

Let us now look further at the female imagery contained in the passage. We have already noted that the Hebrew word transcribed as 'made' or 'created' can mean to 'give birth to'. In this case proverbs 8:22 would read: 'The Lord gave birth to me at the beginning', followed by v.24; 'when there were no depths I was brought forth'. The female aspect is evident and turns us back to ponder upon the nature of God. We can also see a similar suggestion in the Book of Job. In describing his works of creation, God asks Job: 'Has the rain a father, or who has begotten the drops of dew? From whose womb did the ice come forth and who has given birth to the hoarfrost of heaven?' (Job 38: 28–29). There is no clearer statement of both female and male elements in the creator.

The Book of Job also tells us (28:27–28) that God in his work of creation – seeing everything under the heavens, creating the rain and the lightning, understood the way of Wisdom . . . then he saw it, he established it, he searched it out' (v.27).

Thus we have another spin of the prism. One interpretation of its contents shows Wisdom there, in the cosmic order, waiting to be 'found' by god, 'searched out' and 'established', and introduced to humans as a mediator of the ways of God with them; another shows her as a female child of god, given birth to by 'him'. Yet another suggests she is the almighty who herself gives birth to a daughter. If God gave birth to Wisdom, he was using the female side of 'his' nature.

Wisdom and the world

We can now look at another major statement in the text Proverbs 8:22–31 that has enormous consequences and possibilities. Verses 30 and 31 say that Wisdom, at the time of creation and presumably after it, was 'rejoicing in his inhabited world'. So she is not only 'beside him' but takes part in the world of humans, and finds it good. These verses hold that the inhabited world, created by both Wisdom and God, is a matter of rejoicing. I have to stress the word 'inhabited'. It is not a case of the beauty of the world being sullied by humanity, but rather a clear statement that the world with people in it is a good, joyful creation, and at the same time we see in Wisdom a bridge, a mediator between God and the creation. This is carried through in the subsequent verses. Proverbs 8:32–36 specifically instructs human beings to listen to Wisdom, for instruction, for happiness, and for even more. She sings out in these verses: 'The one who finds me, finds life.' It is implicit that 'life' can mean a good everyday life, and also a good spiritual life. Whether spiritual, material, or both, Wisdom suddenly shows a side of her nature which is different to that of the cosmic law. She rejoices with us – and most important – instructs us. Wisdom thus conveys the immanence of the divine to the human being – and finds both good. There is no guilt, no Fall, no sin. Being alive, and aware of Wisdom among us, is a matter of rejoicing.

If at this point our minds go back to the Garden of Eden stories – Adam the first created being and Eve the second; the disobedience and all that appeared to stem from it, (Genesis 1–3) – we can contrast these with this other, utterly joyful, account of creation. Look again at the verses at the beginning of this chapter. Wisdom is created, or creates herself; the earth with its mountains, its hills and fields; then the heavens (note that here, unlike the first verses of Genesis, earth is created before heaven), then the skies and the 'fountains of the deep'. The foundations of the earth are marked out. Lastly we see Wisdom rejoicing with God, rejoicing in the inhabited world – all are of one piece, there is no hiatus, no break, no allienation of the earth's inhabitants from their makers. All rejoice with Wisdom who is to be found in both earth and heaven.

And Wisdom – no matter how one reads the text – was there 'first' – and was female.

Wisdom is universal

Let us follow Wisdom further in the Book of Proverbs.

> Wisdom has built her house, she has set up her seven pillars;
>   . . . she has set her table.
> She has sent out her maids to call . . .
> Come eat of my bread, and drink of the wine I have mixed
>   . . . walk in the ways of insight. (Proverbs 9:1–6)

Here we have an almost human figure, the Lady of the household, inviting all to eat and drink with her. She is not at this moment the unattainable, unreachable reason of the universe, whom God needed to search out. Here she is a living being, calling on everyone to partake of her hospitality – and further, in so doing, to walk in the ways of insight.

Wisdom does not call upon any particular person or kind of person. She does not call upon only men, or Israelites. She calls upon everybody – her grace, her abundance is universally available, to women, to men, to everybody who hears her.

While she is bringing the divine into human life, and making herself a bridge between each, it is important to emphasise that, unlike God in the early bible narratives, she does not propose a covenant between herself and the people of Israel. Nor unlike the call and teaching of Jesus in the later narratives, does she state that only through belief in her or entry through her door (compare John 10:7–10) may her followers be saved. Her unique and standfast characteristic is that she is available to all, with no conditions attached whatsoever.

What is this 'insight' that she promises? We can compare the word with that found in Proverbs 3:19–20. This tells us that the

Lord, by Wisdom (*bhochmah*) founded the earth, by understanding (*btebunah*) he established the heavens and by his knowledge (*bdaatow*) the deeps broke forth. (The letter 'b' as a prefix indicates in Hebrew the word 'by'.)

The choice of words leads to some further connections. All three 'attributes' are feminine – *Hochmah, Tebunah* and *Da'at*. Tebunah may be translated as 'insight or skill', which links closely with *amon* discussed earlier, while Da'at in addition to 'knowledge' also indicates 'skill', 'perception', 'discernment', 'intimacy', 'association'; perhaps these are her 'hand maidens'. Tebunah and Da'at may be personified aspects of Hochmah, or attributes of Hochmah, much as she herself has been taken by some to be an attribute of God.

Certainly it is from Wisdom that insight, skill and knowledge are obtained. All these words link up with *amon* in one or other of its meanings, but especially in the context of ordering, building, being a crafts person, a creator, an architect, of creation, of the world, and then being in a position to instruct the world. She – Wisdom – knows how the universe was created and all its secrets – and she is available to humans to share this knowledge with them.

For us today there is a need to understand that the Wisdom figure was not only creator, was not only a sustaining and nurturing womb, but was the source of intellectual endeavour and challenge, understanding and action. We must also not avoid the fact that the texts make much of her as a woman whom a man may marry, or at least with whom he may enjoy intimacies.[6] That men are directed to have sexual intercourse with Wisdom is a way of depicting intimacy on their own terms. It is also a reflection of the masculinity of God whom men want to resemble. Put the other way round, man becomes as God when he unites with Wisdom.

Wisdom has in this respect become much changed from her former status, existing not as a divine architect of creation, not as a joyful companion of both God and humanity, but as a means by which the human man can retain both spiritual and mundane benefactions. Sexuality is here expressed by the heterosexual male gaining power from the dowry of female Wisdom, and naming it for his own through the medium of physical intimacy. Here transcendent Wisdom, who from a cosmic law existing for all eternity, uncreated by God who must learn from her, has first become a personification of a divine female figure but later a sexual partner for the human male.

Elsewhere she is named as the Tree of Life (Proverbs 3:18); she is a unity between the transcendental and the mundane; she is both creator and created; she is not only divine but a woman, and a woman in this world. This is the female being who was 'there' in the beginning, beside God; the being that has all knowledge, skill and insight and will teach these blessings to human beings; who in fact in some ways is indistinguishable from God, and raises the question of God's female nature.

Wisdom and Torah

What, then, were the monotheistic Hebrews to do with this Wisdom? How could they incorporate her into their overall concept of the patriarchal unity of God? They found an ingenious solution. Wisdom, in Judaism, became the Books of the Law, the first five books of the bible, the sacred Torah. No longer to be found in the cosmos, she is contained in the pages of a document, which itself then assumed an immense sacredness. The Wisdom now offered is part of a pure monotheism, with the world and the heavens created only by God. Lady Wisdom has been forgotten. Within these texts, the laws of Nature can be, and will be, altered at any time to cause punishment to 'sinners'. Righteousness, the good behaviour of the individual and the community, that is, obeying the commandments and living within the ethical principles set down, is now set out as the primary purpose of human beings' relationship with God and with the world he created.

Here there is no symbiosis between the actions of humans and the course of nature. Rather, it is an expression of the division between the Creator and the created; the division remains even for the righteous, for they will be 'rewarded'.

As this change took place, two streams of thought emerged. Wisdom as Torah, and Wisdom who retreated from the world into heaven. An early writer to identify Wisdom with Torah appears to be Ben Sirach (Ecclesiasticus), living around the first century BCE. Wisdom herself, in his book usually found in the Apocrypha, describes her genesis and her journeyings. (24:3-12) She 'came forth from the mouth of the Most High' (v.5), 'alone I made the circuit of the vault of heaven' (v.5), 'in the waves of the sea and in every people and nation I have gotten a possession'. From the mouth of the Most High she is his 'word' – the creative word; she lives in every part of the world. But the creator commanded her: 'make your dwelling in Jacob, and in Israel receive your inheritance'.[7] Her universalism is depleted by this instruction. Ben Sirach's idea of the association of Wisdom with Israel alone, contradicts the more general view of his period and earlier that Wisdom is available to all peoples everywhere.

After a magnificent description of her beauty – resembling all the most precious and desirable phenomenon of the natural world – she is identified paradoxically: 'I am the mother of beautiful love, of fear, of knowledge of holy hope; being eternal I therefore am given to all my children.' (24:17) Immediately following this passage, however, she is placed in a new perspective: 'All this is the book of the covenant of the Most High God, the law which Moses commanded us, as an inheritance for the congregation of Jacob' (v.21). Wisdom has become the Torah. The Torah itself following this, however, then becomes transformed into Wisdom.

The Rabbinic literature known as the Talmud tells us that the Torah existed before the creation of the world, although prior to the creation of time it is a creation of God. A second-century writer, Moses Almosino, declared that the Torah encompassed the concept of the 'eternal now'. It existed before time and is not encompassed by time but is in the eternal present for those who fear God. There is a blessing concerning the Torah, which says 'eternal life has thou planted in our midst', and this reflects the 'eternal now'. The Torah is the Word of God. It is above history and the action of God in History. It is both God's promise and concrete reality. The Word is also identified with Wisdom. When Israel was ruled by kings, they were God's representatives on earth; the kings' foremost task was the study of the words of the Torah.[8]

Since the earliest Jewish tradition, studying the Torah has been the foremost religious duty of men. This has taken precedence over all other activities in life and the status of a man who is able or who chooses to spend his whole life studying the Torah is still the highest that Judaism offers. It is important to understand that this study is the duty of *men*. Women for various reasons not only did not do this but were actively discouraged from doing so.

Enoch's account of Wisdom

Wisdom's journey from earth to heaven is chronicled by a first-century writer who claims the name Enoch and is the author of a book of that name.[9] This is not found in the bible or Apocrypha but is a part of inter–testamental literature known as Pseudepigrapha. A well known passage traces Wisdom's withdrawal from the world.

Wisdom found no place where she might dwell; Then a dwelling place was assigned to her in the heavens.

Wisdom went forth to make her dwelling among the children of men and found no dwelling place.

Wisdom returned to her place

And took her seat among the angels. (The Book of Enoch. 42:1–2)

Enoch has moved her from Jerusalem, where Sirach placed her, into the world itself. But she is disappointed by the world and moves away from humanity. In this account she left because she was not able to make her home in our world. In fact it was a constructive banishment. Once she has gone Enoch sets out on a journey to heaven, to enquire about the workings of Nature, not from her but from the holy angel Uriel who provides him with some fundamental instruction on the nature of the universe. Significantly he tells Enoch to write this down. Enoch finds out how 'the sun and the stars bring in all the years exactly, so that they do not advance or delay their position by a single day until eternity, but complete the year in perfect justice in 364 days' (Lxxiv:12). More didactic material concerning 'the four quarters of the world, the seven mountains and the seven rivers' is part of a body of knowledge presented to the writer. In other circumstances this would have been the domain of Wisdom.

For Enoch at this point, as for his contemporary who was the author of the Book of Wisdom, (see chapter 3) such rational enquiry was part of the divine heritage given to humankind. The road in Enoch's journey, however, takes a sharp turn. He moves from the encyclopaedic mode into the strictly judgmental.

And in the days of the sinners, the years shall be shortened
   . . . And all things on earth shall alter
   . . . And shall not appear in their time
   . . . And the whole order of stars shall be concealed from the
      sinners
   . . . And punishment shall come upon them
   . . . So as to destroy all (Lxxx:2–8)

Punishment is taking the place of Wisdom's unalterable natural laws; sinners may no longer rely on the patterns of the universe. Only through repentance and 'righteousness' can the cosmos return to its normal working. What 'righteousness' is and how it can be achieved then becomes the subject matter of texts, of commentaries. Certainly the focus will move from the study of Wisdom as Nature, to study of sin, or, at best, study of how to avoid sin.

In the meantime Enoch has discovered how to go about his tasks. Of primary importance is that the laws are written down.

Observe, Enoch, these heavenly tablets,
And read what is written there
And mark every individual fact. (Lxxx1.1)

The written text has become the repository of knowledge, as distinct from Wisdom's abundance, which in addition to texts includes 'searching out', independent study, oral tradition and the whole kaleidoscope of Nature. Wisdom is identified with a new cast of thought, which looks to a book and those that expound it in their own way of thinking, rather than to the glory of nature and the universe. It is identified with 'righteousness' and rewards and punishment.

Monotheism was saved; mystical appreciation of the Torah could be allowed; ordinary people now turned away from the observation and worship of Nature to seek understanding from documents and judgements.

Wisdom had to be dislodged from her divinity and glory, as did Nature. The 'human sphere' became one dominated by interpreters, teachers, priests and law-makers. Yet despite these attempts to push Wisdom up into heaven and there forget her, or turn her into a 'manageable' set of texts, she was not so easily disposed of. Well into the first years of the Christian era she was venerated and praised. In particular she shone radiantly among Jews in the Hellenistic age.

In this chapter I have tried to trace the trajectory of Wisdom in ancient Israel. She appears in the Book of Proverbs as an aspect of

God, or possibly his first creation. The texts are not clear and these are matters of profound speculation and exegesis. Those scholars who read the texts as showing that Wisdom is God Herself, or an aspect of God, also suggest an even more challenging idea. This is that she exists independently of God as a cosmic force in the universe which He Himself must seek out. From there we move to descriptions of her part in creation, and the insistence on her as an 'architect' or 'builder' of the world. The point is clearly made in biblical texts that she exists alongside God as a divine being. She is also seen as a mediator, and it is emphasised that she rejoices in the world of human beings and lives among them as well as in Her divine sphere. She is universal and her appeal is to all.

Because this picture of her raised enormous questions about monotheism in the Hebrew religion of the time, religious writers and leaders found a way out of their difficulty. Rather than have a figure beside God, or even a distinct part of God, they shifted the concept of Wisdom into her being the essence of the Torah, the Books of the Law. The Torah, the first five books of the bible, became more sacred than any other part and were deemed to have been written by God Himself. Wisdom as a female being became lost within them, as did her universality and her relationship with Nature. Rather, wisdom was seen as compliance with commandments and subject to reward and punishment, rather than the origin and sustainer of the natural universe.

While leading religious figures promoted this idea, which eventually became the accepted notion of Wisdom, it did not, however, become ubiquitous for a long time. The author, or authors, of the Book of Wisdom of Solomon, written shortly before the arrival of Christianity, stayed with, and elaborated fully on, the position of Wisdom as a divine female being.

3. The Book of Wisdom of Solomon

For it is He who gave me unerring knowledge of what exists
To know the ordering of the world and the working of the
elements
The beginning and end and middle of time,
The turn of the solstices and the changes of seasons,
the cycles of years and the positions of the stars,
the natures of animals and the tempers of beasts,
the forces of spirits and the reasonings of men,
the species of plants and the virtues of roots.
And whatsoever is secret and manifest I learned to know
For Wisdom the contriver of all taught me. (Book of Wisdom of
Solomon 7:17–20). (RSV.)

Here I shall follow the development of the figure of Hebrew
Wisdom as she was perceived in the Hellenistic period after the end
of the writing of the Hebrew bible. Her presentation is in the Book
of Wisdom of Solomon. This is a book written in the first century
BCE by Jewish sources concerned to help co-religionists resist the
attractions of Hellenism. It is to be found today together with
similar texts in the Apocrypha, if we use a Protestant bible, or
within the contents of a Roman Catholic bible. It does not,
however, appear in the Hebrew bible as such.[1]

The Book of Wisdom of Solomon (BWS) was written in Greek

in Alexandria, the highpoint and meeting place of Hellenistic civilisation, where a large number of Jews had settled. It contains an account of Wisdom (Sophia) who is very close to the Hochma of the Bible, but whose powers are extended. In this text she offers us a close-up picture of the female divinity who appears to be part of God, even God Herself, and certainly in many chapters takes over the powers and functions of God. At the same time the BWS also traces Sophia's downfall, showing how she was downgraded into becoming a possession of men, a vehicle for men's aggrandisement, and eventually how she disappeared altogether.

It is in this book that Sophia (Wisdom) reveals how women might become identified with, and be inspired by, her. Above all it is here that the pronoun 'she' is used extensively to describe the divine figure in creation, sustenance, understanding of nature and intellectual activity.

Who wrote the BWS?

It is interesting to look at questions surrounding the authorship of the book. Usually it is taken to be a male Jewish writer concerned to bring the Hebrew tradition and religion into the forefront of Alexandrian Jewish life, in contrast to the prevailing Greek and Hellenistic practices and philosophy. Nevertheless, one scholar over a hundred years ago and others today[2] make an exciting suggestion: Was at least part of the book written by a woman or women? The context is a description, by the first-century Jewish philosopher Philo, of communities called the Therapeutae. Contemporary with the better-known Qumran groups who produced the Dead Sea scrolls, they differ in one important respect: it appears that most of the Qumran groups were composed of men only, while the Therapeutae not only included women but women who were very active in the outer world. They were said to reach into the everyday life of the Jewish community around them, they conducted the Sabbath services, and provided influential commentaries on the scriptures. One modern scholar certainly goes further. Dieter Georgi (1988) suggests that the work of the Therapeutae could have been even more extensive than simply commenting on scripture – they could have been writing it, or something like it. He draws attention to Philo's descriptions of women Therapeutae and sees no reason why it should not have been those same women who composed at least part of the BWS. This brings into play the question of what Judaism was like at that time. There is certainly evidence of different sects – we know from the New Testament of Sadducees and Pharisees, we are aware of the work of the Essenes and others, all of whom except the Pharisees were destroyed by the Romans in the wars of the first-century CE. Among these sects it seems clear that there were some who had women leading services and acting as religious teachers. There is also evidence indicating that the female nature of God, understood as Wisdom, was part of this sect's view of Judaism.

It is suggested that this non 'traditional' type of Judaism is at the heart of the BWS, and is part of its Hellenistic background, a background now discarded or obscured and seldom referred to in Jewish religious circles. I want to prise out this strand of Judaism and follow its course. We can do this by examining the BWS in some detail set against its background and relay again the voices of Jews and others who were part of it, or those who have commented on this strand of Judaism, which incorporated a much wider band of belief than is usually realised.

Wisdom and God

The first five chapters of the BWS introduce a number of conflicting themes and raise important questions. In essence these concern the relationship of Wisdom with God. The notion of Holy Spirit is also introduced, which may be Wisdom or God.

The book, starting with a call to the rulers of the earth to love righteousness, proceeds to pose startling and difficult questions concerning the identity of Wisdom.

. . . Wisdom will not enter a deceitful soul
nor dwell in a body enslaved to sin
For a holy and disciplined spirit will flee from deceit (1:4–5)
. . . For Wisdom is a kindly spirit
and will not free a blasphemer from the guilt of his word;
because the Spirit of the Lord has filled the world (1:7a) (RSV)

In these verses, is Wisdom the alter ego of God? She appears to be identified as a 'holy and disciplined spirit', working alongside the Spirit of God.

It is as if both God and Wisdom are part of each other, operating in unison.

In the BWS Wisdom is firmly presented as divine, with power to judge the wrong-doer. She is the mediator between God and humanity. While Wisdom is part of the divine, and divine in herself, she is also part of the human order. Since she will not live in a body enslaved to sin, it must be conjectured she will indeed live in a body that is dedicated to righteousness, that is, she becomes a part of humanity in the world.

Do we understand Wisdom as Spirit, as God, possibly as Holy Spirit? Modern scholars continue an age-old controversy. While some contend that Wisdom is identified with God's Holy Spirit, others declare they are separate, yet tend towards indicating one reality. Perhaps, it is suggested, Sophia and Spirit are different aspects of God. Often Sophia and God appear to be quite indistinguishable. For example, we read (1:6a) that Wisdom is a kindly spirit, while (1:7a) states that the spirit of the Lord filled the world. Are these spirits identical? We meet a holy disciplined spirit in line 5 – it is not clear if this is Wisdom herself or the spirit of a person who is said to flee from deceit.

We can associate the word 'spirit' – (Greek *pneuma* with Hebrew *ruach*) – the breath or spirit, or wind, of God's power (Genesis 1:2; I Kings 19:11). Wisdom can be understood as the moving wind of creation, the spirit of God whom we meet in the creation narrative.

This is very surprising. We are dealing with a female entity, a divine being, within a Jewish context. We are reminded of the Hochma of Proverbs, but find that here her realisation is more extensive, in many ways quite literally breath-taking. The author has introduced the identification of Wisdom with Spirit, and with God, and followed it with some material not usually contained within Jewish religious texts.

for blessed is the barren woman who is undefiled
. . . She will have fruit when God examines souls . . .
Blessed also is the eunuch whose hands have done no lawless deed.
(3:13–14)

Here there is a break with biblical texts which emphasise the overall importance of child bearing. Certainly there is little history of favourable acceptance of childlessness, and such verses had to have been written by a sect at odds with what has come to be known as 'normal' Jewish tradition. We may suggest they could have been written by women, active in the community and not over-anxious to perform the role of motherhood that is usually cast for them. And sympathy for the male who possibly through no desire of his own is made infertile, also seems to be part of a more liberal viewpoint than was customary.

While it is the conviciton of most commentators that the purpose of the BWS was to encourage Jews to hold fast to, and remain in, a faith that appears to be contained in the commandments of the Pentateuch, the concepts noted above may be seen to be a radical departure from today's accepted views of 'traditional' Judaism.

Chapters 6:12—9:18

These chapters of the BWS introduce us to Wisdom in all the majesty of her divine forms – as spirit, radiance, light and the spark that is in humans, and in the wholeness of Nature. Above all it shows her as creator, and because she made the world she understands it and is prepared to share her knowledge with humanity. The verses at the beginning of this chapter on p. 37 make this very clear. It has been pointed out that, 'if the claims of this text about universal knowledge could be transposed into contemporary idiom, the author would speak of his [her] knowledge of earth sciences, meteorology, astronomy, zoology, demonology, psychology, botany and pharmacy.'[3] Wisdom in this passage is architect or fashioner of all things, replete with the knowledge of Nature and all its workings and in a position of being able to communicate and teach this to human beings. The problem of the identification of Wisdom with God is clear. While God is precisely identified as the source of knowledge, it is also equally precisely stated that the source of knowledge was Wisdom. Scholars have tried to get round the problem by posing relationships between God and Wisdom – God as creator, Wisdom as intermediary. In most instances they are concerned not to identify Wisdom as the actual creator.[4] Wisdom in these verses is also the great teacher, reminding the reader of a similar role in Proverbs (8:6–11) and elsewhere. She is concerned with the world as humans live in it and understand it. She is teaching them about the nature of the universe.

It is important here to note that no ingredient of this passage refers to the Sage acquiring knowledge from the Torah, or from any inherited tradition or biblical text. Wisdom taught her/him 'the structure of the world' as it is, as it can be perceived, in its own right, in no way mediated through scholastic, religious or doctrinal tradition.

While Wisdom is teaching the Sage in v.18 about the 'beginning and end and middle of time' it is not too speculative to suppose that such a description also evokes echoes of deity, a deity involved in time and the world.[5]

The knowledge that Wisdom teaches here is universal. All peoples and all beings in Nature experience alternations of solstices, changes of seasons, and so on. Here is a view of Wisdom that integrates the world.

The reference to mathematics, geometry and astronomy remind us that in the first centuries before, and of, the Christian era these sciences were well established, particularly in Alexandria. It was there that the great library housed all the knowledge of the ancient world, unhappily to be destroyed in the fifth century CE.

Commentators on these verses also point to the science of numerology, which they see reflected in them. Numerology was of enormous interest in the Hellenistic age, and in the Jewish tradition the science was carried forward by the Kabbalists, those men who concentrated on the mystical aspects of the religion. This interest was manifest in the philosopher Philo, who devoted a great part of his philosophy to sacred numerology and its significance.

It is of major significance for us today that in reading the Book of Wisdom of Solomon we find that the great repository of knowledge is female Wisdom. This is offered as our introduction to her qualities which further include radiance, spirit and identification with God. In looking at her as intellect, as pure activity of the mind, we are able to reclaim our intellectual status as women. It is a well-established canon of patriarchal thinking, only recently becoming dislodged, that women's brain power is inferior to men's; that women are less able than men to encompass intellectual enquiry and synthesis; that women's discoveries and achievements are on a lesser scale than men's. Women scientists and artists over the centuries have either been forgotten or are assumed to be of less worth than their male counterparts. There are many explorations of this subject. Margaret Alic (1986) and Sandra Henry and Emily

Taitz (1983) have surveyed intellectual women of antiquity and
more modern history, who have, as the title of the latter book puts
it, been 'written out of history'. They point out that women's
intellectual achievements, often made in the face of enormous
difficulties, are forgotten or are assumed to be the work of men.
Women themselves have many times felt discouraged by this
climate of opinion and have internalised the accusations that they
are unable to understand abstract questions of science, or mathematical and logical problems. Today women will sometimes
decline to take part in such study, claiming it is alien to them.[6]

I suggest that in reading these verses describing Wisdom's
creative genius women can regain a sense of our own intellectual
worth. Rather than concentrate solely on the purely intuitive to the
exclusion of the rational thought processes, we can integrate the
two. To achieve this the mind-set of academia will have to change
– and much has already been called for by feminist academics. But
change may take place not only in schools and colleges; women
everywhere may start to feel confidence in their reasoning and
reclaim their minds along with their bodies and their spirit.

With this in mind, we can look at some verses in chapter 6.

Wisdom is radiant and unfading
and she is easily discerned by those who love her,
and is found by those who seek her.
She hastens to make herself known to those who desire her.
Those who rise early to seek will have no difficulty
For they will find her sitting at their gates . . .
    . . . she goes about seeking those worthy of her
and she graciously appears to them in their paths
and meets them in every thought. (BWS 6:12–16.)

Here we see Wisdom in the world, making herself available to us
all. We need have no difficulty in seeking or finding her. Indeed she

herself seeks us. She is with us in the here and now, and available to us. The first sentence, 'Wisdom is radiant and unfading', sets her in the divine sphere. In these few lines Wisdom is strongly delineated as bridging heaven and earth. It is the first statement of a eulogy which continues for most of the three ensuing chapters of the BWS.

We are presented with the word *lampra* – radiant or bright – indicating 'the luminous nature of Wisdom which renders her easily obtainable in the gloom of ignorance'.[7] (Note this scholar's possessive implication – we are to 'obtain', not seek or find, her.) The unconventional scholar E R Goodenough, who in the early years of this century suffered disdain and denial on the part of his contemporaries for his perception of the female divine in Judaism, takes the word to be associated with the 'light stream which is the stream of creation'. He writes: 'It is not the sun, yet it is in a sense of the projection of the sun to us, or was so regarded by the ancients ... Sophia is not to be confused with physical light, since that can fade away ... she is the light stream of God's glory.'[8] He even goes so far as to identify this light stream as the 'Female Principle in the Universe'.

Much more has been read into the concept of Wisdom as radiance. Scholars, poets and theologians for thousands of years have argued over the concept of the divine spark within the world, within Nature, and whether, therefore, the created was distinct from the creator or that all were part of divinity, and having some part of divinity within each. Although traditional monotheism does make a clean separation between God and humanity, yet many sects and mystics have in fact suggested union with God and related to this John's gospel contains a famous disputed verse.[9]

In the BWS text there can be no doubt about the identification of God and Wisdom – they seem to be part of each other. It seems to me that there is a great similarity between discussions about Wisdom's relationship with God and that of the early Church

Fathers who discussed the nature of the Trinity, particularly the nature of the relationship between the Father and the Son. Is She the same as God? Is She consubstantial with God? Does She partake of the same Nature as God? Is She 'like' God? All these ideas are implicit in our verses. They duplicate the contentious disputations of the third and fourth century–Christian Fathers which for many years, even generations, dominated theological enquiry.[10]

The Sage says that she prefers Wisdom to sceptres, thrones, wealth, priceless gems, gold, silver, health, and beauty. (7:8–10.) Referring to Wisdom's radiance, the passage continues:

All good things came to me along with her
and in her hands uncounted wealth
I rejoiced in them all because Wisdom leads them
but I did not know that she was their mother.(7:11–12.)

Wisdom is therefore the 'mother' of all the good things of the world and of humanity, including the riches of nature as well as human-made authority and prominence.

Here it is worthwhile quoting a sidelight on the use of the word 'mother' by the Jewish philosopher Philo, who remarked that the architect who made the universe was at the same time the father of what was born, while its mother was the knowledge possessed by its maker.[11] I do not propose to analyse this cryptic statement, only to point out that 'architect' and knowledge go alongside Wisdom, and that fatherhood and motherhood seem to be part of the same divinity.

Chapters 7:22b–8:1
This text presents Wisdom to us in all her glory.

For in her there is a spirit that is intelligent, holy, unique, manifold, subtle, mobile, clear, unpolluted, distinct, invulnerable, loving the good, keen, irresistible,

Beneficent, humane, steadfast, sure, free from anxiety, all
   powerful, overseeing all and penetrating through all spirits that
   are intelligent and pure and most subtle.

For wisdom is more mobile than any motion; because of her
   pureness she pervades and penetrates all things.

For she is a breath of the power of God, and a pure emanation of the
   glory

of the Almighty; therefore nothing defiled gains entrance into her.

For she is reflection of eternal light, a spotless mirror of the
   working of

God and an image of his goodness.

Though she is but one, she can do all things; and while remaining in
   herself, she renews all things; in every generation she passes into
   holy souls and makes them friends of God, and prophets;

For God loves nothing so much as the [one] who lives with wisdom.

For she is more beautiful than the sun, and excels every constellation
   of the stars. Compared with the light she is found to be superior;

For it is succeeded by the night, but against wisdom evil does not
   prevail . . . She reaches mightily from one end of the earth to the
   other and she orders all things well. (RSV.)

The first really important word is 'her'. It is in *her* that all these
wonderful characteristics are to be found.

I remember the intense joy I experienced when I first read this
text; at last, I, a female, could identify and be identified with
divinity – and within my own tradition. Since then, on reading this
text with other women, I have found that many have experienced
similar feelings. On one occasion a group of us on an expedition in
Wiltshire entered a small country church. As usual there was a big
and rather beautiful bible exposed on the lectern. I went up to it, to
see if it contained the Book of Wisdom of Solomon, and found that
it did. I began to read out this text. Its effect on my friends and on

myself was almost too intense to describe. Here we were, in church, reading from the bible, and what we were reading was this wonderful hymn of praise to the female divine. One woman, weeping, said it cleared away for her a lifetime of guilt and inferiority, although she and others expressed anger that it was not read widely and not made readily available.

To obtain some idea of the character of the Wisdom of the BWS I will repeat the twenty-one adjectives that describe her, and will then discuss some of these in detail.[12]

Her spirit is: intelligent, holy, unique, manifold, subtle, mobile, clear, unpolluted, distinct, invulnerable, loving the good, keen, irresistible, beneficient, humane, steadfast, sure, free from anxiety, all powerful, overseeing all and penetrating through all spirits that are intelligent, pure and most subtle.

Intelligent (Gk. *noeron*)

Noeron literally means 'possessed of mind'. Reider says it is a term used by the Stoics to describe the spirit of reason in the universe.[13] Reese points out that there is a saying preserved in Plutarch that God is 'an intelligent mind and body'.[14] Here we set the scene for Wisdom's approach to women today. Her first characteristic is to do with intelligence and reason, the power of the mind and rationality. Wisdom is possessed of mind and her message is that we too are possessed of mind, and we do not have to give our minds away in pursuit of the growth of our spirit. Despite the bizarre distortions that 'mind' has been subjected to in so-called objective scholarship and the conservative academic method, we have no business to discard our intellects. She is intelligent; we are intelligent.

Holy (Gk. *Agion*)

There is no contradiction in Wisdom between intelligence and holiness. Wisdom's spirit is holy, and some early commentators have believed she is a manifestation of the Holy Spirit. In being holy, she links up with descriptions of God, and, in contrast, to those holy women who served in the temple with their sacred sexuality (see pp. 133–34), Winston (1979) points out that Isis is called holy,[15] and Reider says the word *agion* has a moral significance.[16] The word 'holy' takes us into the dimensions of the sacred; it begins, when set next to 'intelligent', to build up a many–faceted character of Wisdom and also to cause us to reflect that these various aspects of the prism are in ourselves and make up our own holiness and wholeness.

Unique, Manifold (Gk. *monogones*, Gk. *polymeros*)

Monogones is a strong and sacred word, used rarely. We meet it in the Orphic hymns in addresses to the goddesses Demeter, Persephone and Athena.[17] It can mean 'only born sole offspring', or it may indicate 'unique in kind'. Reider calls it 'singly born' and sees it as 'corresponding to Stoic belief in one world soul'. This links it with the adjective 'manifold' (*polymeros*) and Clarke[18] stresses that the two should be taken together as 'unity within a diversity of manifestations'. Reese picks up 'manifold' as a term linked to magic and used to describe water as an element.[19]

A shock wave hit me when I first read the description of Jesus as *monogones* – only begotten – in the Prologue to the Fourth Gospel (John 1:14) The bible writer transfers the description, 'singly born' and 'unique in kind', always until then applied to the female divine or semi-divine being, to the male human presence on earth of Jesus Christ as the 'only begotten Son of God'. Here is an early indicator of the process of Wisdom becoming absorbed into Jesus Christ.

Subtle (Gk. *lepton*)

Lepton means thin or fine. It can be physical or metaphorical, in the sense of subtle, or refined, ingenious. Clarke[20] reminds us that it was used of the manna that came from heaven to feed the Israelites in the desert (Exodus 16:14ff.). Winston shows that some Greek philosophers saw the soul as subtle.[21] Deane tells us that *lepton* conveys the sense of 'beyond the ken of natural man'[22] and Reider feels that it means 'ethereal or spiritual in essence'.[23] Let us stay with subtle. Wisdom combines mundane and abstract, manna and the spiritual; shall we say bread and roses?

Mobile (Gk. *eukineton*)

Eukineton is traditionally applied to fire. We have here the heat, the movement, the passion of flames. In context it brings forward a great deal of Greek commentary on fire – it was thought to be the motion of the universe, the life force within it. 'Mobile' and 'fire' associated with each other became a way of thinking about life, its movement as it burns, its spendour, then its ashes and finally its renewal. Certainly the use of the word places the text firmly in its Hellenistic background.

We have seen that she – the Sage – places the 'spiritual' and the 'material' together; they are differentiated only in so far as they are separate qualities, without any hierarchy. Where commentators have often considered that the order of the adjectives has no significance, or is arbitrary, it is quite possible in fact that they are in the order they are precisely to ensure that these qualities are understood as equal in importance, and that the jumble of earthly and heavenly descriptions evokes the concept that the female deity combined both kinds within herself.

Clear, unpolluted, distinct, invulnerable, loving the good, keen
(Gk. *tranon, amolunton, saphes, apemanton, philagathon, oxu*)

These six attributes emphasise previous statements. She is whole and her direction is towards the good. Keen and clear, of her intellect and herself. Invulnerable is translated by Reider[24] as 'unharmed', with the comment that it means 'I am not liable to suffering'. This is explained by Clarke, as an attribute of God who is not liable to suffering,[25] though this is a much disputed theological point. Winston translates it as 'unsullied'[26] and this appeals to me more than the other suggestions as it is in keeping with *monogones*. This group of adjectives provides a clear direction for women in the world: this is how we may think of ourselves, and change our understanding and conditioning.

Irresistible, beneficient, humane, steadfast, sure, free from anxiety
(Gk. *akolyton, euergetikon, philanthropon, bebaion, asphales, amerimonon*)
These words form a model which has inspired me for two decades and continues to do so. Let all women be the same. She is steadfast, sure, free from anxiety. That is how we could and should be, free from the burdens that have been laid on us for so long of guilt and responsibility for faults not ours. We should be able to proceed in our way as free beings.

The description 'all powerful' follows, and I feel it could well have been written by a woman, since if we are free from anxiety, steadfast and sure, we are able to get into our power – not 'power-over', not domination, but, as Starhawk puts it,[27] power-within, power to fulfil ourselves and our potential. So Sophia is all powerful, which itself is an adjective that describes God (omnipotent).

'Overseeing all, and penetrating all spirit . . .'
(Gk. *panepiskopon, kai dia pantonchoroun pneumaton . . .*)
She is not only all-powerful, she oversees all but not like a tyrant. She is part of all spirits that are quick of understanding, pure and subtle. Who are these spirits? Deane provides one answer. They are, as humans, the intelligent; as angels, the pure.[28] Clarke[29] agrees with this in a modified manner. He says 'spirits in the broadest sense of angels and human beings', and further 'Wisdom enters into those spirits that have an affinity with her',[30] which to some extent begs the question, as no angels have so far been called into being by

the author. We might well read the lines as suggesting that human beings may themselves have spirits that are intelligent, pure and subtle, and that Wisdom will pervade them. That is certainly my view. Yet another commentator, Goodrick,[31] clearly sees the difficulty and takes a strong line. They 'seem almost without meaning, at least as they stand. That Wisdom "penetrates thoughtful minds" is a platitude . . .' (p. 196). Goodrick is not prepared to take on the question of which spirits Wisdom pervades, but accepts that they are human. He discusses minority versions of the text and declares they are not mistranslations, or attempts to attach a meaning to an empty phrase. Eight-and-a-half decades after this clear sighted exegete, who obviously knew what he wanted and was not prepared to deal in what he might have termed absurdities, it is now possible to question this so-called meaningless or empty phrase and to see that its meaning may well indicate an immanent presence of the divine female deity Wisdom within human beings.

In fact, so important are these lines that they are repeated in v. 24. Wisdom is more mobile than any movement, and she pervades and penetrates all things. She is there within all 'by reason of her pureness'. Here we have a definite and repeated statement concerning Wisdom's presence in the world. Like the fire of the Greeks she is mobile and the source of change and renewal and she, the spirit whom we have described in detail in the preceding lines, the identification of God and holiness, the source and disseminator of all knowledge, she herself lives in everything. There is no division here between divine and mundane, heaven and earth.

In the next lines, the pendulum swings back – there is an antistrophe back to God. It is as if the author is explaining exactly how Wisdom does her work of prevading the world and its beings. She is an *atmis* of the power of God, translated as breath, or vapour, or mist.

'Mist' is a mysterious substance, the ancients believing that it came neither from earth nor heaven and was therefore unique in itself and had magical properties. The fact that it can be equated with breath, and breath with wind or spirit, again brings it into the numinous (that is, pertaining to the divine, the presence of divinity in a particular place). In the second Genesis story (Genesis 2:6) God formed man immediately after a mist had come up from the earth and watered the ground, and breathed the 'breath of life' into him so that he became a living soul. Thus mist makes the earth ready for creation, and as breath it is the source of life itself.

Another example comes from the book of Ben Sirach (Ecclesiasticus) 45:3 (to be found in the Apocrypha). Wisdom says: 'I come out of the mouth of the Most High and covered the earth as a cloud.' Here Wisdom appears to be the breath of God. The thinking is very complex. Wisdom is a breath which is life-giving; she is then described as a pure emanation of the Almighty's power, even his breath. Countless scholars have pondered, in the Jewish tradition, about the power of the *Shekina*[32] and in early Christianity about the workings of the Holy Trinity, where such language was used. The author of the BWS takes on a theology which identified the female Wisdom not only as part of God, but as one that lives in human beings.

Moving on to v. 25b: 'nothing defiled gains entrance into her.' This is quite definitely a male/female metaphor; she, the female, cannot and will not accept defilement. How different this from later attacks on women, particularly women as sexual objects of defilement, throughout Western culture. And the implication of the source of defilement is obvious. What, or who, gains entrance into a female? Did the metaphor mean to indicate male sexuality as the source of defilement? In the context as we usually understand it this would appear unlikely, yet it is there quite clearly.[33]

The following verse speaks of Wisdom as a 'reflection of eternal light'. The Greek word is *apaugasma* which has been used as a description of, or metaphor for, God himself, and was certainly used of and by Christ. (For example, John 1:7, 3:19, 5:35, 8:12) The extensive body of research involving light and Christology is not our concern here, but points to the later identification of light with the Immanent Divine. It is useful to point to the Epistle of the Hebrews, where in 1:3 Christ is described in similar terms to Wisdom and the word *apaugasma* is used.

She, 'the spotless mirror of the working of God' is also an 'image of his goodness'. Seen strictly in the context of the Sage writing a vision of Wisdom, the text provides female deity, immanent on earth, identical with God, his image. This is borne out further in the following verse. 'She being one can do all'; the claim is firmly made for monotheism, a monotheism of totality; all things are contained in her and she not only 'is' but can 'do'; she is instrumental, abiding in herself she makes all things new; she can here most easily be related to the Earth and cosmic goddesses who renew creation in the diurnal and seasonal round. But the Sage is not content with that; it is again emphasised that: 'generation by generation she passes into holy souls and makes them friends of God or prophets.'

Again we have the statement that she is creator and part of humans. She, the divine, is there with, and in, humans. In addition she is their spiritual strength and inspiration. In v. 29 She is 'fairer than the sun, above all order of stars, and superior to light', followed by v. 30 which states that light is superior to the night. This is out of line with traditional Hebrew thought, contrasting with the creation story (Genesis 1:5) where evening and morning together make a day, and also contradicts the Greek notion of night from which all inspiration and creation arises.[34] The connection of darkness with evil is to be found, however, in later texts, notably the Fourth Gospel.[35]

'She reaches mightily from one end of the earth to the other and she orders all things well.' (8:1)

This first verse of chapter 8 is still a description of Wisdom. In telling us that she reaches mightily from one end of the world to the other conjures up a vision of wings. This is all the more interesting since it recalls Genesis 1:2 where *ruach* the 'spirit of God' hovers (the Hebrew word, *merachepet*) having the sense of 'flapping wings like a bird'.

All these concepts and symbols associated with divinity may be distinguished in the BWS 8:1, noting that here again is an identification of creator with spirit and with guarding and protecting the world.

The second half of the verse makes the same point clearly. She orders all things well. She is the regulating force of the world, she is its design and its designer, she is the source and instrument of cosmic activity, and within her great wings[36] all things are ordered well.

This verse satisfactorily rounds off the section 7:17–8:1. Wisdom and God are so interrelated that they have become indistinguishable. Wisdom is the source of all knowledge; she is spirit, both divine and human. Or rather it has been argued here that she is the divine spirit that is also available to, and part of, human beings. She is within the part of all things in the cosmos, the essence of change and of mobility, and at the same time she is a representation of God and holds within herself the power to do and to order all things.

The figure presented in the text owes much to Hebrew and to Hellenistic thought, but is 'unique in herself'. The author of the BWS has assimilated the various elements and has envisaged a female aspect of deity and of creation that resonates with both Hebrew and Hellenistic cultures.

We have here a clear picture of Wisdom, presented as identical with, and working on behalf of, deity. She is spirit, yet in the world; the essence of goodness against which no evil can prevail, yet a compendium and teacher of everyday practical matters. Above all, she, as aspect of deity, can be present in human beings and in the cosmos.

She, deity or an aspect of deity, is the all-pervading force of nature of which she is the source and which she orders and rules. It is the task of humans to understand and acknowledge her, to receive her, be inspired by her, to come into their own divinity because of her. In the summation of her work, 8:1, the whole world is under her wing and ordered by her.

The universalism is absolute; there are no exclusions and no individual favourites, no special relationships with any one person or people. In this text there is no reference to eschatology, or to spiritual redemption. She is available to all, and her works are to do with the world and the spirit. It is a world where, if human beings follow the vision presented, harmony is achieved with both divine and human interrelating and becoming part of each other.

Sophia–Wisdom is cosmic activity of the divine, working in the world but being of the order of the transcendent. This female figure identifies and re-identifies with God, assuming a universalism beneficial to the whole of creation.

Chapters 8:2–11:1

After this remarkable laudation of the female Sophia, the mood changes significantly. The Sage now speaks as a man, approaching Wisdom as a woman whom he wants to marry and have live with him for his own advantage.

However, he still eulogises Wisdom's divine qualities, and describes Her as 'the fashioner (*technites*) of what exists (v.6). She is still a teacher to humans of 'self-control, prudence, justice and courage' (v.7), possibly reminding the Hellenistic reader of the qualities of the Egyptian goddess Isis. She is still the source of all knowledge, v.8, she knows the things of old, and infers the things to come; she understands the turns of speech and the solutions of riddles; she has foreknowledge of signs and wonders, and of the outcome of seasons and times.

All this, however, is required from her by her husband, not as universal teacher but as a useful source of his rise to power.

Because of her I shall have glory among the multitudes
and honour in the presence of the elders . . .
I shall be found keen in judgement,
and in the sight of rulers I shall be admired . . .
I shall govern peoples, and nations shall be subject to me;
dread monarchs will be afraid of me when they hear of me;
among the people I shall show myself capable, and courageous in
    war. (8:10–15.) (RSV.)

He has turned from a description of Wisdom to her effects upon
himself. Wisdom has become an object to be possessed by the Sage,
an object which will grant him his fantasy of power and success,
and comfort and happiness at home. (v.16) Indeed, because of the
advantages to his worldly life to be gained from her, he 'went about
seeking how to get her for myself' (v.18).

A very great change in the perception of Wisdom has taken
place, and a crucial change of emphasis from the universal aspects
and divinity of Wisdom to the centrality of the Sage and *his* needs.
Among the first of his needs is for him to conquer his enemies, have
domination and be remembered for posterity.

In his eulogy of himself and of Wisdom, the emphasis is
exclusively on of what use she will be to him. She is there to bring
him victory, to conquer enemies. It is at this point that the concept
of domination is expressed in the BWS in relation to Wisdom,
providing a climate in direct contrast to that pervading the earlier
chapters.

When the Sage manages to capture Wisdom, he immediately
uses all her resources for not only his aggrandisement and worldly
success but for victory over his enemies and the allegiance of 'dread
kings'. All her riches are there, her riches of spirit, of creation, of
knowledge. But she is to be his slave and the use he makes of her is

totally within the concept of power over others.

There are other verses within the text which to some extent contradict this. For example, the Sage praises Wisdom for her own sake; in 8:18 he expresses 'pure delight in friendhsip with her', but he immediately counters this with a statement about expecting to gain from 'the labours of her hands, unfailing wealth'. The Wisdom of chapter 7 has been coerced into the service of greed and war. And the woman he marries has to yield all her physical, intellectual and spiritual resources for him to plunder for the success of his selfish and warlike ambitions.

The closing chapters

There are still some puzzles and paradoxes. Wisdom appears in the place of God and then disappears entirely.

Chapter 10 provides an overview of the history of the Israelites from creation to the Exodus, duplicating the material in the book of Genesis with one enormous difference; throughout this chapter it is not the Lord, or God, or the Lord God who is instrumental in the salvation of his people, it is Wisdom. A few verses from the chapter indicate that she has here taken on the identity that in the Pentateuch belonged to God.

> Wisdom protected the first formed father of the world
> When he alone had been created
> She delivered him from his transgressions
> And gave his strength to rule all things. (vv.1–2)

The chapter also records:

When the earth was flooded . . . Wisdom . . . saved it. (v.4)
Wisdom also . . . recognised the righteous man and preserved him blameless before God. (v.5)
She rescued a righteous man when the ungodly were perishing. (v.6)

Those who were not saved 'passed Wisdom by'. (v.8)

It was Wisdom who became (to holy men):

a shelter to them by day
and a starry flame through the night.
She brought them over the Red Sea
and led them through deep waters. (vv.17, 18) (My italics.)

This is in contrast to the biblical Exodus story (Exodus 13:18, 21) which makes it quite clear that it is the Lord who is in the pillar of cloud and in the pillar of fire and who led the people through the Red Sea.

The end of the BWS chapter 10 has the righteous praising the Lord: 'because Wisdom opened the mouth of the dumb and made the tongues of babes to speak clearly.' (v.20, 21.) Chapter 11 opens with a verse which continues Wisdom's instrumentality in Israel. She enables their works to prosper by the hand of 'holy prophet' (v.1), and this verse closes the account of the history of Israel in the light of Wisdom's nurture and protection.

From here onwards we hear no more of Wisdom. God returns as the source of help and salvation. There is a theological sermon about crime and punishment, a condemnation of idolatry (chapters 13–15), and a sermon that rewards the righteous and punishes the sinners. Wisdom is not called upon here. The BWS ends with the verse:

For in everything O Lord, thou has exalted and glorified thy people, and thou has not neglected to help them at all times and in all places.

The universalism of the earlier chapters has made way for what was to become the traditional tribal relationship between Jahweh and his people. Wisdom has been discarded and hidden. She is no longer part of God or of humanity. She disappears, and does not exist.

Did the Therapeutae women write the first part and some conventional (male) sage the second? If so, why were both parts, so contradictory, retained? The mystery has still to be solved.

The early praise of Wisdom and her divine status, however, her role as mediator between heaven and earth, and above all Wisdom as a free female holding and sharing universal knowledge, speaks to us now. This is how she was, this is how she shall become again. And as she, so we. No longer to be captive, no longer to be plundered, no longer to be used and discarded; as women our own female divine. Wisdom cries out within us, and now it is our time to listen and to act.

We turn back to the Wisdom of the twenty-one adjectives, mother of all good things, teacher, deity while yet protecting the world and ordering it well. Wisdom is in Nature and is Nature.

We have seen that as architect and contriver of the universe she knows its secrets and will share them with humanity. This is the picture that the Sage presents to us in the early chapters. We have seen that she is the alter–ego of God, that she is mother of the universe, and yet she also lives in us. Women may turn to her for spiritual and intellectual inspiration. Yet, half way through the book, the brightness of this depiction begins to fade, and we see her taken over as a possession by the man who wants her good things for himself. Eventually she sinks away and we hear no more of her.

This swing from an acknowledgement of, and veneration for, the female in the divine towards a patriarchal monotheism is characteristic of its time. It is not possible to explore this in this book, but it should be noted in a background where the Hellenistic goddesses are also both worshipped and become neglected, and the female deities of the Ancient Near East are eased out of their position – although still revered widely. The appearance of the

Book of Wisdom of Solomon at the time of the birth of Christianity
seems to be at a hinge point of civilisation: the old world with its
concepts of goddesses as well as gods, of female divine power as
well as male, and all the associated notions of wholeness and
balance, is in transition. The terminus it will meet is a total
monotheism aligned on male concepts. But its journey is in a
terrain that still contains the deities that have been important to
humans for many thousands of years. It is those that we shall be
looking at in the next chapter.

4. Greek Classical and Hellenistic Goddesses and Wisdom

Divinely honoured, mother of the deathless gods, nurse of all.
Look in our direction; accomplishing Goddess, thou Lady, be with us.
Your fast running chariot is drawn by bull killing lions.
You carry the sceptre of command, the famous axis of the sky, thou, many named, majestic.
Your throne is in the centre of the world, and therefore.
Yours is the earth, gently granting nourishment to mortals.
From you the race of immortals and mortals poured out.
From you grew mighty rivers and all the oceans.
Once you were called Hestia, now we name you Giver of Prosperity.
Because you graciously provide all good things to mortals.
Attend our Mysteries, Lady who loves the drumbeat.
All subduer, Phrygian, Saviour, Bedfellow of time.
Celestial, ancient, life-gathering, frenzy loving.
Come in joy, Agreeable one, to our holy celebrations. (Orphic Hymn *To the Mother of the Gods*.)[1]

'For all things are from you, who unites the cosmos, You will the three-fold fates, you bring forth all things, Whatever is in the heavens, and in the much fruitful earth and the deep sea ...' Orphic Hymn *To Aphrodite*.[2]

So far I have discussed the figure of Hebrew Wisdom on her own, but in fact she takes her place in the context of the many other female aspects of deity which surround her. These include classical Greek and Hellenistic goddesses and deities from Egypt and the Ancient Near East and other ancient Hebrew Goddesses. In this chapter I look at some goddesses from the classical Greek and Hellenistic tradition.

A reflection or echo of the Mother goddesses of the Ancient Near East and Hellenistic cultures is found in the Hebrew Wisdom, and of her in them.

The Hellenistic world begins with the rise of Alexander the Great (330 BCE) and lasts until the Roman conquests of the first four centuries CE. Alexander's sweep from the Western Mediterranean to India brought cities, countries and cultures under a single authority. They intermixed and were drawn into intermingling parts of the Hellenistic empire with Greece as its centre. 'Greek' philosophers often in fact lived and taught in the country we now call Turkey (then Thrace or Anatolia), in Crete, Cyprus, Rhodes, and in the whole of the former Persian empire which took in Babylon and beyond.

Ideas flowed and reflowed throughout this vast area; deities moved and took on new names. Often, as happens more frequently than conquerors like to remember, people of lands apparently defeated in fact superimposed indigenous beliefs on the new names and ideas and languages.

The Orphic Hymns
These associations and relationships can be clearly seen in the set of ancient hymns which have the name of Orpheus attached to them.[3] The collection is of about eighty short poems of praise to various divinities. While their date is unclear, it is accepted that they were used in ritual and sacred practice from at least 300 BCE to 500 CE,

that is, for nearly 1000 years, and the material in them comes from earlier sources.

I found the Hymns extremely important when I was considering the ties between Wisdom and the Hellenistic goddesses. In particular, I came across the work of the great early twentieth-century scholar E Goodenough, whose controversial results of in-depth comparison of Jewish and Hellenistic thought and mythology alienated him from the traditional body of scholarship at the time.[4]

In discussing Jewish 'Wisdom', Goodenough points out that Sophia (Wisdom) is the same 'female principle in Nature' that Orphic hymns celebrate. He writes: 'There is a common notion applied to all this list of goddesses. However different they were in details, each is the Great Mother, the Female Principle, the Universal Queen . . . with this Female Principle goes the notion of bisexuality of the female with power to impregnate . . . here the Female Principle has been dissolved in a conception of Deity that combines the notion of the universal genetrix with the power of impregnation.' Goodenough points out that Nature is also referred to as eternal Life, while the God Dionysus is hailed as male and female. He continues: 'within this composite conception was included the notion that it was the Fire or Light Stream' and, later, specifically identifies Sophia, the wisdom figure, with the 'Light Stream' which is also Nature.[5] This pointer to the connection between Wisdom, Nature and the Hellenistic goddesses excited me. I felt that a clue to the mystery of the female divinity in Judaism and to her apparent disappearance had been given me.

It is the reason I chose my title. The goddess riding 'in a chariot drawn by lions' is usually depicted as the Great Mother, Cybele, of the ancient world. But I could also see that there was no hard and fast division; much of what is attributed to her and to the other goddesses praised in the Orphic Hymns applied to Hochma–Sophia as well. Above all, it is resemblance of Hochma–Sophia to the

'Nature' goddess of the hymns that made clear to me the connections between the various strands of Hellenistic thought and the Hebrew goddess.

Looking at the Hymn to the Mother of the Gods, (quoted on p. 62) we see that she is 'divinely honoured ... nurse of all'. Wisdom's divine honours have been discussed in the preceding chapters. The description 'nurse of all' can be linked with the mysterious word *amon* of Proverbs, discussed above, where one translation is given as 'nurse'. The word I have translated as 'accomplishing' (Gk. *Kranteira*) is given in the dictionary (Liddell and Scott's) as 'one who goes, performs, accomplishes', and this links up particularly well with the alternative translation of *amon* as 'artificer', 'fashioner' and with the BWS description of Wisdom as *technites* – craftsperson, fashioner, accomplisher. The feeling throughout the descriptions of Wisdom, both in the BWS and often in Proverbs, is that she is the one who *does*. She links heaven and earth, and accomplishes on earth and through human beings everything from creation itself and the maintenance of the workings of nature, through to the orderly manner of conducting individual lives. In addition, she is responsible for imparting knowledge and guidance.

The fast-running chariot, drawn by lions, of the great mother can be seen to have a direct link with the 'chariots of fire' in the vision of the biblical prophet Ezekiel. These drew the 'appearance of the Lord' across the heavens. (Ezekiel 1:26–28) and gave their name to a strand of Jewish mysticism named *merkavah* (Heb. chariot) which persisted throughout history. It has been a source of Gnostic speculation, and of later Kabbalistic study and praxis. In this book of Ezekiel the chariot wheels are actually under the throne and the suggestion is that the Lord God is riding in the chariot. In connecting this with the chariot of the Great Mother it is worth while looking at the question of the date of the book of Ezekiel. It is supposed to describe events at the end of the sixth century BCE, at the time of the exile of the Jews to Babylon. In fact internal evidence has been cited to show it must have been written considerably later, and may even have been as late as the time of Alexander the Great.[6] If this is so it would have been contemporary with the Orphic hymns, and the large concentration of Jews in Alexandria and other parts of the Hellenistic world would have been sufficient to have brought the ideas of Ezekiel into the world of the Orphic hymns, or vice versa.

On the one hand we have the Hebrew prophet declaring that God himself is riding on a throne in a chariot (or that the chariot is the throne); on the other we have a description of the Great Mother doing the same. But whereas the former is drawn by 'living creatures with their wings stretched out' (Ezekiel 1:23), and with whirling flames, the other has her chariot drawn by lions. Now I have seen many lions depicted in the Ancient Near East, including Israel; often they have eagles' wings. Lions are royal beasts, frequently associated with goddesses, including those in the Hebrew background, from the Ishtar gate at Babylon to an ancient statue of a lioness with a wheel of fate, now standing in the Israel Museum and labelled 'Nemesis'.[7]

Perhaps the most important reference to lions in the context is that made by the author of the book of Ezekiel. In the description of the 'four living creatures' with wings who drew the Lord's chariot, they had, 'on the right side', the face of a lion. Later, (Ezekiel 10:14) one of the living beings had the whole face of a lion.

I propose therefore that the chariot of the Great Mother, the Mother of the Gods, can be seen to be in close relationship to Ezekiel's chariot which drew God along; and Wisdom, the female aspect of God, or the Goddess herself, may be the occupant of the chariot drawn by the lions of the Orphic hymn.

There are more connections which can be described from the Orphic Hymn quoted at the beginning of this chapter. She carries the sceptre of command (line 4) which is the axis of the sky. This is her symbol of authority and shows her to be divine. We may be reminded of Wisdom's description of herself as 'beside Him', when God established the heavens and made firm the sky. (Proverbs 8:27–28).

She is 'many named', liked the goddess Isis who greatly resembles Wisdom (see chapter 5) and she is the earth, gently granting nourishment to mortals. Here I see a strong reference to Wisdom as we meet her in the BWS 7:21ff. who teaches us the ordering of the world, and the working of the elements . . . and all the multifaceted workings of Nature. She is also the one who reaches from one end of the world to the other, and orders all things well (BWS 8:1). A similar thought comes from the Orphic hymn to Aphrodite, she 'who unites the cosmos' and brings forth all things.

The Orphic Hymn to Nature
We turn now to the Orphic Hymn to Nature. In it we have the clearest indications of Wisdom's identification with her, and can trace them, step by step.

To Nature
O Nature, mother goddess of all, artificer mother,
celestial, venerated, goddess of richness, sovereign,
all subduer, untamed, steering, lighting all,
almighty, nursing mother of all,
Undecaying, first born, legendary, enabling us,
Born of the night, all wise, light bringing, powerful in restraint
The track of your feet is whirling and silent motion
O sacred one, cosmic mother of the Gods,
unending one, bringing all to completion, common to all, but
    belonging to yourself alone
self-fathered, yet without a father, beloved, gladsome, great,
flowerlike, garlanded, beloved, accessible and wise,
leader, accomplisher, life giving, all nourishing maiden,

Self-sufficient, justice, combining in yourself all the Graces,
   presiding
Goddess of earth, air and sea,
bitter to the worthless, sweet to those who honour you,
all wise, all giving guardian queen of all,
Bringing food, freely endowing us with ripening plenty,
Thou, father, mother of all, with us as nourisher and nurse,
swift birth giver, blessed one, rich in seed, begetter of the seasons,
Creator of all, shaper, source of all richness, sea goddess,
everlasting, setting in motion, all wise, full of care,
Never failing, you whirl with quick force.
All flowing, circular in motion, shape shifting,
on your fair throne, you are honoured, alone you perfect your
   design,
Loud thundering you sit above the rulers,
Fearless, all subduer, you are destiny fiery goddess of fate
You deathless, are everlasting life and know the future.
You are the all and you alone create.
But Goddess we pray you in good season lead us to peace, health
   and
increase of prosperity. (Orphic Hymn *To Nature*, translated by
   A P Long and D Scott.)

This thirty-lined hymn addresses Nature as Mother of all, as
'artificer', an idea repeated several times, as almighty, completion.
One of the most startling concepts occurs in line 11 which states
that she is 'self-fathered, yet without a father' an idea which is
repeated later in addressing her as 'father, mother of all', who is a
'swift birth giver . . . rich in seed'. This idea of nature creating from
herself has been the source of much controversy. For here, in
comparison to the account of Wisdom in Proverbs 8:22, Nature
cannot be understood as engendered by a father God but is herself
the source of the universe. She contains the male as well as the

female within herself. We have seen that Goodenough asserts that this is the meaning of the great Female Principle which includes both female and male. He also makes the point that her light–bearing character identifies her as the Light Stream, and he points to Wisdom herself, so often called a lamp, lightbearer and radiant with light. He turns to the Book of Wisdom of Solomon to show Wisdom as 'fine, mobile, clear, unpolluted' and asserts these are descriptions of her as light itself.[8]

At the same time we see that the Hymn to Nature does not concentrate exclusively on light. Nature is 'born of the night' (line 6), and she is the creator of all, shaper and source of all richness (line 21). It is important that the line which asserts she was born of the night is also the one which calls her light bringing, thus making a whole of dark and light, night and day.[9] In this line too she is called 'all wise'.

The many words which identify her as creator, artificer, architect acomplisher emphasise her similarity to Wisdom who is described in this way many times. Like Wisdom, she belongs to herself alone and yet is available to all (line 9); she is deathless, and knows the future, she is almighty, and is Justice. In addition to being named 'all wise', she has these and other characteristics of Wisdom. She 'sits above the rulers of this world' (line 25), and is 'presiding Goddess of earth, air and sea' (line 13). All these ideas are to be found in descriptions of Hochma, whether as attributes of God or as herself alone.

We can see that there is a strong identification of Wisdom with Nature, or Nature with Wisdom. And there is a total identification of the divine with Nature, who is described in terms that show that not only is she the creator but also sustainer of the universe. There seems to be some idea of the circularity of the world in the lines which describe how she sets it in being and then whirls it in circular motion (line 24). Like Wisdom she is not a remote creator, but one ever present with the world she has made, which is dependent on her for its prosperity.

This Hellenistic view of Nature is all encompassing. It leads me to believe that in the many varied aspects of Greek philosophy and religion this view of Nature is never lost, and indeed unites antagonists.

Greek 'objective' science

It is generally believed that Greek scientists were the first to view the world 'objectively' and to do away with supernatural explanations for everyday events, even for the creation of the world. Their work was based on observation of the natural world and exploration of the meaning of their findings. Benjamin Farrington, for example, suggests in his work on the character of early Greek science (1936) that these activities led to exact measurement, geographical precision, more precise methods of navigation and other first-hand observation of far off lands and seas. Such knowledge and observation contributed to the Greek feeling that the whole inhabited earth is part of the same family. The science was formidable. Dicacarchios, a pupil of Aristotle (died 322 BCE) measured the size of the earth and knew of its spherical shape. In the mid-second-century BCE Seleucus deduced that the earth and the planets moved round the sun. Mathematics, mechanics, the natural sciences and medicine were all the subjects of extensive objective observation and research. Scientific methods usually labelled as 'Greek' owed much to the cultures from Egypt and Asia Minor that gradually became part of the Hellenistic empire. In the old bronze age civilisations of the valleys of the Nile and Euphrates practical knowledge was passed on orally to apprentices by the farmer, the potter and the smith. But larger-scale enterprises, such as the control of water supply, redivision of land, erection of great buildings were in the hands of the ruling and literate classes and gave birth to sciences which were emerging from the purely practical stage, sciences such as positional astronomy and mensuration.

Among others, Farrington points to the 'rationalism' of such philosophers and scientists, particularly relating to those following the third-century BCE thinker Epicurus known as Epicureans.

A recent commentator, Koester (1982), believes that these Greek thinkers postulated that it was meaningless to worship the gods. He suggested that the Epicureans drew the consequences from their atomic materialism, the course of natural events determined by laws which derive from the movement of atoms; hence there was no need for the gods. 'There are also no spiritual realities outside of the material world as constituted by the atoms, and even the soul is nothing but a part of this world.' Epicureans appeared human enough to treasure happiness and friendship however; 'community and pastoral care were understood as religious duties, while the regular common meals of the members . . . were liturgical celebrations' (p. 147).

I understand that no form of supernatural or divine agency was to be contemplated, yet it is vital to realise that although the Epicureans and the other 'objective' thinkers discarded deities as such, they continued to see in Nature the source of understanding of the universe. They looked to Nature to provide them with all knowledge and, in eschewing her divinity, they still needed to reverence and venerate her. In this I understand they sought to listen to Wisdom as Nature and to follow her.

Hellenistic magic

In contrast to the methods of the objective scientists, Hellenistic thinkers were much preoccupied with magical means of under-standing and controlling the cosmos. Betz (1986) points out that while condemned by many philosophers as 'illict, fraudulent and superstitious, magic was an essential part of daily life at all levels of society . . . magic was presupposed in all forms of the miraculous, and in medicine, alchemy, astrology and divination.' He continues: 'over the course of history, magic changed in appearance, scope and importance from being an element of simple rituals to becoming highly complex systems claiming the status of science and philosophy' (p. 93).

Primary sources include amulets, magical gems, curse tablets, spells, figurines, sculptures, tools and finally handbooks of magicians who collected the materials they used (especially the Greek magical papyri).

Secondary sources include those from literature and art and philosophical discussion. For example, Luther Martin (1987) in his analysis of the magical journey of Lucius narrated by the second-century CE author Apuleius in his work called *Metamorphoses*, but known pupularly as *The Golden Ass*, has surveyed magical beliefs of the period. Magic involves 'power over the order of nature'. A person who has this, witch or magician, is able 'to bring down the sky, to bear up the earth, to turn the water into hills and the hills into running waters, to call up the terrestrial spirit into the air and to pull the gods out of the heavens, to extinguish the planets and to lighten the very darkness of hell.'[10] By similar means, 'the swift rivers might be forced to run against their courses, the sea to be bound, immovable; the winds to lose their force and die; the sun to be restrained from natural journey; the moon to drop her foam upon the earth; the stars to be pulled down from heaven; the day to be darkened; and the night to be made to continue forever.'[11]

There is also a magic that can be called upon for specially 'good' purposes, and this too presupposes power to manage events in nature. Martin believes that all magical practice and investigation assumed a finite cosmos in which all things are related to one another through a cosmic sympathy (in Greek, *sympation*) and quotes Plotinus. 'But how do magic spells work? By sympathy and by the fact that there is a natural concord of things that are alike and opposition of things that are different, and by the rich variety of the many powers which go to make up the life of the one living creature.'[12]

Such sympathetic forces can be used for medical and healing purposes, or for charms to bring victory in war, love or even on the racecourse. A late Hellenistic magical papyrus with some Jewish affiliations (though not by an Orthodox Jew) can be seen in the Paris Magical Papyrus (300 BCE): 'For those possessed by daemons, an approved charm by Pibechis. Take oil from unripe olives, together with the plant mastigia and lotus pith and boil it with marjoram . . . saying "Joel, Ossarthiomi, Emori, Theochipsoith . . . come out of such an one (and the other usual formula)".'

Such papyri echo very long lived methods of healing by magic. For example, the Ebers Papyrus, from Egypt, dated about 1500 BCE, contains 875 prescriptions for everyday ills. A remedy for headaches, said to have been made by the goddess Isis for the god Ra, mixed berries from coriander, the Xaset plant and juniper with wormwood and honey, the resultant mixture to be placed on the head.[13] While this appears to have been a medical prescription with no recourse to 'supernatural' assistance, it is assumed that the practical remedy would be facilitated by spells or charms. When the god Osiris is being raised by his sisters, the goddesses Iris and Nepthys, they chant:

> This is our brother,
> Come let us lift up his head,
> Let us rejoin his bones
> . . . May the moisture begin to mount on his spirit
> Osiris live! Let the great Listless one arise.[14]

In these examples of Hellenistic magic there are a variety of attitudes and methods. Nature can be forced to change its normal course; the charm calls upon daemons to leave the body of the afflicted person, naming the daemons is a powerful weapon. While the headache remedy's potency mainly lies in its ingredients and can thus be called 'scientific', the ability of the goddesses to revive and bring Osiris back to life goes beyond human endeavour and calls upon their innate divine regenerative powers.

This renewal of life is linked to the renewal of life on earth, after winter barrenness and drought. Philo, the first-century Jewish Philosopher in Alexandria, speaks of the magical beliefs and practices of the Babylonians as being based on 'harmony between things on earth and things on high, between heavenly things and things earthly. Following as it were the laws of musical proportion, they have exhibited the universe as affinity between its parts, separated indeed in space, but housemates in kinship.'[15] This view was widely held and long–lasting. In the twentieth century, Jung, for instance, would not have disowned it.[16]

Returning to the materialism and atheism of the Greek scientists, we can see that there is in fact a bridge between their attitudes and those of the magicians. Nature is the source and 'mater' of all material, just as in her design and activity she expresses a panorama of order that pervades the universe. Within Nature, Greek philosophers grappled with enquiry into the existence of divinity, especially in relation to the problem of welding together the things on earth and things on high and explaining their relationship.

What we now call the 'scientific method', employed by the philosophers and scientists of the time, started in every case with the exploration of natural phenomena and events, followed by a listing or gathering of all known observations. The Greek scientists looked at nature and devised means of obtaining information about 'the structure of the world and the activity of the elements' and all the varied sciences deriving from this first base. Where the Epicureans found it 'meaningless to worship gods', since there are 'no spiritual realities outside of the material world', the major philosophical schools of Plato, Heraclitus and the Stoics endeavoured to make sense of, and explain, a universe that included the divine and the material, in relation to Nature as a living entity and with a background of Nature as 'mother of all'. Although they disagreed with each other and with other schools of thought it appears to me that the ancient philosophers, whether objective or magical or a combination of both, were united on this fundamental principle.

The numinous sixth-century BCE Heraclitus, acclaimed as father of science and philosophy, complained about the methods of the 'materialist scientists'. He wrote: 'Wisdom is one only . . . they will not find wisdom by running to the ends of the earth and trusting to their eyes and ears which are bad witnesses to men if they have not souls that understand her language.'[17] When he finished his great work concerning the workings of Nature, he placed a copy of it on the altar of Artemis, goddess of his native city Ephesus.

The Great Mother

A very long-lived veneration, born in the very earliest stages of the human history and classified as one of the major religions of the Hellenistic world, was that of the Great Mother. She existed as a goddess to be worshipped with splendour and awe well into late Roman times and challenged the young and expanding Christianity of that era.

Her full title was Great Mother of the Gods, known in early times as Kubaba, and later as Cybele. Phrygia in Anatolia (Turkey today) was the central site of her worship, but this spread throughout the ancient world.

The Great Mother has much in common with Nature as a deity, but has an over-arching theme that transcends even Nature. She was able to procure for humankind the promise of redemption, salvation and an after life, especially in her later phases. This was done partially through a 'baptism of blood'. A system of ceremonies was instituted at a three-day spring festival, named the Taurobolium by the Romans, where a bull was ritually sacrificed and devotees washed away their sins in its blood and became sanctified. This was believed to offer the chance of spiritual renewal and immortality.

Apart from the aspect of salvation, the Great Mother is not only parent of the gods but also of all creation. She is particularly identified with the welfare of animals and humans and with the earth itself and its topography. She is a source of healing and renewal. She is named 'great parent of all nature' rather than Nature, and in this respect resembles Wisdom as creator who brought all into being. She has dominion over seas and winds and is especially associated with mountains, where she was worshipped in frantic excitement. A recent author, Giulia Sfameni Gasparro in a study of Cybele (1985) suggests that the violent ceremonies in these places were methods of fusing with the deity and attaining salvation and that the frenzy, 'displays the features peculiar to a mystic cult in its quality as a ceremony re-evoking the significant moments of a divine vicissitude characterised by deep pathos but also orientated towards a positive outcome.' She compares the worship of the Great Mother to that of the Eleusinian mysteries and points to 'the profound "participation" in the interaction between the divine, cosmic and human levels'. She emphasises this interaction, where the goddess in her mysteries becomes part of the world and fuses with her worshippers. Gasparro also refers to the goddess' 'medical and cathartic qualities' and her capacity to infuse *mania* which turns into a beneficial possession which puts the worshipper 'into a state of bliss and in an immediate relationship with the deity' (p. 122).

We see therefore that the Great Mother of the Gods takes on an additional similarity with Wisdom. Not only is she of this world and matters pertaining to human life within it, but also the means whereby her worshippers can fuse with her divinity, can themselves become at least part divine and can attain salvation. While the religion that sees Hochma–Sophia as divine did not in fact use the actual practices of the Great Mother, in fact Hochma in the BWS is certainly the means of salvation, and is associated (in a rare moment in Jewish theology) with the means of obtaining a good afterlife (BWS: 6:18).

Like Wisdom, the Great Mother also brings to her devotees a dimension of spiritual life, although expressed differently. The orgiastic rituals and frenzied dancing of her followers, together with the three-day festival of mourning and then renewal that was celebrated alongside it, conveyed purification of one's sins and new birth. Her cult involved communion with the divine through frenzy; co-relationship of the deity and the natural round of the seasons was expressed in the acts of her worshippers.

Although parts of the cult of the Great Mother are abhorrent to modern notions of behavioural conduct, nevertheless the cult stated quite clearly that the Nature Goddess was creator and sustainer of this world, was goddess of the dead and, that with the baptism of her worshippers, they would achieve spiritual regeneration and, in some cases, immortality.

The wildness of Nature was reflected in these frenzies. Through the myth and ritual contained in them, humans attained the character of the divine and took part in the divine round of nature, causing the crops to grow and the fruit to ripen, while the dead, through the sowing of seed, were regenerated. At crucial points in the ritual humans united with the divine and took part in divine powers. It must be stressed that these powers are essential to the character of the Great Mother in her Nature aspect. It was through powerful communion with Nature that humans were able to achieve sustenance of life in this world and in the spiritual domain.

These practices demonstrated two major religious assumptions of the ancient world. First, a unity of the divine and human could be achieved that both influenced the round of Nature and provided a dimension of spiritual renewal for the human being. There is also another dimension. The Great Mother of the Gods is depicted at these 'frenzies' as being surrounded by lions and wolves and hymned as 'howling and roaring'.[18] The Goddess at the feast 'delights in drums' and is the frenzy-loving, joyful one.'[19] I feel the importance of this very strongly as it has been denied us for so long. When it emerges it is so often distorted and turned against us or against others who do not deserve it and whom we do not wish to hurt. We have the capacity for orgy, for frenzy, for demonic release, and we can use this safely if we have space for it, and if it is sanctioned and in the service of our deepest feelings. How many women are locked up in psychiatric hospitals, or at home in the prison of valium and other anti-depressants, only because they have nowhere to work out their life-loving frenzy? In love there is space, but because of the age-old tyranny of patriarchy frenzy can so often only manifest itself in male violence. This is perverse and depraved. Loving space between people is almost all we have to work on. Where we are able to link it up with the world of the Great Mother and apply it and ourselves to Her I am sure we will have her strength and inspiration. If there is frenzy, it should be safe and non-violent, life loving, not a killer and despoiler. I would like to think that in the future a safe and life-loving frenzy may be possible, but this demands an enormous cycle of change in us all.

Summary

In this chapter I have set out to show that at a time when the Book of Wisdom of Solomon was written, and the idea of Wisdom as female deity or certainly an aspect of deity in Judaism was most profoundly presented, the Goddess of Wisdom did not stand alone, even though she was distinct from other deities. She can be identified with Nature, and as creator of Nature.

There is major agreement that Nature is the source of cosmic law and harmony, although there is ambivalence about the relationship of such cosmic harmony to deity, whether in fact the harmony (Nature) is the deity or takes the place of deity, or whether it is through the action of deity that such harmony exists.

Cosmic harmonies permitted the Greek materialist scientists to establish understanding through exact observation and measurement, without recourse to any supernatural explanation, while the same harmonies could also be seen as ideals created supernaturally which could be followed or achieved in some part by human beings. The magicians called upon Nature's laws and harmonies to give them power to achieve control of events, whether beneficent as in the case of medicine and healing, or malevolent if they wished to cause destruction. An understanding of Nature was necessary for magicians and scientists alike, as well as for artists and musicians. Eventually this led to a concept of spiritual salvation.

For many, Wisdom, like Nature, is a fashioner, who either creates the world or is used by the deity to create or help create the world. At no point do any of the thinkers doubt that Nature's laws are there to be followed by humans, or that they are good, or that they are the source of knowledge and of well being. The divinity of Nature becomes Wisdom, as it is seen to mediate between earth and heaven and heaven and earth.

Wisdom goddesses are of Nature, in Nature, create Nature, or are created by Nature. They also become part of the world, literally and metaphorically. They are divine and they are of the world itself. The great Mother of the Gods is seen as Nature and the source of all activity, both spiritual and mundane, because she shares herself with humankind which is thus united with the divine in her. The Great Mother and other Hellenistic goddesses show specific characteristics associated with creation, sustenance, teaching and healing. Many in addition to having the gift of life, are also able to confer the immortality of renewal of life after death.

Renewal of life in the world is achieved through religious behaviour. But this, reflecting again the union of the sacred with the mundane, is not enough. Humans also have to understand that to obtain good harvests, good health, and even a good afterlife, they must behave in a manner that reflects the order and justice of nature. Thus orgiastic behaviour is to be combined with an appreciation of truth, justice and the necessity for just conduct – whether towards the earth or towards fellow human beings. I suggest that the goddesses surveyed show this to be a characteristic of Wisdom.

5. Wisdom in Egypt

'You see me here, Lucius, in answer to your prayer. I am Nature, the universal Mother, mistress of all the elements, primordial child of time, sovereign of all things spiritual, queen of the dead, queen also of the immortals, the single manifestation of all gods and goddesses there are . . . though I am worshipped in many aspects, known by countless names, and propitiated with all manner of different rites yet the whole round earth venerates me.' (Apuleius *The Golden Ass* – the Goddess Isis speaks to Lucius.)[1]

In this chapter I survey a common factor in the long religious history of ancient Egypt. The very long period of some 3000 years, in spite of all the changes that take place in that time throughout, offers us the figure of the Goddess Isis, Mistress of Wisdom, creatrix and sustainer of peoples. I look at Isis and her sister goddesses in the ancient world and also at their later influence. I see in the documents recovered this century from the sands of Egypt, now known as the Gnostic Gospels, which are dated to 200 BCE– 200 CE approximately, a reflection of those ancient Egyptian Goddesses, and also of Hebrew Wisdom, now called Greek Sophia.

Isis, Ma'at and Wisdom
The religion of Isis, Goddess in Egypt from the second millenium BCE, became widespread in the Hellenistic world of the first

centuries of this era. R E Witt (1971) states that: 'She took possession of the traditional centres of Greek worship, Delos, Delphi and Eleusis and she was well known in Northern Greece and Athens. Harbours of Isis were to be found on the Arabia Gulf and the Black Sea . . . she found faithful followers in Gaul, and Spain, Pannonia and Germany. She held sway from Arabia and Asia Minor in the East, to Portugal and Britain in the West. Shrines were hallowed to her in cities large and small: Beneventum, the Pireaus, London.' (p. 21) Witt sees her as 'a formidable foe to Jesus and the oecumencial Paul' (p. 20), as during the formative years of Christianity the religion of Isis was drawing its converts from every corner of the Roman empire. Her priests were dedicated missionaries crusading on hallowed service.

Howard Clark Kee (1980) sums up the attraction of this religion: 'In the Hellenistic period, Isis, whose earlier mythic role was that of consort and rescuer of Osiris (god of the Nile and symbol of fertility of the land) assumed a universal significance as the embodiment of wisdom, as agent of cosmic order, and as saviour of the needy . . . it was in her capacity as goddess of wisdom and as mystic healer of the blind and the ailing that she was revered throughout the Graeco-Roman world and that her influence on both Judaism of the post-exilic period and nascent Christianity is most readily apparent' (p. 145ff.).

The appeal of her religion and of the Goddess herself appeared to lie in a combination of spiritual and material features. She was 'Mistress of Magic' and 'Great Physician', in which aspect she is able to heal Osiris, and to become the mentor of physicians. She goes further for she is able to breathe the breath of life into the nostrils of Osiris' corpse which she has re-assembled to revive him, thus bringing the idea of immortality into the practical sphere. There is the point, emphasised by Grant Showerman (1901) that 'the resurrection of Osiris through the efforts of Isis symbolised the rebirth of the soul and it was this that made the Isis cult the greatest of all Egyptian religions' (p. 302). But although venerated and adored as a means of the soul's salvation, Isis is also very much of this earth.

Plutarch (born 45 CE) refers to her as 'the Mud of the Nile' as well as 'the universal principle of Nature'. He posits Isis as the essence of beneficence as well as its practical application. That she is the actual mud of the Nile makes it clear that she is the very earth itself. Yet she is also the essential spiritual principle. She instructed humans in the arts of agriculture, and she is called 'Mistress of the Seasons, Goddess of Earth and Water, Queen of the Earth'. At the same time she is 'Queen of the Stygian Realms' and 'Protectress of the Dead'.[2] Towards the end of the famous account by Apuleius of the journey of Lucius towards salvation, Isis speaks of its attainment: 'Thou shalt live blessed in this world, thou shall live glorious by my guild and protection, and when after thine allotted space of life thou descendest to hell, there thou shall see me in that subterranean firmament shining . . . and if I perceive that thou art obedient to my commandment and addict to my religion . . . know thou that I alone may prolong thy days above the time that the fates have appointed and ordained.'[3]

Lucius also praises Isis as Goddess of all:

Thee the gods above adore, thee gods below worship. It is thou that whirlest the sphere of heaven, that givest light to the sun, thou governest the universe and tramplest down Tartarus. To thee the stars respond, for thee the seasons return, in thee the gods rejoice, and the elements serve thee. Thy nod the winds blow, the clouds nourish [the earth], the seeds sprout, the buds swell. Before thy majesty the birds tremble as they flit to and from in the sky, and the beasts as they roam the mountains, the serpents hiding in the ground, and the monsters swimming in the deep.[4]

Thus she is creatrix, goddess of nature, giving 'light to the sun', as well as immanent in the world as provider of essential instruction to humans, and in the afterlife as source of immortality to humans and protector of the dead. More, in her aretalogy (hymn of self–praise) dated about 200 CE found in Cyme, she gives fifty-seven descriptions of herself. Twelve are concerned with her activities as creator: 'I divided the earth from heaven, I created the ways of the stars'. Seventeen are concerned with lawmaking and herself as instigator and maintainer of justice and mercy on earth: 'I gave laws to human kind which no one is able to change . . . I made the right strong . . . I decreed truth was to be called beautiful . . . I made nothing more fearsome than an oath . . . I established penalties for those who practice injustice . . .' In an even more down to earth manner, she proclaims 'I arranged for the ten–month child to be brought into the light by the woman' . . . 'I decreed that parents be loved by their children' . . . 'I arranged punishment for unloving parents', and in the world of day-to-day dealings, 'I devised marriage contracts' . . . 'I betrayed the unjust trickster into the hands of those he tricked.' Isis who 'makes the seas rage, and also be gentle' is, of course, 'mistress of all things to do with ships', and finally, when she has declared that she has 'brought islands out of the waves into the light' and is 'mistress of the rains', she made her pronouncement that she is above fate and controls it. 'I overcome Destiny [Fate], those things that are decreed [Fate] harken to me.' Yet the last line praising this creatrix, all powerful deity who makes and rules the world and is as knowledgeable about the individual as about the universe, comes home and sets up a harmonic balance, 'Hail to Egypt who nourished me'.[5]

Isis' power permeates everything. There is no division into 'masculine' or 'feminine' roles, or even any hiatus between a transcendent and an immanent deity. She divides earth and heaven, she overseas childbirth and childcare, she is involved with ships and laws and justice, with rainfall and punishing trickery.

Isis as a figure of Wisdom combines everything within herself.

Alongside her is a sister goddess, often identified with her. She is Ma'at, goddess of truth, right and order. Her name is the same as that of a measure – an ell – of land. The overriding importance of exactness and precision of measurement in the land of the Nile must have been especially felt when every year the river's inundations obliterated the boundary marks between fields. Ptah, lord of the ell, wears a Ma'at emblem, a feather on his head.

Howard Clark Kee (1980) believes that the Egyptians recognised a divine order, established at the time of creation. This order is evident in nature in the orderly phenomenal processes; it is manifest in society as justice, and appears in human life as truth. Ma'at is this order. Thus we understand that she is the embodiment of the powers immanent in the world by which ordered creation functions.

In addition to her function of ensuring precise order in the world and the continuance of the order of nature, Ma'at has the responsibility of judging the souls of the dead, and is so seen depicted in many Egyptian tombs. The heart of the dead person, which symbolises conscience, is balanced on one scale, and on the other Ma'at's feather of justice; sometimes Ma'at herself, is shown balanced on the scale. Ma'at is also inclined to defend the suppliant. The *Book of Breathings* has her saying to the deceased person: 'Hail, thou enterest the Underworld . . . the Goddess of Justice and Truth maketh speech on they behalf.' The soul then makes a Negative Confession: 'I have not committed iniquity . . . I have not oppressed the poor . . . I have not defaulted . . . I have not caused the slave to be ill-treated . . . I have not in aught diminished the supplies in thy temples . . . I have not murdered . . . I have not made any to weep . . . I have not falsified the beam of the balance . . .'[6] The Negative Confession embodies ideals of human justice and links them both to a very human compassion and to exactness and precision in every-day dealings.

While Ma'at links exactness and right dealing with the judgement of the dead and the after life, Isis continues her work in the practical world. She has among her many titles that of Goddess of Life and Healing, and was also Mistress of Agriculture, credited with the discovery of wheat and barley. She declares: 'I was the first to reveal to mortals the mysteries of wheat and corn.' She was named 'Lady of the Green Things', 'Green Goddess whose colour is like unto the greeness of earth', 'Lady of Bread', 'Lady of Beer', 'Lady of Abundance'. She is called 'cornfield', and is described as 'She who has given birth to the fruits of the earth'. Among her many titles are 'Queen of the Field', 'Goddess of Earth and Water', 'Magician'.

As well as these attributes Isis is Mother of Medicine.[7] In her service Egyptian women trained in medicine in the House of Life in Heliopolis. They are shown in illustrations conducting surgical operations. They are particularly concerned with gynaecology and had a wide knowledge of this subject.[8] Much space in the papyri is devoted to pregnancy tests and management, as well as to methods of contraception. The temple priestesses appeared to run a birth control clinic; there they prepared for their patients a pessary made from crocodile dung. Pat Whiting, a modern commentator, remarks: 'This kind of pessary would have had a dual contraceptive effect – that of blocking the cervix, and also a spermicidal action as the warmth of the body released acid from the pessary.'[9] This, as well as another kind of pessary made from acacia leaves, released lactic acid which has spermicidal properties. As Whiting points out, such properties were not rediscovered until the end of the nineteenth century of our own era.

We are reminded here of the Wisdom of BWS, where she taught humankind 'the nature of animals . . . the varieties of plants, and the virtues of roots', among all the rest of the 'unerring knowledge of what exists' that she was willing to share with us (BWS 7:20). Isis, Ma'at and Sophia are Wisdom goddess siblings in the world of

Egypt in intertestamental times. They are witnesses to the longevity of the concept of female deity.

It may be no coincidence that contemporary documents have revealed so much of an alternative religious system which grew for a time side-by-side with early Christianity. Such texts, scanning a period of four hundred years, were buried by so-called heretical groups of Christian hermits in the sands of Egypt in the fourth century of our era.

Wisdom, the Gnostic dimension

Material discovered in Egypt at a place called Nag Hammadi in 1945 brought an entirely new dimension from out of the desert to the religious scene surrounding the birth and infant growth of Christianity. These were documents which have been popularly known as 'The Gnostic Gospels'.[10] Until this discovery, little was known of Gnosticism or Gnosis, which was familiar only through isolated texts and through the attacks on them by a number of the early Christian Fathers. Today, there is a whole school of scholarship devoted to deciphering and interpreting the material. Elaine Pagels (1979) and Rose Arthur (1984) have illuminated feminist understanding of some of the difficulties.

There is strong evidence that Gnosis or Gnosticism was prevalent throughout the ancient world on a far more comprehensive basis than was previously surmised, and that it was not simply a breakaway Christian sect. The secret knowledge that is both Gnosis and Gnosticism involved the figure of Sophia, Wisdom, as well as other female synonyms for Wisdom: Ennoia and Protennoia. To place Sophia of the Gnostics in context, it is appropriate to turn to G W Macrae whose study of *The Jewish Background of the Gnostic Sophia Myth* (1970) provides a starting point. Macrae first discusses the background of the Sophia figure in Gnostic literature and points to the disputes. Sophia, he suggests may be a 'Gnostic adaptation of the personified Wisdom of Jewish apocalyptic' (p. 86) or influenced by a more Ancient Near–Eastern myth; or Judaism and Gnosticism may have a common background but with essentially independent traditions. He lists fifteen similarities between Jewish Wisdom and Gnostic Sophia. These are that Wisdom, whether Hebrew or Gnostic is (a) personal, (b) joined in intimate union with God, (c) brought forth from, or the beginning, (d) dwells in the clouds, (e) attends God's throne or is herself enthroned (f) is identified with a Holy Spirit, (g) was 'at least instrumental in the creation of the world', (h) communicates Wisdom and revelation to humanity, (i) descends into the world of humans, (j) re–ascends to her celestial home, (k) protected, delivered and strengthened Adam, (l) is referred to as 'sister', (m) is associated with a seven–fold cosmic structure, (n) is identified with life and (o) is a tree of life (pp. 88–94). Macrae comments that this long list of parallels makes it virtually impossible to rule out all influence of Jewish Wisdom on the Gnostic Sophia. His essential point is that Gnostic Sophia and associated female divine figures have close commonality with Hochma. While the Gnostics formulated various theological systems around these figures, their similarity of origin and characteristics of Sophia with Hochma is too noticeable to be ignored.

Another suggestion has been made that a different female figure in Gnostic speculation is nearer than Sophia to Jewish Wisdom. This is Barbelo. She is described in the Gnostic Apocryphon of John. (James Robinson (ed.) *The Nag Hammadi Library in English*, 1977.)[11] In this document the world, which is evil, is set against a Supreme Spirit who is described as 'invisible spirit of whom it is not right to think of him as a god or something similar. For he is more than a god . . . he is eternal . . . he is total perfection . . . ineffable . . . unnameable . . . he is immeasurable light which is pure, holy and immaculate' (p. 106).

From this Supreme Spirit came Barbelo. 'His thought performed a deed and she came forth, namely she who had appeared before him in the shine of his light. This is the first power which was before all of them and which came forth from his mind' (p. 101). There is a clear comparison here with Proverbs 8:22 where God created Wisdom, 'the first of his acts of old'. In this Gnostic document the female is created by the male. It is his 'thought' rather than a physical act which created Barbelo.

'She is the fore thought of the All, the light shone like his light . . . the glory of Barbelo, the perfect glory in the aeons, she glorified the virginal spirit and it was she who praised him, because thanks to him she had come forth. This was the first thought, the image; she became the womb of everything, for it is she who is prior to them all' (p. 101).

Barbelo requests foreknowledge, indestructibility, eternal life and truth, to all of which the Supreme Spirit gives his assent (pp. 107–8). Barbelo then conceives 'through the pure light which surrounds the invisible with his spark'. The child is the 'only begotten of the Mother–Father. It is the only offspring, the only begotten one of the Father, the pure light' (p. 108). The thought 'which brought forth Barbelo' is Ennoia; the foreknowledge she requested and was granted was Protennoia and the child is the only begotten (*monogones*). Both Ennoia and Protennoia appear as divine female knowledge; Protennoia appears in the texts with her own section, as seen below. Her name indicates 'primal thought', and that of Ennoia means 'understanding'.

   These personages ring with many echoes of the Wisdom we have already encountered in BWS and proverbs. In this document Barbelo is the highest aeon, reflecting the light and eternity of the Supreme Spirit; created by him, she becomes the 'womb of the world' with no pejorative associations attached. She is contrasted with 'our sister' Sophia who created and who was at fault in her manner of creation.

In these accounts of two female entities associated with Wisdom one – Barbelo – is created by God and remains perfectly pure and good, becoming the womb of the world. The other, Sophia, because she created her child autonomously and disregarded the male, is shown to have done a wicked thing, and one for which she must suffer and repent, and from which, although forgiven, she never recovers her former place. Her 'fall' and her journeys through repentance and suffering have been compared with the fall of Eve. The idea of the female declaring and pursuing an independent course from that of the male is delineated as the origin of evil in the world.

These two contrasting aspects of a divine female figure have been discussed by Kurt Rudolph (1984). In his study, *Gnosis, the nature and history of an ancient religion*, of Barbelo he says, '[she] represents the female aspect of the Father and is a kind of Gnostic Mother Goddess. Probably she was from the beginning one person with Sophia' (p. 80). For Rudolph, however, Sophia's uncontrolled passion was a violation of the 'unity of bisexuality'. He comments that: 'for the gnostics, bisexuality is an expression of perfection; it is only the earthly creation which leads to a separation of the original divine unity' (p. 80). Sophia's violation of this has 'fateful consequences for herself and the cosmos'.

I dispute this however. There is another Nag Hammadi document which draws together the two aspects of the female. This is the 'Thunder Perfect Mind'.[12] Rudolph states: 'there is reference to two sides of a female figure . . . behind her is evidently concealed Sophia, but also the soul, both in their manners of existence: as perfect divine and redeeming power, and as fallen phenomenon exposed to deficiency' (p. 81). Yes, but here is shown a total, wholy female figure, containing all within herself. Here are some of the lines of the text:

Thunder Perfect Mind

I am the first and the last
I am the honoured one and the scorned one
I am the whore and the holy one
I am the wife and the virgin
I am the mother and the daughter
I am the members of my mother
I am the barren one
and many are her sons
I am the mother of my father
and the sister of my husband
and he is my offspring

I am the silence that is incomprehensible
and the idea whose remembrance is frequent
and the word whose appearance is multiple
I am the utterance of my name

I am knowledge I am ignorance
I am shame I am boldness
I am shameless and am ashamed
I am strength I am fear
Give heed to me
I am the one who is disgraced and the great one

I am she who does not keep festival
and I am she whose festivals are many

I am the wisdom of the Greeks
and the knowledge of the barbarians
I am the one whose image is great in Egypt
and the one who has no image among the
     barbarians
I am the one who has been hated everywhere
and who has been loved everywhere

> I am the one whom they call Life
> and you have called Death

Here we have an amazing picture of a female divinity whose place in the world is one of paradox and opposites, who is loved yet reviled; who points to a polarisation between the 'they' who call her 'Life' and the 'You' who call her death. She has all within her, she 'is and is not'; everything that can be. Far from being apart from the fear and misery of the world she is part of it, endures it, yet also remains its opposite. I find her a glorious image to reflect upon; we are all her, and she us.

Let us also look at a sister document. This is a speech by Protennoia,[13] 'First Thought', a female divine being.

She begins with a statement of her position in the cosmos.

I am Protennoia, the Thought that dwells in the Light.
I am the movement that dwells in the All,
she in whom the All takes its stand,
the first-born among those who came to exist,
she who exists before the All . . .
Called by three names, although she dwells alone (since she is
    perfect).
I am invisible within the thought of the Invisible One,
I am revealed in the immeasurable, ineffable, I am
    incomprehensible, dwelling in the incomprehensible.
I move in every creature . . .
I dwell in those who came to be.
I move in everyone and I delve into them all.
I walk uprightly and those who sleep, I awaken.
I am in the Invisible One within the All.

It is I who counsel those who are hidden since I know the All
    that exists in it.
I am numberless beyond everyone, I am immeasurable, ineffable.
Whenever I wish, I shall reveal myself of my own accord.
I am the head of the All.
I exist before the All and I am the All, since I exist in everyone.

This is another moving account of a supreme female divinity. Rose
Arthur (1984) draws attention to the Protennoia to show the
contrasts and unity of opposites declared in her position:

I am the thought of the Father
I am mother and the light which she appointed as Virgin
I am their Father and I shall tell you an ineffable Mystery[14]

Again we see a 'Mother–Father' figure in divinity. Rose Arthur
writes: 'The goddess of the Trimorphic Protennoia truly belongs to
a higher order of pantheism. She partakes of opposites as does the
goddess of the Thunder. She is frequently called the voice but she is
silence as well. Although apparently the Mother of the Universe,
she also says that she is the Father as well as the Son' (p. 168).

Rose Arthur has chosen eight Nag Hammadi documents to
illustrate her view that there is a relative decline in the prestige of
personified Sophia (Wisdom) from the earlier non-Christian
documents to the later Christianised and Christian documents. She
raises questions about Sophia, seeking to show that in the
documents in which Sophia is a personage within Jewish or Gnostic
myth she is not a tragic figure in need of male redemption. Rather,
the fallen Sophia appears to be a specifically Christian motif. She
believes that the Thunder and the Trimorphic Protennoia are the
high points of feminism among the Nag Hammadi documents, and
that they seem to stem from a pre-Christian Barbelo cult featuring
a lofty pantheistic vitalism.

Elaine Pagels (1978) is another scholar who has written widely on the Gnostic texts. She believes the Thunder and Protennoia 'celebrate the feminine powers of Thought, Intelligence and foresight' (p. 55). Of the androgyny or, rather, gynandry,[15] described in the Thunder, Pagels asks 'What does the use of such symbolism imply for the understanding of human nature?' (p. 56), and then relates the material to the Genesis creation story, suggesting that Genesis 1:26–27 'narrates an androgynous creation'. She examines the thought of some Gnostics that 'humanity, which formed according to the image and likeness of God (Father and Mother) was masculo–feminine' (p. 56). Pagels also quotes Theodotus (CE 160) who states that Genesis 1:26–27 means that 'the male and female elements together constitute the finest production of the Mother, Wisdom'. Pagels comments: 'Gnostic sources which describe God as a dyad whose nature includes both masculine and feminine elements often give a similar description of human nature' (p. 57).

Both Pagels and Arthur agree that the two texts are descriptive of feminine divinity, while Rudolph's pointer to the unity of opposites confirms a relationship with what he calls 'the oldest and most important elements in the structure of Gnosis' (p. 83).

There is a huge gap between these concepts and those of the 'fall of Sophia' outlined by the sect of Gnostics known as Valentinians. Before describing this process I need to reiterate that my understanding of the Thunder is not a dualism contrasting the perfect with the deficient but is a total concept where examples of divinity and human experience are presented as facets of each other, expressed through the female.

The date of the Thunder is apposite when considering the text. Arthur believes that while the extant copy is dated to the fourth century it is probably earlier and perhaps even pre-Christian (p. 157). In this connection she quotes the view of Quispel (1975) who has commented on survivals in the Nag Hammadi Library of very old views, which he believes were suppressed and can help us recover unknown and forgotten aspects of Judaism.

The 'Thunder' combines elements of Jewish, Christian and Hellenistic religions. With the first line we are reminded of the statement by the Lord God in the Book of Revelation (1:8, 21:6., 22:13), 'I am the First and the Last', also resonant with the inscription above the temple of Isis and Neith at Sais, Egypt: 'I am all that ever was, is or will be.' This is a declaration of eternity and divinity.

The following lines describe contrasting human conditions – whore and holy one, wife and virgin, mother and daughter, barren with many sons – which can be construed as a totality of experience. We are reminded of earlier goddesses, for example the lady Anat,[16] who with many lovers retained or regained her virginity annually; or who was both mother and daughter; the 'mother of my father, and sister of my husband . . . and he is my offspring' remind us of the Nature Mother–Father figure previously described; of the wife–sister relationship of biblical female personages such as Sarah and Rebecca for example, (Genesis 12:14, 20:12). 'The whore and the holy one' certainly evoke memories of the *quedeshim*, the 'holy ones', servants of the temple who performed acts of sacred prostitution in the furtherance of a fertile and prosperous society.[17]

She who is both 'the silence that is incomprehensible' and the 'word whose appearance is multiple' and the 'utterance of my name' brings forward twin concepts of divine power – through silence and utterance of the word, and in letting her name be known she shares her power with humans. She who is 'the wisdom of the Greeks and the knowledge of the barbarians'; who has been hated and loved everywhere, recalls Isis, the many-named Goddess revered throughout the known world of that time; while the one 'whom they call life and you have called death' can be seen to be intimately connected with the Sophia who starts as giver of life –

and then by the Valentinians is held to have caused the fall and brought evil to the world.

The 'Thunder' text would appear to make a definite statement about a Wisdom divinity, with many echoes of Hochma and the Sophia of BWS while also picking up a relationship with the earlier goddesses of the Ancient Near East. The Goddess demonstrates an attitude to female divinity that may even link her with the far-off figure Tiamat, whose characteristic was totality and wholeness, a Chaos which contained All.

Rose Arthur's examination of the contrast between non-Christian and Christian views of Sophia expressly emphasises that 'the Christianised erring Sophia . . . appears to be a re-mythologisation as well as a devaluation of the creative female principle of the universal goddess of the Hellenistic world' (p. 96), and points out that: 'in the documents in which Sophia is a personage within Jewish or Gnostic myth she is not a tragic figure in need of male redemption; rather, the fallen Sophia appears to be a specifically Christian soteriological motif' (p. 4).

Arthur has summarised the Christianised texts in which Sophia is fallen and is in need of salvation through the male. These include Exegesis on the Soul, where the Father assists her when fallen into adultery by turning her sexual organs, exposed like male genitals, back to the inside; she is then able to 'receive her consort . . . and produce good children' (p. 4). In the 'Sophia of Jesus Christ', the feminine element is 'inferior and in need of the great light of the male' (p. 5), while the 'Hypostasis of the Archons' has varied a previous account (on the 'Origin of the World') of Sophia as a saviour figure. She is linked to the 'Mother of the Abyss' and creates the 'foolish Samauel, Ialdebaoth'.

Extracting information concerning the position of female divinity and her relationship to humanity from the many faceted mass of Gnostic material is of expanding interest to many feminist researchers. Perceptions of Sophia and other Wisdom figures vary from Female Divinity to Fallen Woman; from a source of universal religious symbol for the soul's journey to apologetic for Christianised dogma concerning the Fall and the origin of evil; from feminist appreciation, not only of female divinity and spirituality but also of an egalitarianism between the sexes in Gnostic circles, to a concentration on the disobedience of Sophia and her necessary subjection to male dominance.

The Apocryphon of John[18] is concerned with the action of Sophia who conceived and brought to birth a child without the consent of her consort. The moral appears to be that if a female acts without male approval the result is faulty.

And the Sophia of the Epinoia being an aeon, conceived a thought from herself with the reflection of the invisible Spirit and foreknowledge. She wanted to bring forth a likeness out of herself without the consent of the Spirit – he had not approved – and without her consort and without his consideration. And though the personage of her maleness had not approved . . . she had thought without the consent of the Spirit and the knowledge of her agreement, [yet] she brought forth. And because of the invincible power that is in her, thought did not remain idle and a thing came out of her which was imperfect and different from her appearance, because she had created it without her consort. And it was dissimilar to the likeness of its mother for it had another form. She cast it away from her, outside that place, that no one of the immortal ones might see it, for she had created it in ignorance. And she surrounded it with a luminous cloud, and she placed a throne in the middle of the cloud that no one might see it except the holy Spirit who is called the mother of the living. And she called his name Yaltabaoth.[19]

It is important to note that the 'thing' which she brought forth was imperfect, and the tractate continues with a description of her son's imperfect creation of the world, leading to the evil within it. This son, Yaltabaoth, 'possesses himself of the Mother's light and called himself God' (p. 111). But the world he created was 'deficient', God was 'arrogant' and 'ignorant', the mother recognises that it is her sin of conceiving without consent and aid of her consort that has produced this imperfection, and she 'repents with much weeping' (p. 112). She was then 'taken up', but not to her own abode, 'until she had corrected her deficiency'. The offspring of the Mother who created without male consent and co-operation is deformed and deficient, leading to a deficient world; Sophia needs to weep and to be punished.

Further, there is an identification of an imperfect creator and a deficient world with the action of Sophia–Wisdom. In earlier texts Wisdom creates and sustains the world and brings the light of her teaching and her spirit to it. Now, although still integral to the world, she has changed from beneficence to error, and her error is reproduced in the cosmos. She is not condemned entirely, but her salvation is dependent on her repentance and on the male deity's charity. But she stays, forever, in a lower and less esteemed position than formerly.

At this point it is possible to trace the significant part of the trajectory that Wisdom has performed. In the BWS Wisdom starts as an identification of the Spirit of God, is described as an effulgence of eternal light, the mother of all things, creator, ruler, and the one who dwells in the cosmos and orders all things well. From there, she moves into the world, and the author attempts to grab her for his own benefit, requiring that she shall bring him personal success and grandeur. The transit of Wisdom continues when she ceases to be universal, and the book speaks of her paying particular attention to the care and salvation of the Hebrew people. Eventually, in the closing stages of the work, BWS refers not to Wisdom, but to God.

The next stage on her journey is chronicled by the authors of the

Book of Enoch and Baruch, and Ben Sirach, as well as by Philo and other Jewish writers of the period, followed by rabbinic tradition. Wisdom becomes the Torah.

It is possible to see within the Judaism of the period a conflict concerning Wisdom herself, a conflict which may also be perceived in Jewish struggles to define monotheism and to discard all forms of female deity.

The Gnostic philosophical conflicts were eventually dissolved in the acid of history. The monks who buried their scrolls in the desert at Nag Hammadi in Egypt in the fourth-century CE were on the losing side. It was only through the polemic against them on the part of the Church Fathers that Gnostic beliefs and insights were later known at all. (Although there is some evidence that minority neo-Gnostic sects continued and renewed themselves for many hundreds of years.)

Yet in Valentinian Gnosticism we see the ground work that the Church was later to build into a mighty edifice. The divine female is not only demoted from her previously consubstantial position with God but is the source of the error and deficiency of the world itself. Consequently her rejection not only brings her humiliation, but much worse to follow.

The explanation of the imperfections of the world is at hand – they are her fault. With the biblical story of Eve to reinforce this view, the scene is set within Christianity not only for an anti-material world viewpoint but for punishment of the female who is said to have caused the harm. Further, since the world and the material encompass the mischief, a separation takes place between the divine within the world and the divine outside it. The Gnostic sages may nurture a secret spark of the divine, but pluck it away from nature to a purely spiritual concept. Nature, always identified with the female, also becomes part and parcel of her deficiency. She is to be ruled; she may not act autonomously. No longer a divine guide and teacher, Nature is to be controlled and dominated; the spiritual has moved away from her, and from women generally.

Isis and Ma'at are forgotten, it seems, together with the ancient Egyptian heritage of the divine female who was both Lady of Heaven and the mud of the Nile.

6. Wisdom Goddesses in the Ancient Near East

The position of the goddesses of early antiquity, in this context 5000 BCE to 2000 BCE, is contained within the concept of their identity with Nature. Early people saw the earth, the sun, the sea, as life-producing, life-enhancing and life–destroying. From the earth in particular came all that was needed to nurture and sustain life. The earth accepted death by whatever means, encapsulated it and produced renewal of life. The goddesses seemed a reflection of this process and were venerated accordingly, some being particularly associated with creation and instruction.

Common to all the goddesses is the notion that the cosmos is born from them. They are the givers of life, and the source not only of the cosmos but also of other divinities and creatures. They have the gift of being able continually to create new beings. They are also sustainers. There is a clear comparison with the woman who gives birth and then mysteriously produces the vital fluid that will keep new beings alive.

Throughout antiquity wisdom goddesses were associated with the earth on which all life depended – but not solely on the earth. In very early times it was observed that women's menstrual periods coincided with the cycle of lunations in the sky.[1] This enigma appears to have powerfully borne out the idea of female divinities encompassing not only the earth but also the moon. In some cultures the sun, too, was seen as female and this idea was encapsulated in the notion of the 'Queen of Heaven'.[2]

Thus we have a picture of a divine Mother, or Mothers, who give birth to the universe, and maintain life and know its secrets. They are goddesses of the earth, the moon, the sun, rhythmically renewing themselves; creators of the pantheon of the gods in the heavens. They are also Ladies of the chaotic, formless sea, source of life and living creatures.

These goddesses are the originators of the whole round of creation, to be seen in the earth and heavens and also in the oceans. Humankind, in recognising this divinity, also has intimations of its own shortcomings and ignorance. Only the Goddess who is Nature herself understands her own ways, such as the cycle of the seasons, the courses of the stars, the progression – as it seemed – of the sun, and of the seas and the winds that so greatly affected the puny lives of human beings.

These ancient goddesses who create, maintain and renew are the sources of wisdom and understanding. Humans may be instructed by them, they share this knowledge, they teach the world knowledge of its own nature, and by the proper application of this knowledge humans are helped to survive and renew themselves both physically and spiritually. The arts that enhance life – agriculture, medicine, domestication of animals, handicrafts, architecture and building, meteorology, mathematics and astronomy – are encapsulated by the goddesses and brought to humans for their edification.

In the Ancient Near East background to the bible we can recognise these goddesses as they show three distinct traits. They are addressed as authors of creation and as Wisdom deities; they are addressed initially as creator deities, with the title of Wisdom added later, they demonstrate the characteristics of Wisdom, for example, healing, inventiveness, teaching, even though they are not specifically addressed as Wisdom.

A Wisdom goddess occurs in early Mesopotamia, in the ancient Babylonian Epic of Gilgamesh,[3] the hero who sets out to obtain immortal life. Pursuing this quest he finds the Paradise Garden, which he may enter only because of divine blood inherited through his mother. There he finds the Goddess of Life and Wisdom, Siduri Sabatu, seated 'by the throne of the sea' and underneath a vine. He asks her for the gift of life. She is the 'Keeper of the Fruit of Life' and she sits in a garden of 'dazzling beauty'. Similarities with the Genesis story of the Garden of Eden are immediately apparent, as well as great differences. In the bible, the fruit of the Tree of Life is not in the keeping of a goddess (apparently), and eating the other fruit – that of the knowledge of good and evil – is said to bring death, not life. But we can certainly understand that the changes made by the writers of the bible narratives specifically deny the goddess, and in the bible we are told that Wisdom–Hochma is a tree of life (Proverbs 3:18).

A famous commentator on the religion of the Ancient Near East, F N Albright, in his paper entitled 'Goddess of life and wisdom' (1920), has taken the figure of Siduru Sabatu and traced echoes of her throughout biblical and post-biblical times; he sees her in Homer's Odyssey, where he points out that the nymph Kalypso is also able to bestow immortality and 'dwells veiled, surrounded by grapeladen vines at the source of four streams (p. 258).

Siduri Sabatu has also been described as a 'barmaid', by scholars anxious not to take her too seriously. This is a reference to her association with the vine. Yet the vine appears throughout ancient history and the bible texts as a symbol of life and prosperity. So important is this symbol that we find Jesus himself declaring 'I am the true Vine'. Wisdom herself has been described as a vine by the inter-testamental writer Ben Sirach (Ecclesiasticus) in his panygyric on her qualities (Ecclesiasticus 24: 13–17). Siduri Sabatu sat in the Paradise Garden of the Babylonians. Albright traced her through mythology, changing with the centuries but never forgotten, until she reaches the Gnostic Barbelo, and suggests that this name is related to the Aramaic *bulbala* (chaos). And we can see affinities with the major Mesopotamian creation and wisdom goddess Tiamat.

Tiamat, Mummu and the Formless Creating Sea

Among the ancient cuneiform poems that have been discovered in the last century and a half, the Babylonian Creation Epic (dated about 2500 BCE) caused excitement among biblical commentators in our late nineteenth and early twentieth centuries. They were able to use this poem to show extraordinary similarities with the Genesis creation story. Today feminist theologians use it to review material that until recently has been overlooked or discounted. The creation myth, named the 'Enuma Elish' (When on high), like Genesis begins with an account of pre-creation.

When on high were not raised the heavens
And also below on earth a plant had not grown up
Alone there existed primordial Apsu, who engendered them
Only Mummu and Tiamat who brought them all forth
Their waters could mix together in a single stream
In the depths of their waters were the gods created[4]

There are references to 'the chaos Tiamat' who was 'the producing mother of all of them'. She is referred to as a sea monster, a chaos monster and 'the deep'. There is a Babylonian depiction of her as a dragon.

The Epic describes her story. Creation of the gods comes first, from her body; then there is dissension between them. Eventually her descendant Marduk with his various friends manages to kill her and tear her apart. He gives the various divisions of her body to his friends and each of these becomes master of some part of the universe created from Tiamat.

Whether Tiamat 'alone' created the world, or with the help of Mummu, an enigmatic figure – sometimes female sometimes male – and with Apsu, god of the sweet waters as engendering father, depends on the text. Mummu, whose name is related to the word for mother in almost all languages, appears to be an aspect of Tiamat described as a 'chaos monster'. The primaeval sea, her home, has been understood by numerous ancient writers to be the origin of life.

The concept of Tiamat as a dragon indicates a vision of totality, thus encompassing the four elements – a dragon is amphibian, living in both sea and on land; it breathes fire and air. The formless deep which is the body of Tiamat contains everything within it necessary for life – and she herself creates various forms and monsters during the battle with Marduk.

In addition to this totality – a wholeness without form – Tiamat is described as 'holding the Tablets of Destiny' which appear to symbolise supreme knowledge of the world and its future.

The Enuma Elish describes how the god Marduk assembles a force to overcome Tiamat and Mummu, in order to become lord of the universe and possess the Tablets. After a horrific battle he is successful. How he kills Tiamat and the way he disassembles the various parts of her body and builds the different areas of the universe from them have been widely commented upon, as has the possible relationship of Tiamat to the Hebrew *Tehom* (the 'void', Genesis 1:2), and the idea that she was an alternative source of creation which must, in the Hebrew bible, be shown to have been vanquished.[5]

Until recently, there was general consensus among scholars that the dismembering of the 'chaos dragon' brought about what Jacobsen (1946) called 'the fundamentals of world order'. The separation of her various parts and labelling them, as areas of the world, and putting them under the dominion of various lords has, Jacobsen suggests, contributed to the orderly control of Nature (pp. 180–83). Today, this is no longer a unanimous view, owing to reappraisal by female scholars. Mary Daly (1979) uncompromisingly names the Tiamat–Marduk story as a 'sado-ritual syndrome enactment of goddess murder'. Ruby Rohrlich-Leavitt (1977), documenting the consolidation of the state into the hands of a male elite in Sumer during the fourth millenium BCE draws attention to the relevance of the murder of Tiamat and its methods to ways in which force and violence were used to enslave women of the period.

In fact, Tiamat stands out not, as Jacobsen believes, as a symbol of passivity and inaction, but of wholeness and totality. She is the creator goddess from whom all beings emerge, and, further, she is the keeper of the tablets of destiny. The later Babylonian priest Berosus, naming her as the 'woman Omoroka', praises her as Mistress of Incantations and Mistress of the Moon. 'The Coil of Tiamat' is part of certain Kabbalistic doctrines, reflecting echoes of ancient mysteries. N K Sandars (1971) points out that the Babylonian hymns, whilst recounting Tiamat's defeat, also intimate that she is never really destroyed. The Hymn of Praise exhorts Tiamat to 'recede into the future . . . till time of old'. Durdin-Robertson (1975) reflects that the zoomorphic beings of Tiamat's creation are probably considered to be prototypes of the present Western zodiac, and connect with the well-known Chaldean (Babylonian) skills of astrology and astronomy.

Thus Tiamat comes well within the definition of a Wisdom goddess; creator of the gods, possessor and keeper of the Tablets of Destiny, repository of magical and intellectual powers, and with even a hint of immortality. That she lives in, and is godess of, salt water gives the idea of the sea as the source of life.

Nisaba–Nidaba, goddess of the reeds, writing, music and mathematics
Where Tiamat is the great creating goddess, who contains everything including destiny within herself, Nisaba–Nidaba is a

prototype of the wisdom goddesses who, being nature themselves, share their knowledge and essence with the creation. She is a Sumerian deity of the third to second millenium BCE, and is goddess of the reeds. Jacobsen in Frankfort (1946) writes:

It is quite clear that . . . in themselves they [the reeds] were never divine. Any individual reed counted merely as a plant, a thing, and so did all reeds. The concrete individual reed, however, had wonderful qualities . . . it was capable of amazing things such as the music which would come out of a shepherd's pipe, or signs which would take form under the scribe's reed and make a story or a poem . . . these powers combined into a divine personality, that of the Goddess Nidaba. If she were not near, the shepherd could not soothe the heart with music from his reed pipe. To her the scribe would give priase when a difficult piece of writing had come out from under his stylus and he saw it to be good. The goddess was thus the power in all reeds: She was one with every reed in the sense that she permeated it as an animating and characterising agent; but she did not lose her identity in that of the concrete phenomenon, and was not limited by any or even all existing reeds. She is shown in human form as a venerable matron, but the reeds also are there. They sprout from her shoulders – are bodily one with her and seem to derive directly from her (pp. 132–33).

Nisaba also appears as the Goddess of Wisdom from whom the hero takes counsel in the Sumerian heroic poem 'Enmerkar and the Lord of Aratta'. She is referred to as goddess of writing and accounts in another Sumerian hymn. One of her titles is 'She who teaches the decrees'. Others refer to her as an architect and the 'most learned of deities'.

In an account of the 'Vision of Gudea' we are introduced to a goddess presenting herself in a dream to the king who wishes to build a temple. She is Nisaba, who holds a reed stylus and a writing tablet. She makes a drawing of the temple in his presence. He is later able to build the edifice completely successfully, using the plans she created.[6]

That Nisaba has not been entirely forgotten is manifest in the title of the religious Texts Translation series of a present-day European learned press, E J Brill of Leiden, Holland. Named *Nisaba*, the inscription on the title pages of the series reads: 'Nisaba is the name of the Sumerian goddess of vegetation and writing whose symbol is the calamus (the instrument with which the writing was impressed on the soft clay) on an altar. The Sumarians were the first people to use writing for keeping accounts, and by extension, *inter alia*, as a substitute for the oral tradition. For this reason, the goddess has been given pride of place here.'

The identification of the deity with herself as a divine entity, with the material of creation, and her inspirational powers for human beings appears to be a paradigm of ancient wisdom goddesses. These goddesses were also the source of useful knowledge. Yet their activities were never wholly mundane. Always divine beings, they had powers of life and death. They knew the secrets of poisons as well as of cures, and as immanent beings of the sun and moon they could burn and freeze as well as heal. They were prepared to share knowledge with human beings. Throughout the ancient writings we find temples of healing which are also temples of learning and instruction.

Gula, queen of physicians, lady of healing
Gula, also known as Gula–Bau, is a goddess of great longevity, whose worship is recorded from the oldest Babylonian period 3000 BCE through the times of Hammurabi 1500 BCE down to the reign of Nebuchadnezzar 600 BCE. Another name of this goddess was Nin-din-dung, signifying the lady who restores to life. The designation well emphasises the chief trait of Gula-Bau which is that of physician. She was spoken of as 'the great physician'. The

temple of Gula in Babylon, says S H Hooke (1953), functioned partially as a hospital of the goddess Gula, who was much sought after as a healer. The elaborate arrangements of corridors and side chambers (of the temple) suggests provision for the attendance of the sick and for the ministrations of the priests (p. 48).

Gula's medical and surgical arrangements were a prominent part of Babylonian life for over 1000 years. Records exist of treatment methods which antedate the Laws of Hammurabi (1800 BCE), which codified the respect and payments due to doctors. The cities of Uruk and Borsippa were particularly notable for their schools of medicine. Normal remedies included the straightforward use of beneficent herbs, and surgery, leavened by more magical means. Incantations, spells and, above all, the calling on the name of the divine healers were powerful ingredients in the cure. Gula-Bau 'mother of humankind' and the 'great physician' was chief of the healing deities. Her symbol was the 'Ningizzida' with which she was usually portrayed. This is the staff round which are entwined two serpents, which became the caduceus (wand) of Mercury, the symbol of a physician, from then to this day.

It was said of Gula-Bau, Queen of Physicians, that in her the internal fire burnt, both of vital heat and painful fever. The diseases associated with fever only the Lady of Healing could assuage. She was further associated with heat by the layout of the corridors of her temple – which were in an eight-rayed shape for reflecting the sun at its height.[7] A ninth-century BCE cylinder seal shows a deer and a dying man in a reed hut with attendant figures, and dogs sacred to Gula who is obviously in medical attendance. Her position as 'mother of humankind' and her titles of Lady of Healing and Queen of Physicians indicate her status as a Wisdom Goddess.

Other Mesopotamian healing and wisdom goddesses
That Babylonia and ancient Mesopotamia were the homes of healing, astronomy and mathematics is generally accepted. It is

useful here to pick out a few other goddesses associated with these sciences, as well as of magic. The epics tell us that Ninhursag, mother goddess, created eight goddesses of healing, one for each major part of the human body. The goddess specially designed to care for the body's ribs was Ninti. According to the Epic of Creation, she healed the rib of the god Enki (himself a wisdom god) in the Paradise Garden. The biblical echoes are strong and the Hebrew creation stories show a reversal of roles.

Inanna, Lady of Heaven, held comprehensive away over the pantheon of the Ancient Near East for many centuries, if not millenia. As 'Queen of Heaven and Earth', she was entitled to hold the insignia and regalia of the *me* – the insignia described as 'that set of universal and immutable rules and limits which had to be observed by gods and men (sic) alike . . . The *me* keep the cosmic entities and cultural phenomena operating continuously and harmoniously without conflict or confusion.'[8]

When Inanna prepared to descend to the underworld, the myth tells us:

she gathered together the seven *me*
She took them in her hands,
with the *me* in her possession, she prepared herself

Thus equipped with the means of keeping the world order in being, 'she took the lapis measuring rod and line in her hand'.[9] These tools indicate the goddess' sovereignty over calculation, computing, building and measuring. As with her Egyptian counterpart, the goddess Ma'at, whose name denotes a measure of land, Inanna's association with measuring also carries with it the connotation of justice, and by extension, truth, right and wisdom. What is measured correctly establishes a true picture; measurement provides exact methods that can be checked to discover falsity.

In one myth Inanna needs to have the experience of descent and sojourn in the underworld, where the dead live and are judged. Similarly, Ma'at, goddess of the underworld, judges the souls who descend there, by virtue of her ability to weigh and measure exactly. The practical association of day-to-day activities with abstract virtues is typical of the 'wholeness' of a world view aligned to the goddesses. Correct behaviour, good day-to-day practice, and divine judgement and justice are intimately linked to the concept of a deity who is not only creator and earth goddess but ruler of the underworld and judge of the dead.[10]

Inanna's possession of the measuring rod and line, as goddess of practical exactness and of the *me*, the divine symbols of order and sustenance of the world, indicates that she holds the universe together. There is no separation between the mundane and the divine. This echoes the wholeness and totality of Tiamat.

Canaanite myths and the natural world

While the deities are responsible for the creation of the universe and of life, in antiquity it was thought that humankind had to join with the supernatural powers to keep creation in being. Suppose the goddesses and gods tire, look away to another creation in another part of the universe, become diverted or just go to sleep? Would then the rain not flow, the mist not rise, the sun cease to move, and the earth burn or dry to death? To remind the powers of their responsibilities, and to help keep creation in order, humans had to be constantly aware of the seasonal and diurnal round. In addition they had to devise rituals that would assist the sun, the moon, the wind, the earth, the sea and the heavens in their task. While doing this, humans themselves became attuned to the part they had to play in the universe; they were not odd, singular creatures, different from the rest of creation. They were part of it, of its family, and had to behave accordingly.

This type of relationship with Nature is amply set out in a range of myths and religious procedures which form the Ras Shamra texts, dated about 1400 BCE.[11] Found early this century in northern Syria, they provide a massive, if disconnected and fragmentary, corpus of knowledge about the life and thought of the Canaanites. John Gray in *The Canaanites* (1964) described the worship of a triad, possibly El and Asherah, the creator and the Mother Goddess and Baal–Hadad the young, vigorous god, primarily of rain and storm and secondarily of vegetation. Asherah is also 'Lady of the Sea' and plays a powerful part in the myths, alongside Baal's sister, the goddess Anat, on whom he depends for assistance and on whose power he relies. Gray believes that the myths describing the vicissitudes of Baal relate to the rituals throughout the agricultural year, being orginally designed to make the significance of such rites explicit and to double their efficiency. They complemented the rite itself by influencing the deity.

Baal is also Hadad, god of storms, thunder and lightning and, above all, of rain. One tablet tells how Baal–Hadad, seized by monsters and then escaping into a bog, is a absent from the earth for seven years during which time there is no rain. In addition, all normal activities on the earth have ceased:

The king had ceased to judge, the woman drawing [water at] the spring had ceased. He that frequents El's house and she that plays in the house of confinement had ceased.

Baal–Hadad's disappearance caused not only drought and suffering but almost brought all life on earth to a standstill. The situation could only be put right by a goddess: the Lady Anat.

It is in a cycle of myths concerning Baal–Hadad's death that the power of the female deities is strongly shown. He has been challenged by Mot, the god of death who eventually kills him. Anat finds him dead in the fields. Because of his death the sun burns without ceasing, and rain disappears. In the meantime Anat determines to find Mot and regain her brother and bring him back to life. In her rage against Mot, who deceives her, she seeks him out and attacks him. 'She seized Mot . . . ripped him open with a sword, winnowed him in a sieve, burnt him in the fire, ground him between two millstones, sowed him in a field. Verily the birds ate pieces of him, verily the sparrows made an end of the parts of him piece by piece.' The pieces cried out that the victor Baal has died, that the prince of the earth has perished. 'But then, as Mot is completely overcome by Anat she rejoices; and lo, the victor Baal is alive and lo the prince lord of earth exists . . . the heavens rained oil, the ravines ran with honey.' Later the myth addresses the Lady Anat:

> And thou, o virgin Anat,
> do thou fly over the hills . . . and tell . . .
> that the downpour of rain will come down
> for the victor Baal is alive
> . . . the dead will come to life
> . . . and the herbs will be saved
> . . . for he will graciously send rain from the
> clouds and give plentiful showers of rain.

The many themes here include a telling of a universal theme of death and ressurection in connection with the harvesting of crops and their processing into grain and seed, leading to a renewal of life. It is through the agency of the Lady Anat that this process can take place. The two male deities, Baal and Mot, fight and trick each other, but it is Anat who kills death and renews life. When Baal comes to life again he is able to send rain, but he depends upon Anat for his ressurection.

Another theme within the cycle again demonstrates the dependence of Baal on the goddesses. Despite his greatness he has no palace or court or temple. He asks his sister Anat for help. Together they approach their mother, Lady Athirat (Asherah)[12] of the Sea. They entreat the mistress of the gods for her assistance in getting the father god El to grant Baal a temple. The party sets out to tackle El, together with the goddess Elat 'and her band'. El, at first unwilling, asks, 'so I am to be serving as a lackey of Athirat? So I am to be serving as one that handles the hod?' but then agrees. 'Be gladdened Baal, I have brought thee glad tidings. A house shall be builded for thee . . .' It is Anat who conveys the knowledge to the supplicant.

These myths offer the opportunity of perceiving the ambivalence in attitudes to female and male deities which took place at that time. We see that a goddess has the power of life, death and resurrection of the dead and thus qualifies as a Wisdom goddess, also that the mother goddess is in the process of being shifted from an all-powerful position to one where she is at times subordinate to El the male creator, but yet retains her older, recognisable identity and, to some extent, her power.

Integral to these myths is the concept of the strong and powerful goddesses, who although not given a primary position in fact act as if they are all-powerful. Although one may perceive Anat's importance to be diminished it can also be seen that her role is crucial. And while Athirat needs to ask El for permission for Baal's house, El's remarks as he yields indicate he appreciates the power struggle between them.

The goddesses – Anat, Asherah (Athirat), Elat, and Shapash the sun goddess – play powerful roles but are seen in the context as serving the gods and putting their own power at the gods' disposal. Even so, the power of life and death is Anat's; it is she who brings about Baal's resurrection and it is she who thus brings back life and fruitfulness to the earth.

As we look at the perfect identification of nature, divinity and humanity described in the Ras Shamra myths, we perceive that the goddesses throughout the cycle represent energy, movement and life itself.

Baal-Hadad, a divine being, is implicitly part of the world of humans. His life and death are mirrored in the events of the world. Such myths, it is conjectured, are acted and told and retold in ritual settings in order to assist nature.

Another Hittite myth confirms this.[13] It is the story of Hanna Hanna, a Grandmother Goddess. She does not appear in the Ras Shamra texts but is contemporary with them. The myth is of the disappearing god who walked out in anger. He was god of the weather, and when he disappeared nature came to a standstill: wheat and barley no longer grew, cattle, sheep and humans could not give birth, and springs, meadows and woodlands dried up. Everybody and every creature goes to search for him unavailingly. When the king asks the Grandfather God for help he is told that the whole affair is his own fault and that the god will investigate; if the king is guilty he will be killed. In despair the king approaches the Grandmother Goddess Hanna Hanna (her name means Mother Mother). She tells the king 'if it is not your fault, I will put it straight. And if it is your fault I will also put it straight.' She sends out a bee, who finds the weather god sleeping in a grove. The bee stings him and he wakes, angry, but eventually stamps back home. All is returned to normal; all is set straight through the agency of the Grandmother Goddess.

Hanna Hanna was understood as a direct descendant of the more ancient goddesses of the land, those who were Nature herself. By her time the god had taken control of the weather, and yet nothing could be done when things went wrong until the ancient goddess put them right.

Continuing this theme, there are attributes of the goddess Atargatis, also Mistress of the sea. The first part of her name duplicates that of Athart (Astarte–Asherah). Atargatis in the Canaanite pantheon is the wife of Baal–Hadad. She is another deity of exceptional longevity, from the second millenium to the second century BCE at the very least. Atargatis' connection with the sea is extremely powerful. She is Mistress of the Sea and is occasionally represented either as a fish or as having a fishtail. As goddess of the sea she is said to typify the function of water in producing life. Thus she is associated with the creation of life through water and she has been accepted as goddess of generation and fertility. She is Goddess of Nineveh. Another of her titles, with apparent incongruity, is 'Inventor of useful articles' and yet another, 'Goddess of Oracles'.

Again there seems to be no inconsistency in a deity with cosmic, creative and magical powers also having the mundane as part of her activity, so that in addition to her role as the producer of life and mother of the gods, the oracle is also the inventor of useful articles.

The importance of this marrying of the cosmic and the mundane in terms of creation cannot be overstated in our appreciation of the characteristics of Wisdom goddesses.

Another goddess who revives and raises the dead is depicted in the story of Keret in the Ras Shamra texts. He, a just king, becomes sick, and is dying. Offerings are made so that Baal will send rain and the land will flourish, for a good harvest and the supply of necessities of life depend on the continuance of the king's health. (This concept is in line with much ancient thought and the source of widespread ritual and cult practice.[14]) The divine being that is able to cure Keret is the female Shataqat. The text reads: 'Shataqat went into the house of Keret. She did weep as she penetrated therein. She did shriek as she went therein . . . release the plague from his head she came back and washed him clean. She opened his throat for food . . . for truly death had been shattered, truly Shataqat was victorious.'

Athirat–Asherah–Atargatis, Anat and Shataqat are a few only of the goddesses to be found in the Ras Shamra texts. The last named does not seem to re-occur elsewhere, but the first four dominate the Ancient Near Eastern world over many centuries. All appear in various forms and under various names. All are in their various aspects an integral part of the kaleidoscope of the Wisdom goddesses who were to be venerated over a vast area of time and space.

In this chapter we have been able to look at only a few of these Wisdom goddesses, and have concentrated on their creative, regenerative and healing powers. It is these powers which in particular define such goddesses as being in the category of Wisdom. It is often suggested that Mother Goddesses of antiquity are solely symbols of fertility, but it will be seen from the diverse material which spans long eras of time that much more is involved.

Siduri Sabatu from Babylonia in the third millenium BCE held the gift of life and of immortality; she is followed by many through the centuries, female divinities or semi-divine figures such as Kalypso of the Homeric legends, all of whom have similar powers. Gula is Queen of the Physicians, and again healing and restoration of life are shown to be in the hands of Wisdom goddesses from varied cultures.

Life, immortality, and medicine are joined by care for justice, which itself is associated with the order of the cosmos and the everyday running of worldly matters. The Wisdom goddesses, like Inanna who carries the means of keeping the world in order in her hands, or Ma'at, Egyptian goddess of order, justice, and the underworld, make it clear that the divinities are closely concerned with proper behaviour in the world.

This indeed is closely linked with the order of the universe. One might say that heaven and earth are connected here: human behaviour is part of the functioning of the universe; and good behaviour consists of balance, harmony and truth, both among individuals and in relation to the world and to participation in the course of nature.

If things go wrong, as in the case of the Hittite god who does not return to his duties of helping the seasons to perform their natural round, it is the goddess Hanna Hanna who is called upon to set things to rights. Added to this is the enhancement of human life by the gifts of music, mathematics and writing associated with Nisaba.

The Wisdom goddesses are a source of inspiration to humans as well as to their creators, nurturers, teachers, and the very ground from which all are born and all return.

7. Ancient Hebrew Goddesses

In this chapter I want to look at those goddesses in the Hebrew bible who for so long have appeared to be hostile entities, yet who were never expurgated from the texts. Indeed we can see that they are truly, both as goddesses and as demons, part of the Jewish tradition.

Such goddesses who are condemned by its authors as abominations, shameful,[1] and certainly as alien to the true Hebrew religion, actually formed part of it over a long period of time. There is evidence of an unbroken cult of this nature from the time of monarchy to the destruction of the second temple (c. 1000 BCE–70 CE), and we can recognise these female deities who appear throughout the Hebrew bible.

The Hebrew goddesses are even more enigmatic and ambivalent than Hochma–Wisdom, and commentators and readers have had very great difficulty in explaining them. I am encouraged by the remarks of Peter Ackroyd, in *Goddesses, Women and Jezebel* a distinguished contemporary biblical scholar, who questions the traditional view that such goddesses were alien to the Hebrews. He writes: 'The hostile biblical portrayal of such goddesses and wicked queens such as Jezebel were part of a polemic. This was designed to demonstrate that such religious practices did not belong in Israel – in fact that they were alien.' He infers that such polemic may well have distorted actual records or historical fact, and that it is at least arguable that the foreign women and 'stranger' goddesses were not in fact foreign and not strange to the people of Israel and to the Hebrew religion.[2]

Let us first of all look at the queen of Heaven narrative in the Book of Jeremiah, the events of which at the end of the sixth-century BCE take place at the time of the exile from Jerusalem. The Hebrew women now in Egypt tell Jeremiah that far from having brought their doom on themselves as he suggests, by backsliding into alien polytheism, this doom has happened because they no longer continue their Jerusalem rituals of baking cakes for the queen of heaven offering incense and pouring out libations to her.

'Seest thou not what they do in the cities of Judah and the streets of Jerusalem? . . . The women knead dough to make cakes for the Queen of Heaven' (Jeremiah 7:17–18).

'Then all the men which knew that their wives had burned incense unto other gods, and all the women that stood by, a great multitude, even all the people that dwelt in the land of Egypt, in Pathros, answered Jeremiah, saying . . . we will certainly . . . burn incense to the Queen of Heaven . . . as we have done . . . in the cities of Judah, and in the streets of Jerusalem: for then . . . we . . . were well, and saw no evil . . .' [and the women said] 'when we burned incense . . . and poured out drink offerings to her, did we make her cakes to worship her . . . without our men?' (Jeremiah 44:14–19).

This Bible glimpse lights up a time when Hebrew women led religious ritual, in contrast to their later exclusion from it. They were free and independent and members of a society in which men were happy to accept this. The picture illuminated in the Book of Jeremiah opens up a possible panorama which has been entirely hidden from us. This society appears to be founded on ancient tradition and is similar in ideas and practice to those of neighbouring peoples in the Near and Middle East.

I suggest that the description of the cake-making ritual for the Queen of Heaven in the book of Jeremiah can be seen to be of great significance. First it is a communal and sacred activity by women in honour of an autonomous female deity, whose representatives they are; the activity is also part of the society in which they live, and is accepted and honoured by the men; further, sexual independence on the part of the women can be inferred from the ritual. I suggest that the women are the inheritors of a tradition of collective female power, that there is a social and spiritual female unity reflected in divine images. Women are not divorced from society's approval or from male companionship, if they desire this.

I have mentioned the episode as part of Hebrew women's herstory. Most people would dismiss it as paganism and definitely not part of Judaism – and something against which the prophets of the Bible were always warning their people. It is such practice that seems in traditional thinking to be exactly the opposite of true Judaism. I propose that a re-thinking is necessary.

The idea that the Hebrews were quite distinct from their neighbours does not mean that they did not take part in the same kind of religious activities as the Canaanities, Phoenicians, Egyptians and others; rather, that these activities had a specific flavour. It is clear, though, that one section of the Hebrew religion certainly disapproved of them. And it is that section that was preserved by the rabbis after the Roman holocaust in the first century CE and which forms the basis of the Jewish religion we know today. It was, though, only one part of a very varied and flexible religious life.

The story of the Jewish women in Egypt at the end of the sixth-century BCE provides a tiny pinpoint of light that breaks the dark occluding curtain, and suggests there may be quite a different patterning to women's past. To have an idea of what this might be, we have to look at the context of the queen of heaven bible excerpt more closely.

Jeremiah and the Jewish people in Egypt
Jeremiah is one of the many Old Testament prophets who inveigh against idolatrous practices.

'The word which came to Jeremiah concerning all the Jews which dwell in the land of Egypt, at Migdol, at Tahpanhes, and at Noph, in the country of Pathros' (Jeremiah 44:1) sets the scene. A good deal of scholarly research has gone into suggesting the strong probability that Noph was the city of Memphis, capital of Lower Egypt. Migdol (the word means tower) was on the frontier on the route from Egypt to Asia, and Tahpanhes, Tell Daphnes, where the prophet stayed, was on the eastern branch of the Nile. The country of Pathros appears to have been the Nile Delta. Further to the south was the town of Elephantine from which we have papyri dating to the fifth-century BCE (100 years later than Jeremiah), and we know there was a Jewish colony there which was obviously akin in practices to those described by the prophet.

The goddesses named in the Hebrew Bible are Ashtaroth and Asherah. The queen of heaven as such, however, is not given a name. Scholars have identified her with the Semitic goddess Astarte, who has been called the great female principle. Astarte is another form of Ashtaroth, and also of the Mesopotamian Ishtar, who is often referred to as Astarte–Ishtar.[3] Astarte was worshipped throughout the Near and Middle East over a period of something like 3000 years. She had the quality of creatrix and universal motherhood of all animate and inanimate life. She was the All-Begetter and All-Nourisher. One of her titles is Mother of the Blest. She has been called 'the great fruitful kindly earth itself'. Most of her sanctuaries were on high places in groves of green trees, but she was also worshipped in caves and in temples.

There are numerous invocations, inscriptions and records relating to the queen of heaven or 'queen of the sky', Specifically Astarte–Ishtar is identified with the bright planet Venus, which has always been associated with the archetypal feminine. It is her astrological symbol that gives us our women's sign today. She was called 'queen of the royalty of the sky'. One text declares:

> The mass of stars cluster in the sky
> O Ishtar you are their queen
> O Innin you are the brightest among them,
> you are called Ishtar of the stars.
> among the gods no one is like you
> and all people adore you.[4]

Astarte–Ishtar is also invoked as 'Lady (Beltia) of heaven and earth'. Innin and Inanna are variants of her name.

The planet Venus rises about three hours before sunset and then sinks below the horizon and is not seen until about three hours before sunrise, except at high altitudes. This apparent 'descent' has been thought to provide an explanation of the journey of Ishtar (Inanna) into the underworld which is chronicled in Ancient Near Eastern texts,[5] and of the various accounts of how she rises and is renewed again. This journey has provided many women with deep insights into the renewal and reclamation of their identity and spirituality.

For women it is important that the queen of heaven, of the stars, is also goddess of earth and of the body, of sexual celebration, childbirth and creativity of all kinds. Here is part of another hymn to Ishtar:

Praise to the Goddess, most awesome of goddesses
She is clothed with pleasure and love
She is laden with vitality, charm and voluptuousness
The goddess – with her is counsel
The fate of everything she holds in her hand
At her glance is created joy
Power, magnificence the protecting deity, and the guardian spirit

She pays heed to compassion and friendliness
Besides, agreeableness she truly possesses,
Be it slave, unattached girl, or mother, she preserves her.
One calls on her; among women one names her name.[6]

There is no separation, no division; the goddess whose 'name is named' among women is magnificent, queen of heaven, yet also agreeable and friendly. She combines 'above' and 'below' in herself, and all are good. There is no uncleanliness, no tabu on women's functions. The Sabbatu of the Babylonians, the day of rest, from which our word Sabbath may derive, was said to be the day when the goddess was menstruating; everyone had to cease work in her honour and rest with her, so that she would be strengthened by their support.[7]

The Queen of Heaven can often be identified by the particular emphasis placed by her worshippers on baking and offering cakes to her. And this was the case amongst the early Christian women's sect of Collyridians who baked cakes in honour of Mary, Queen of Heaven. Such cake-making was a feature of goddess worship throughout the Near East. A hymn to Ishtar includes the lines: 'O Ishtar I have made a preparation of milk, cake grilled bread and salt, hear me and be kind.'[8] Another hymn to her states: 'O Ishtar, I look on your face, and I make an offering of pure milk with a baked cake . . .'[9] 'Cakes baked and offered to the Queen of Skies may have had an image of the goddess on them.'[10]

The cakes so disliked by Jeremiah are called *kawanim* in Hebrew which has been linked with a Babylonian cake called *kamanu*, made of figs and honey and cooked 'under the ashes'. Others see the cakes as prepared in a vase or cauldron and baked in an oven at the sanctuary. We know that the cakes were pierced with holes, and there has been a great deal of discussion about whether they were made in the image of the goddess or as 'round moons'. It has been suggested that linguistic evidence provides for the cakes to be idols, that is, sacred images of the goddess, made communally and then sacramentally eaten. One scholar refers to them as 'rude idols'[11] and believes they resemble a cake called *hais*, made to be used in a ritual to Arabic goddesses in pre-Islamic times by the women worshippers. The recipe consisted of dates kneaded with butter and sour milk. However the *kawanim* and *kamanu* always appear to contain grain, usually barley. It is known that from its appearance (look at a grain of pearl barley) barley symbolises the female genitalia.

It appears that the cakes for the queen of heaven 'made in her image' were possible made in the image of women's bodies, and in particular of the vulva. That these were communally and eaten sacramentally in the worship of the female deity gives ground for assumption that the women who led these rituals were sexually free. The cakes are sacred offerings by women; the men take part by lighting the fires and the children by gathering the sticks. But it was the women who led the ceremonies and partook of the mysteries. Throughout the ages such mysteries have been expressed in rituals associated with life, death, and the renewal of life – as with Ishtar, the queen who shines in the evening, goes into the dark, and shines again in the morning, apparently miraculously renewed.

So far it has been supposed that the Queen of Heaven is Ishtar and is identified by the cake ritual. There is another view: that she is the lady Anat and possibly consort of Jahweh. This suggestion is based on documents and other material found in the town of Elephantine in Egypt, dated to about 400 BCE, about 100 years after the narrative in the Book of Jeremiah. There is mention of the temple of Anat–Jaho, and even of dues from this temple being paid to the main Hebrew temple in Jerusalem – and accepted by it.

The temple of Anat-Jaho is surprising because it clearly links the Lady Anat with Jaho (Jahweh) and this is not questioned; which leads us to believe that this was certainly at least a recognised strand of Jewish life at the time. Further, the material from this temple links with letters and inscriptions of the same period from various temples in Egypt. In the same area, one at Syene was dedicated to 'the Queen of Heaven'. This is known particularly from a letter addressed to the temple but found at Memphis. It starts: 'Salutations to the temple of Bethel and to the temple of the Queen of Heaven.'[12] The temple there of Bethel – the word in Hebrew means 'house of god' – is very fully recorded as a temple of a goddess associated with both 'the Queen of Heaven' and with the Lady of Fate or Fortune. Her name, SIMA, means, 'The Name', an appellation later of God, whose divine name was never to be spoken. Bethel gives classicists their name of a round meteorite, often shown on coins and reliefs in the Ancient Near East; it is called a *baetyl*. This is a sacred stone believed to contain the living deity, and is particularly seen in representations of a goddess, often in a chariot, and sometimes showing the astrological sign of Venus – Queen of Heaven. Clearly, the words 'Bethel' and 'baetyl' are connected in form and in meaning, and indicate a presence of divinity – in the *baetyl* a goddess, in the *Bethel*, God.[13]

Alongside the temples at Elephantine and Syene, there are two more at Memphis, those of Anat Bethel and Asham Bethel. Anat seems to me to refer to the Lady Anat, whom we have previously met in the Ras Shamra documents and who was instrumental in reviving her brother's corpse to bring life to the parched world. Here she is twinned with Yaho – Jahweh – in a temple from whom dues are accepted by the temple in Jerusalem. This can only mean that the worshippers in this outlying area are considered part of the Jewish 'household'; they were not disempowered, excommunicated or relegated to near or non Judaic communities. We have to face the strong possibility that Anat–Jaho (that is the Lady Anat and the Lord Jahweh) were considered as a couple, and notice that the female name is placed first. The couple is of female and male aspects of God, if you look at it from a strongly monotheistic standpoint, or of Anat and her consort, or Jaho and his consort. The idea of Jahweh and a divine consort is not as revolutionary now as it would once have been, owing to fairly recent archaeological finds and inscriptions.

The name of the temples are Anat Bethel and Asham Bethel, and we need to consider further the inner meaning of Bethel. It is familiar to us from the story of Jacob who meets an angel of God while he is sleeping on a stone (Genesis 28:2,19; 35:15–16) and names the place Bethel, that is, House of God. The implication of the narrative is that the very essence of God is present in the stone.[14] By the time of the fifth century in Egypt, the Hebrew Bethel has developed in the ancient Greek world and becomes the classical *baetylus*, the meteorite or 'black stone' which falls from heaven containing within it an essence of the divine Queen of Heaven. The literature on the subject confirms . . . that a stone 'falling from heaven' may contain the essence of the divine; . . . in all cases the divine indwelling in the sacred stone is female; . . . this divine female is stated to be the Queen of Heaven, and has such titles as Mistress of the Skies, of the Stars.

Thus Anat Bethel's temple can reasonably be translated as the temple of that same Queen of Heaven to whom cakes and libation were offered by the Hebrews in Jerusalem and in Egypt.[15]

There is significant confirmation in an inscription found when a great temple to Astarte was excavated at Kition (Citium) in Cyprus, dating to the time of the Phoenician occupation. A tablet records payments to various servants of the temple. One reads: 'For the bakers who baked baskets of loaves for the queen [of heaven].'[16] The word used for loaves is not the *kawanim* of Jeremiah, but *halloth*, the plural of the familiar Hebrew word for the Sabbath loaf: *hallah*. *Halloth* occurs in the Bible always to denote a sacred offering of bread. David distributes *halloth* (II Samuel 6:19) when the Ark of the Lord comes into Jerusalem. Twelve *hallot* must be placed on the altar of the Lord in the temple at Jerusalem as 'shewbread' or 'bread of the Presence' (Leviticus 24:5, Exodus 35:13 and 39:36). They are to be made of grain wheat, oats or rye. Cereal offerings are 'laid down' and not consumed by fire as are the later animal sacrifices. Very early peoples believed that the grain contained the very life or spirit of the deity; by Biblical times grain, still the support of life itself, was given a specific place and sacrament.

Jahweh and Consort?

While the Queen of Heaven reigns in her own right, it has recently been suggested that she be recognised as the consort of the King of Heaven, that is, the Lord, Jahweh. And this raises the topic of God's one-ness; does it include the female aspect as goddess or does God have a consort, worshipped with Him, or separately? While it is usual to think of God's biblical relationship with Israel as that of husband with wife, this is a theological polemic. Today it is being suggested that God's consort or wife, as much a deity as he himself, was acknowledged in the person of the Lady Asherah, whom we have already met in the Canaanite tradition.

The names of Ze'ev Meshel, William Dever, Z Zevit and Robert Oden[17] are among those modern scholars who have identified and commented upon inscriptions and shrines which couple Jahweh with Asherah. Perhaps the most dramatic find is that of Ze'ev Meshel. In a communication published in 1979 he asked 'Did Jahweh have a consort?', and described his findings at a site in Northern Sinai named Kuntillet Ajrud. A shrine possibly used by travellers on cross-country routes and guarded by keepers, it contained a series of drawings and inscriptions, both on its walls and on *pithoi*, which were large jars used to store commodities such as oil. The murals show a series of pictures which included a seated female on a throne playing a musical instrument, attended by male figures. An inscription beside her asks for blessings from 'Jahweh and his Asherah'. Some scholars read these lines as Jahweh and

Asherah, but all see that the names ar linked. Other drawings include a cow and suckling calf and other humans and figures.

References are made to the presence of two ovens which Meshel finds somewhat 'overlarge' for what appears to have been a modest edifice and fragments of linen material The invocations to Jahweh 'and his Asherah' caused a great deal of surprise when reported, as did the important position occupied by the seated female figure and the presence of the cow and suckling calf, always in the Ancient Near East a symbol for the Mother Goddess. The implications were clear to Meshel that here at least, dated about 700 BCE, Asherah was a particular deity, female, and apparently the consort of Jahweh. Dever (1984) suggests that 'his Asherah' is an incorrect reading and that the inscription should read 'by Jewish and Asherata'. This ties in with a discovery by Zevit (1984) who called attention to a similar inscription of similar date on a pillar in a burial cave at Khirbet el Qom. The worshipper who inscribed them, or caused them to be inscribed, has the Jewish name of Urjahu – we note that Jahu or Jahweh is part of his name. The inscription translates as: 'I blessed Urjahu to Jahweh, and from his enemies, O Asherata, save him.' Zevit goes into some detailed linguistic analysis of the form Asherata and compares it to Meshel's inscription. He too suggests with Dever that Asherata is a form of Asherah, and indicates that Asherah is not a possession, that is, 'his' of Jahweh, but is a power in her own right.[18]

Asherata is also mentioned in a report of finds of tenth–century shrines at Tell Taanach. A suggestion offered by Dever is that the shrines probably attest to the presence of another cult of Yahweh and Asherah, this time at the headquarters of the fifth district of King Solomon.

At this point we need to enter into the world of the Goddess Asherah, who is named at these places in connection with Jahweh. What do we know about her? She is met with in many texts of the

Hebrew bible, all of them hostile to her, and she is conflated with the goddess Ashteroth.[19]

Setting aside for a moment the implacable hostility of the writers of the narratives, what do we find they have actually said about her? First, she is always connected with trees. She is worshipped 'beneath any green tree, on any high hill'. Groves of trees are sacred to her. In many cases she seems to be worshipped as a tree or part of a tree, a branch or pole.[20] For a long time commentators were content to imagine that an *Asherah* was a 'cult object', a wooden stick or branch or statue that people worshipped. But with the material from Ras Shamra and all the evidence from background sources it becomes very difficult for them to stick to this view, though some do try to do so. Asherah, as goddess, a tree, a grove of trees, part of a tree, like Nisaba of the reeds offers a far more acceptable solution: while she is in every tree, every branch or pole, she not merely one of them. The tree is her symbol and emblem, and contains her. The tree which stands strongly in earth, is nourished by rain, air and sun, gives shade in the heat, provides fruit to eat, often medicine to heal, is an ancient and universal symbol of life. Are we not all familiar with, and moved by, the expression 'The Tree of Life'? This was barred from humans after they had eaten the fruit of the tree of knowledge of good and evil in the garden of Eden – again a tree. The Lord set a flaming sword against it. Suppose indeed that our foreparents in the land of Israel had understood that the tree of knowledge and the tree of life were part of the grove of the Goddess Asherah. Is it not likely that the biblical writers would, in their need to do away with all aspects of female divinity, take an antagonistic attitude to them? The fruit of one – given to the woman first – is not to be eaten, and when it is consumed 'death is brought to the world'. And in the Genesis story the other may never again be approached by human beings.

And then later, in a land full of desert and heat, where groves of trees are life–giving in every sense, the narratives say that God instructed his righteous people to cut them down, burn them, grind them to dust.[21] We may be sure that Asherah, worshipped among trees and with trees as her symbol in which she in dwelt, was the target of their hostility, even to the point where the life–giving countryside was itself destroyed.

And yet, as in so many biblical narratives, the message is not as clear and straightforward as it seems. For while on the one hand Asherah and Asherim (that is, the symbols of Asherah) were being destroyed, the phrase the 'Tree of Life' came back into it own. Of Wisdom it was said (Proverbs 3:18). 'She is a tree of life to all who lay hold of her'. I think we can see here a connection with Asherah. Also, while we understand that the 'righteous' kings and prophets caused her symbols to be dispersed and her worshippers punished, yet when we follow these narratives, what do we find? That what is called the popular religion continued to be widespread, no matter how stringent the persecution against its participants.

We read in the Book of Kings of the reforms carried out by the 'good king' Josiah (II Kings 23). First the priests had to bring out of the temple the 'vessels made for Baal, for Asherah and for all the host of heaven' (v.4), so from this we know there were vessels sacred to them in Jahweh's temple. Then we are told that the priests who were to be deposed had burned incense there to 'the sun, the moon, the constellations and all the host of heaven' (v.5). Lastly they bring out the 'Asherah from the house of the Lord' (v.6). They burn it – it is of wood – 'beat it to dust, then cast the dust of it on the graves of the common people' (v.6) This is the statue that stood in the temple since the days of Solomon and had been worshipped there.[22]

The holy ones – sacred prostitutes
We learn from the same narrative that in the house of the Lord, where the woman wove hanging for the Asherah there lived the 'male cult prostitutes'. In other places, we are told about female

'temple harlots'. These have a long and honourable history, reflected in the Hebrew word which is translated into English as prostitute, harlot, sodomite, and even dog. The words *qedeshot* and *qedeshem* derive from the word *qodosh*, which means holy. They were in fact the 'holy ones', women and men, who served in the temple.

Their name is linked with that of the Goddess Qodsha or Kadesh, the Holy One who gave her name to a city of which she is likely to have been the titular goddess. She is depicted in the British Museum. Naked, she stands with a lion or panther, she carries a lotus blossom and a mirror, and is attended by two snakes. Other representations of her show her with serpents and with stars. She is described as 'mistress of all the gods'.

These are very powerful symbols. The lions often associated with great goddesses suggest royalty and power; the lotus blossom indicating sexuality and the mirror are frequently shown with goddesses of love. The mirrors are not so much symbols of vanity, as those of being able to see oneself clearly and thus to know the truth. Mirrors were also used to foresee, or to descry, the future. The snakes indicate wisdom, healing, and possibly powers of life–giving and immortality.

Her servants were not always given terms of abuse. In the code of laws instituted by Hammurabi of Babylon, such temple servants, then in the service of Ishtar and called the Holy Ones, were singled out for particular commendation and reward. We read of pensions given to sacred temple women, and of their right to free housing and gardens. Children born to them are to be respected and termed children of the temple – there was no slur on them.

This temple service appears to have lasted from the early third–millenium BCE until the return of the Jews from exile in around 500 BCE or perhaps longer. It seems to be connected orginally with the ceremony of the sacred marriage. This was the heart of the seasonal ritual in ancient Mesopotamia, among many other places. John Allegro in *Lost Gods* (1977) has described it:

A bridal bower was erected and decorated with foliage, there the union was consummated . . . it is the priestess who summons the king to her embrace, and who, representing the goddess, bestows on him through their intercourse, a divine but subservient status in the more creative process. (p. 134.)

This ritual marriage (*hieros gamos*), in which the king represents the people of the earth and the priestess the goddess, was a magical means of helping the land and the people flourish, and also provided the king with his royal authority to rule. It brought rain and sunshine, fertility and creativity. While procreation and abundant harvests were important, the *hieros gamos* seems to have also meant that the goddess in the person of the priestess was sharing her divinity and the king representing the people was accepting it in trust to fulfil their needs. There was participation on the part of humans in the holy, and of the divine in the world itself.

While this union took place between the sacred pair, it was an occasion for love feasts for the whole community. Such feasts of all kinds need not, as their later detractors have alleged, have been depraved orgies; rather, in their own way, even in celebrating their own sexuality, people could be taking part in the union of heaven and earth. Sexuality and sacredness were not divided.

By the time the bible came to be written, these customs were represented by the sacred women and men in the temple of Jahweh. They lived there and were sexually available to strangers. There is no information about their individual sexuality; we may surmise that strangers entering the temple might be of either sex and might choose their partners as they wished. We may also expect that the women and the men living in the temple may have related each to each other. The outstanding importance of the praxis was in terms of sexuality, the union of the human with the divine, which itself represented such communion.

It is as if these underground echoes and reflections throughout the bible, are connected, like water. Like rivers and seas they flow, and in far places break way from each other, yet are totally part of a whole. Let us look again at Asherah and her symbols: trees and sexuality. Where is that connection first made? It is in the Garden of Eden set at the function of four rivers (Genesis 2:10). As a result of eating the fruit of the tree of knowledge of good and evil, the first human beings immediately turn to each other in sexual love. By Christians, this is called 'the Fall', and posited as the first sin – with particularly dire consequences for women (see chapter 8). The Jewish position concentrates rather more on birth and growth, of populating the earth and of ensuing work in the world. My own position, starting from the latter, then sees love and sexuality as inspirational, promoting creativity not only in the sense of procreation, but of art, knowledge and the creation of the good and the beautiful. Asherah, as the Tree of Life and the Tree of Knowledge of good and evil gives her children choice and power. And that same Tree of Life is identified with Wisdom, as indeed are all the aspects of the ancient Hebrew goddesses.

Image worship

We can contrast this perception of Asherah with the biblical insistence that worshippers addressing themselves to idols were sinners. Much is made of the fact that images and statues are carved from trees or stone or bone and are fashioned by human beings. How then, ask Biblical writers, can people worship them? The Psalmist contrasts this with the, to him, vastly superior principle that 'our God is in the heavens and does what he pleases' (Psalm: 115:3) and indeed abhors images, which are totally forbidden by the first commandment.

I suggests this negates an ancient universal principle of the numinous. This principle holds that the deity can be in the heavens, and also be part of the created world and can lend itself to any object made in love and offered in sacred space. Indeed, all objects have to be made from something in the natural world: the wood, the grass, the plant, the bone, the flower, the earth, the rock – and much more, all have the divine within them.[23] This seems to be the philosophy of people of antiquity and those who today have managed to retain something of earlier religions. My opinion is that nothing in this world is too far away from the natural to be denied access to spiritual input. Objects in themselves are not evil as such (for example, napalm or the hydrogen bomb); what is evil is the use of natural materials to make these objects and the design for which they are constructed. Their energy is part of the energy of the universe; the materials, whether directly taken from the earth or indirectly constructed from natural sources, can retain the divinity that is part of them. It is our use and attitude to the materials that denies the divinity.

When therefore the Psalmist tell his listeners and readers that the idols 'have eyes but they see not, ears but they hear not' (Psalm 115:5,6) he is stressing something that is totally irrelevant. The worshippers feel themselves in the presence of the creative divinity within these images, they relate to this divinity, and, indeed, because they recognise it, are less likely to exploit the world's natural resources so cruelly and thoughtlessly as others who reject the resources of nature as divine.

I suggest that it was in this perception of divinity within the earth and its resources, its relationship to the perceived female in terms of birth giving, sustenance and teaching, and in having a totality of life at her disposal, that the religion of the Hebrew Goddess was able to withstand so much attack. Asherah and Ashtaroth continue to be loved throughout the biblical records, no matter how many prophets denounce them, kings order their religion to be ground into the earth, and fiats of divine retribution are brought out. It was the strength of this devotion to the principle of the goddess that allowed Wisdom to remain in the bible, not as an idol or 'abomination' but as a treasured associate of God.

Summary
Throughout biblical times the religion of the Hebrews acknow-ledged and worshipped goddesses already present in the Canaanite background. Establishment prophets and leaders struggled against this with very little success, for a very long time. For example, there was the notion of the marriage of Jahweh in the 'popular' cult with the Goddess Asherah or Anat, and in the established or orthodox notion with Israel as a people or as a nation. This idea of the marriage of Jahweh with Israel has been extensively discussed and surveyed, but the appreciation of Jahweh's marriage with Asherah is only recently coming to the fore, based on new archaeological and scholastic evidence.

That the Hebrews also worshipped a 'queen of heaven' is fully attested, and this queen of heaven is well-known throughout the Ancient Near East and Hellenistic world. In becoming the consort of Jahweh, Asherah remained a personified goddess with her own praxis, and the Queen of Heaven was autonomous in her own right. The two may or may not be identified with each other.

The personification of the goddess Asherah into a tree, or part of a tree indicates the appreciation of the immanent female divinity among her worshippers in the world. The Queen of Heaven, and the ritual of cake–making, libation and incense to her joined humans to the cosmos, and particularly identified the queen of Heaven with the natural movements of the sun and the moon as they appeared to take place – the latter particularly associated with women's menstrual cycle. Both the Queen of Heaven and Asherah–Ashtaroth–Anat were connected with sacred sexual rituals that renewed creation continually, whether biologically or inspirationally. Such sexual celebrations themselves associated with worship, a sense of the divine, became the focus of denunciation in the Hebrew bible, and later converted into a source of evil as Christianity took root.

The theory that when worshipping images people were addressing themselves to lifeless pieces of material rather than to God or any kind of divinity was pursued obsessively; one result of this was to separate the material of the world, the 'mater' or 'mother' substances, from the divine. Following on from this, as Christianity became widespread, humans felt free to exploit such resources. In so far as the material of Nature was identified with the female, and to a large extent with sexuality, these too were subjected to oppression and persecution in pursuit of the solely 'spiritual'.

In the post-biblical period, however, when reform of the Hebrew religion gradually replaced a normative worship of the goddess, a divine female concept which had been continuously present in the Hebrew consciousness was allowed to come to the fore: Hochma-Wisdom.

Hochma takes over the characteristics and symbolical nature of many of the earlier wisdom goddesses, but in the course of time is de-personified. As the orthodox school of religion carries the day, she becomes an attribute of Jahweh, and eventually is converted into the Torah.

The ancient Hebrew goddesses and their symbols and rituals are 'demonised' in the biblical texts,[24] but careful study indicates that they never really were overcome; they lived on in disguise and re-appeared in the practice and theory of mystical Judaism – though this was not available to women. However, it is arguable that in what has now become traditional Judaism, there are strong echoes of a Goddess past. In Christianity women's sexuality was held in contempt, but this was not the case with Judaism – provided it remained strictly within marriage – while later rituals of welcoming the Sabbath emphasised the Goddess as a divine bride.

It can reasonably be argued that there are relics of the ritual of making cakes for the queen of Heaven in both the traditional and current sacred Jewish practices relating to the Sabbath bread.

Early Christianity contained a sect whose name, 'Collyridians' denotes bread rolls, and whose method of worship was making and offering small loaves of bread to Mary, Mother of Jesus, Queen of Heaven. These women were denounced by the Church Fathers as heretics since in fact they worshipped Mary not only as Mother of God but as God the Mother. An undercurrent of this belief continued over the centuries.

Conclusion

Having reached this point, we can look back to see that Wisdom and Wisdom goddesses were part of the consciousness of the peoples of the ancient world, who are in the background of the events compiled in the bible. Looking ahead, we must ask: 'What happened to Wisdom? Where are the goddesses?' They seem to disappear, and little or no sense of female divinity emerges. Rather an entirely different viewpoint takes over, as we shall see. Yet even within such dark ages as were to come, Wisdom was never totally forgotten. We shall follow her lamp, even though it is to a large extent obscured for a very long time.

8. Wisdom and Christianity

I have to preface this chapter with a personal note. For years I have been trying to write it, or something like it, and have come across innumerable and apparently insurmountable obstacles. I see something clearly, but it has taken me a long time to understand that this is not necessarily clear to others, although it might be, or might have been, to some (the great nineteenth-century feminist Matilda Joselyn Gage,[1] for example, or Rosemary Radford Ruether who wrote *Faith and Fratricide* in 1974.[2])

In the cultures before Christianity, the idea of the divine as female was never totally lost. Obscured in Judaism and translated into texts, it moved underground into the *Shekinah* (see chapter 9). With the advent of Christianity the notion of female Wisdom was subsumed into Jesus Christ, subsequently into the Third Person of the Trinity, the Holy Spirit, and eventually into 'Mother Church'. Although in the last two named some semblance of the female remained attached for a while, the Christian religion in all its various forms became totally male–dominated, with the Church acting as a bulwark of male supremacy.

Christianity's influence has been very great in the world over a very long period, and has been the prime mover in shaping the so-called civilisation of the West. I see it to have shaped the domination of male Christians over women, nature and non-Christians (particularly Jews) who were seen as subordinate and inferior. Christianity was also the source of exploitation of resources; additionally, there is a shameful history of slavery which was condoned by this religion.

This is all the more painful since these revelations produce a cruel paradox. Christianity is a religion which claims to have been founded on love. Its chief Founder and individuals, then and now, have been, and are, motivated by love, and indeed have died for love of their fellow humans. Yet for me the religion appears to be unboundedly cruel and hypocritical. I see Christianity – no matter what sect or denomination – as an all–pervasive influence set against the humanity of individuals. Historically it has been the guiding force for the subjugation of women and of all so called inferior peoples.

In the context of the exploration of Wisdom in this book I see that if a hinge or turning point can be identified, it is when female Wisdom was lost to the male form of Jesus Christ. I know that some Christian feminists and others are finding the balance is redressed in a 'Jesus-Sophia' figure, and that some Christian congregations are now actually worshipping Sophia.[3] In my view this shift is good. I want to place the turning point against the divine female Wisdom firmly in its context and to discuss its implications. I will enquire into the various forms of identification of Wisdom with Jesus Christ in the Gospels of the new Testament and then pursue its further development by Paul and, following him, the early Church Fathers. I hope to show that the new attitudes to Wisdom, their growth within the early Church, and the success of their protagonists against many who opposed them became directly linked with the gender issue in terms of control and domination.

Jesus and Wisdom
New Testament material that connects Jesus and Wisdom differs in approach, and scholars have found this a fertile source of disputation. There are three major sets of texts on the issue, each

contrasting strongly with the others. The first set occurs in the Synoptic Gospels, the second in various Epistles of Paul, and the third in the Fourth Gospel – that of John.

The Synoptic Gospels are those of Matthew, Mark and Luke. Much of the material within each duplicates that of the others, or varies in slight detail. But all the material differs considerably from the Fourth Gospel. A wide spectrum of scholarship connects the Synoptic Gospels with a proposed earlier common source, termed 'Q', which is now lost.

It will be helpful to look at some of the quotations which have been assumed to identify Jesus with Wisdom in these Gospels. I have used the RSV translation in all cases.

And coming to his own country, he taught them in their synagogue . . . and [they] said: 'Where did this man get this wisdom and these mighty words? Is this not the carpenter's son? Is not his mother called Mary? And are not his brothers James and Joseph and Simon and Judas? And are not all his sisters with us? (Matthew 13:54–55; Mark 6:2–3).

The Queen of the South will arise at the judgement with this generation and condemn it; for she came from the ends of the earth to hear the wisdom of Solomon, and behold, something greater than Solomon is here. (Matthew 12:42; Luke 11:31).

Then said Jesus to the crowds . . . O Jerusalem, Jerusalem . . . how often would I have gathered your children together as a hen gathers her brood under her wings . . . (Matthew 23:1 and 37; Luke 13:34).

The Son of Man came eating and drinking . . . yet Wisdom is justified by her deeds (Matthew 11:19; Luke 7:35) (Luke replaces the word 'deeds' by 'children'.)

At first glance, these quotations may hardly seem to place Jesus on the throne of divine Wisdom but rather to connect him with her in some way. Many commentators, however, over a very long period of time, have derived from the rather opaque hints a statement that Jesus is indeed Wisdom.

An important and specific point is made by Pierre Bonnard (1979) whose survey is entitled, 'From Wisdom personified in the Old Testament to Wisdom in person in the New'. Bonnard introduces 'Jesus Sagesse' (Jesus Wisdom), having looked at the personified Wisdom of the Hebrew bible, and surveyed Wisdom in creation, Wisdom and humanity, Wisdom personified, Dame Wisdom of Proverbs, and Wisdom and Life. He then discusses the origin and appearance of 'Divine Wisdom'. Up to this point he concludes that Wisdom is a personification of an attribute of God. She reveals herself in God, humans and universe. But humanity, says Bonnard, wants more. Humans are waiting to see the Wisdom of God as an actual, living person in their lives, and believe that one day this person will be among them. This happens in the New Testament. In the Synoptic Gospels Bonnard asserts that Jesus is presented 'more or less directly' as Wisdom in person. Wisdom is walking the earth and is called Jesus (p. 135).

Here we have the theological revolution described as it was initiated by the Christian writers of the Gospels. God, or the divine creator and sustainer, is here on earth as a person – actually as a man – and instead of being a personification, or a deity in heaven, or an attribute, is here, human, among us. So far, so good; this is the Christian message. But it does not seem to be enough. Not only must Jesus, walking the streets of Jerusalem and the shores of Lake Galilee, be a man, he must also be Wisdom in person. Since he is actually a man, then She is actually a man; it follows, then, in all this actuality, that She is lost.

But is She lost? In each of the texts giving Wisdom solely to Jesus, there is a mysterious female element. The first seems merely to identify Jesus' parentage and provenance, asking where he got this wisdom from; we know his humble, ordinary parents (and the rest of the verse identifies his brothers by name and asks 'are not his sisters with us'?) He is a man from a family amongst us; how is it he has these mighty words? It is interesting here that his mother is named; so often we are introduced to people merely by their own and their father's name. It is also interesting that his sisters, although not given their names, are at least mentioned. There is something of the female as well as the male, even though the questioners are doubting that Jesus is anything other than an ordinary person. And commentators who do identify Jesus stress an interpretation that shows he is much more than an 'ordinary' person, and that in some way he has been able to take on Wisdom as part of himself. Mark's version (6:2) actually asks 'What is this Wisdom given him?', which reinforces the notion that Wisdom is something extra to himself, rather than that he is Wisdom incarnate.

The second quotation is much more mysterious. It is generally taken that the Queen of the South is a reference to the story of the Queen of Sheba, visiting King Solomon (I Kings 10:1–13) and testing his wisdom by means of riddles and puzzles. Most commentators concentrate on the last phrase 'behold something greater than Solomon is here' (in Jesus) – that is, they infer it is Wisdom (herself). Bonnard believes, for example, that one can read from this that Jesus carries within his own person transcendental Wisdom (pp. 136–37 and p. 146). But why bring in the Queen of the South? Why will *she* 'arise at judgement' and condemn this generation? The Queen of Sheba in the Solomon story was no more than a neighbouring monarch. How is it that she has become something greater than that, indeed that she has become Judge of the last days? There can be no more direct pointer to a Goddess figure than this. My reading of the text infers that She then judges Jesus too – 'something greater than Solomon is here', and presumably he accepts Her judgement. This is surely a reference to, or a strong echo of, Wisdom as God and an identification of Her as female.

The third quotation, concentrating on the homely image of a mother hen, has in fact a strong Wisdom linkage, something that Jesus as a Jewish preacher could well have recalled. There are many traditional Jewish references to the acquisition of knowledge being like the action of a hen picking up scraps, while the emphasis on Jesus as a mother hen gathering her brood under her wings again stresses the female, and once more like the image of Wisdom is invoked in the reference to her wings.

In the last group of texts, there is a stand-off between Jesus' actions as a human person (indeed, the full text – Matthew 11:16–19 – shows people grumbling about him as a person) and the juxtaposition with Wisdom, who is given female gender. Both sets of verses can be, and have been, taken to mean that Jesus is both behaving as a human and is Wisdom. Various authorities have declared that in effect the verse is saying that the works of Jesus are the works of Wisdom, or that the children (presumably meta-phorical) of Jesus are the children of Wisdom, and there are a number of interpretations that emphasise the connections between Wisdom and 'the tongues of infants'.

Every reference so far to Jesus and Wisdom has brought in a female element, and I think that they need not be read as transferring Wisdom totally to Jesus. It is interesting that a theme of 'Jesus-Sophia' is emerging today which gives Christians the opportunity to regain the female aspect of Wisdom and to reclaim Her more distinctly than was previously possible. That a cult of Sophia worship should be emerging within traditional Christian groupings shows how strong is this desire and need.

Wisdom and Paul

Paul is probably the earliest commentator on the life of Jesus. His works written in, say, the two decades after Jesus' death provide both a picture of the earliest Christians and the foundation of their separation from the Jewish and Palestinian background. Paul's idiosyncratic version of the life, beliefs and aims of Jesus Christ stamped the developing churches into shapes of hierarchy, anti-Judaism and misogyny which were developed by the Church Fathers into a single great edifice in the following centuries.

I wish here to concentrate on Paul's manipulation of the Jewish Wisdom – Hochma – into the service of his new religion.

The major text in which he identifies Jesus Christ with Wisdom is Colossians 1:15–20. The others in his various Epistles, and in those in what is called the Post–Pauline tradition (that is, not necessarily written by him) will also be referred to, but I will quote the main text here. Paul is writing of Jesus Christ:

He is the image of the invisible God, the first-born of all creation; for in him all things were created, in heaven and on earth, visible and invisible . . . all things were created through him and for him. He is the head of the body, the church; he is the beginning, the first-born from the dead, that in everything he might be pre-eminent. For in him all the fullness of God was pleased to dwell, and through him to reconcile to himself all things, whether on earth or in heaven, making peace by the blood of his cross (Colossians 1:15–20 RSV).

Now here a number of matters are made plain. The 'first born of all creation' picks up immediately on Hochma in Proverbs 8:22 'The Lord created me at the beginning of his works, the first of his acts of old'.[4] The fourth-century Christian Father Epiphanius, among many others, makes this clear in the context of identifying Jesus with Wisdom. Among the commentators on this point, a scholar writing some six decades ago goes even further. Not only, says Burney (1922) is Christ the first-born of all creation; but in examining the meaning of the word 'first' (in Hebrew, *reshith*), incidentally the first word of the Hebrew bible ('in the beginning') (Genesis 1:1) Burney brings witness that, in Paul's words, Christ as the 'first begotten of all creation' is more than just that. Burney writes that 'hence in Him' were created all things; yet also he sees this may bear the sense 'by' so that all things were created by or through Him; it may also be interpreted as 'into', while the whole word must also mean 'before' all things, and may carry the meaning 'sum-total', so that all things are summed up in Him (p. 175). Burney thus perceives that Christ is the fulfiller of the meaning of *reshith*, and that He 'fulfils every meaning which may be extracted from it' (p. 176). He has already proved that Wisdom was set up in the beginning – and thus Christ who is the 'head and sum total' of creation (*rosh*, the Hebrew for 'head') also bears relationship with *reshith* is identified totally with Wisdom. He writes (p. 175) 'Proverbs 8:22 ff. where Wisdom (ie Christ) is called *reshith* gives the key to Genesis 1:1 *bereshith* (In Wisdom/In Christ) God created the heavens and the earth.'

So here we see major changes. The female identification of divine Wisdom is entirely lost, while her Jewish–Hebrew origin is absorbed entirely by the Christian. There had to be no element of female in God, and anything the Hebrew religion contained that was attractive and useful to the new religion had to be taken over and made to appear as if it was determined for this purpose from the outset.

Many Christians today might argue with this conclusion; they might say that, even if this was the general view, it was not the view of Jesus himself, or of many devoted believers through the centuries. They might point to the idea of 'Christ within' and suggest that the views of early church Fathers and later commentators do not in fact constitute a personal Christianity for them. And Christian feminists in particular will look to the 'feminisation' of Jesus by the understanding that Sophia is part of himself, and wish to develop this concept. I do not dispute any of this, or similar arguments which may be brought forward.

I do, however, point to the long centuries of history in which the views of the Roman Catholic and Protestant Churches were the foundation of Western society and law, carried throughout Europe to the New World, and to other continents. It may well be that the Church incorporated Roman law and customs, including the untrammelled rights of the father (*Pater Familias*) into their doctrines; it is certainly the case that the Church was not the first organisation to implement male domination. What appears to me to be crucial, however, is that for historical reasons it was the Church that became the ruling power in Western society, and that it is its misogyny that even today has shaped our culture and our expectations.

Paul's declaration moves from Wisdom's identification with Christ to its consequences. He is the 'head of the body, the Church' and in this respect we remember Paul's remarks to the Ephesians: 'For the husband is the head of the wife, as Christ is the head of the church, his body . . . as the church is subject to Christ so let wives also be subject in everything to their husbands' (Ephesians 5:23–4). Here we have a hierarchy introduced which equates Christ with the man and the church and woman with the body; in this case, however, the body, the Church, was in a position to rule itself and others, while the woman had no such chance and was made to feel the rule of her husband as a religious duty.

Paul goes further; Wisdom, as Christ, the first–born of all creation, no longer as in Proverbs 'rejoices in the inhabited world', pleased with the human race rather, the emphasis is turned to the blood of the cross and all its implications.

One of the most distinguished modern commentators on this theme is James Dunn. In a magisterial work (1980) he has read substantial changes into the Christ–Wisdom identification. He accepts that Paul identifies Christ as Wisdom but questions Paul's meaning and intention with such an identification (p. 176). It is not Christ at 'the beginning' and active in creation who is Wisdom, he believes, but as 'the one predetermined by God to be the means of man's salvation through his death and resurrection' (p. 178). Wisdom has changed its meaning. Paul is transmuting the old Israel into the new. Dunn outlines his conviction that 'for Paul God's wisdom is essentially through the proclamation of the crucified Christ' (I Corinthians 20–25), and further that Christ is 'God's Wisdom in its most important expression, salvation'. Thus Wisdom remains as a concept but is totally changed in meaning and in gender, becoming the personified Jesus Christ. His message was to offer salvation to those who believed in him through his ransoming of their sins by his death on the cross and his resurrection. The movement is away from the world, the cosmos and nature in her material form.

While it can be argued that Dunn's is only one scholar's viewpoint, yet it seems to me that it adequately sums up the views of many and points to the enormous change in perception of Wisdom and to the consequences of this. Writings attributed to Paul, but generally accepted to have been written later, follow Paul's Wisdom–Christ identification. For example, in Hebrews 1:3 the Son was the means by which God created the world, reflecting the 'glory' of his nature and bearing the very 'stamp' of his nature. By this time, female Hochma–Sophia has become the Son, and it appears to be no coincidence that in Hebrews 2:9 Paul's viewpoint is acknowledged as fact: Jesus from heaven, and as a man on earth is the means of salvation through suffering. Described first in Wisdom terms, a new religion is created and the notion of Wisdom transmuted to serve its needs. The passage from Hebrews links Wisdom with the Incarnation. This massive theme is to be found in all its magnitude in the Prologue to the Fourth Gospel.

Hochma, a female aspect, or attribute of deity – whichever reading is chosen – is negated entirely, or rather is swept away completely out of sight. Within mainstream Christianity she never again reappears. She is as 'if she never was'.

Alongside her are banished all the great Wisdom goddesses of the Ancient Near East, Egypt and the Hellenistic world. Even the ambivalent Sophia of the Gnostic systems fades from view, appearing briefly in the Book of Acts as a harlot. The descension is complete. We need to look at the Fourth Gospel to follow this journey.

Wisdom and the Fourth Gospel

In the beginning was the Word, and the Word was with God and the Word was God. He was in the beginning with God. All things were made by him and without him was not anything made that was made. In him was life; and the life was the light of men. The light shines in the darkness and the darkness has not overcome it ... The true light that enlightens every one was coming into the world ... and the Word became flesh and dwelt among us ... full of grace and truth ... we have beheld his glory ... and from his fullness we have all received, grace upon grace ... No one has ever seen God: the only Son who is in the bosom of the Father, he has made him known (John 1:1–18).

Usually the Gospel of John, the Fourth Gospel, is dated to some time in the second-century CE, that is, perhaps fifty or more years after the writings of Paul. But the Prologue to this Gospel, parts of which are quoted above, is thought to contain much older material and there is general agreement concerning much of it, although great disputation as to what sources the writer was drawing upon. The use of the Greek *Logos* (Word) to describe Jesus Christ takes up a Hellenistic idea to be found both in Greek and Jewish philosophical writings, in both of which the Logos is a divine order or reason of the universe.

The Prologue contains material that links it with Wisdom, and with the Egyptian goddesses Isis and Ma'at.[5] The echoes of the language of Wisdom are forceful. Logos, like Wisdom, is there 'in the beginning' and can be understood like her as the architect (*technites*): all things were made by him, and nothing would be made without him; He, like She, is life, and like her is the light of human beings – the lampra of the BWS 6:12, Wisdom who is luminous and unfading. Grace and truth belong both to the Logos and Wisdom (BWS 6:15–19). There is a very interesting connection in the use of the word 'dwelt', where the Logos was made flesh and 'dwelt' among us. (John 1:14) The Greek word is *eskenosen* – which links up with the Hebrew word *Shekinah*. Here we have a vast mystery. *Shekinah* is used in the Hebrew bible to denote the dwelling place of God; it is always a feminine noun; it is always associated with glory; and it is an attribute of God, or the female presence of God. And Shekinah and Hochma are closely related (see chapter 9).

One particular word at the end of the Prologue is of great interest – (John 1:18) Translated as 'bosom' of the Father (RSV) and 'at the Father's side' (GNB), the Greek word *kolpe* usually means lap or mother's womb. Again we see a slide from female to male consciousness.

There are many other similarities between the Prologue, Wisdom and Hellenistic goddesses. For instance, the Shekinah may have been used as another name for God, or as a direct reference to God's female presence, linking up with the echoes of Wisdom. The fact that it is immediately followed by a reference to glory quite specifically calls upon the tradition of the glory of the Shekinah. The word translated by the RSV as 'only' Son of the Father is in fact *monogones*, the word applied to Wisdom, only born, unique in herself, and to Persephone in the Orphic Hymns (see above p. 49).

We see that the writer of the Fourth Gospel has confronted the ancient Wisdom and goddess figures with the new Logos and subsumed into it the Wisdom nature and narrative, echoing

Wisdom's own descriptions of herself. In the nascent Christian world of the second century those familiar with these figures will have recognised them; others, and particularly those in the gentile world to whom the Gospel was primarily addressed, would take the description on its own merits. These were the attributes of the Logos, and of the Logos alone. The point is made even more clearly in the opening verses of the Prologue.

The similarities are not in question. What is to be noted here is a succession of stand-offs: the new notion of the male Logos as opposed to female Wisdom, on the point of gender and on the point of a new Christian belief versus the old Judaism and the old Goddess religions. In a brilliant *tour de force* the author of the Prologue has melded all the ingredients to produce an unbroken, clearly decipherable, manifesto for his new religion. Even the disputed verses of John 1:6 and 1:15, whether interpolated later or not, lend credence to this view. John, the man sent from God who comes to bear witness to the light, is not, it appears, referring to the light of the BWS 7:29 to which Wisdom was found to be superior; rather, perhaps, to the 'eternal light' of which she is said to be a reflection in the BWS 7:26, or to the many descriptions of her as a lamp or light to her followers. The man from God prepares the way for 'the light' who in John 1:14 became flesh, and in v.15 is identified yet again by John as the one expected, who, though following him, was 'before him'. That is to say, when Jesus appears in v.29 'coming towards him', no one is surprised that it is a man who is doing so rather than an incarnation of female Wisdom.

John, a man, has prepared his audience for someone else, like himself a man, though greater and more mysterious. He has not suggested that if it is not Sophia it might be Isis, Persephone, or the Great Mother who will arrive, yet he has used symbols and attributes of all of these figures in his introduction.

For the writer of the Fourth Gospel, Jesus is to take over all of these attributes, from the transcendental to the mundane; his hearers will recognise them: the Jews will know Hochma, the gentiles, Persephone and Isis. The writer proceeds to build his overarching theme, to present his vision while clearly and unmistakably laying down the groundwork of unalterable hostility between those who accept the new and those who do not. The notion of 'domination' is introduced, while total exclusivity of salvation is claimed for Jesus.

In contrast to Wisdom who enjoined all to come to her table (Proverbs 9), where her Spirit in the BWS 1:7 fills the world, where she makes herself available without difficulty (BWS 6:14) and is universlly present ordering the whole world (BWS 8:1). Jesus in the Fourth Gospel is made to outline for his disciples and followers a separation from the world, a distancing from it (John 17:1–26). He tells his desciples (v.16) that they and He are not of the world. He does not pray for the world, but only for those particularly given to him (v.9). It is crucial that those who believe are those who can partake with him, and again in John 10:9 only those who go in by his door will be saved. While the words of Jesus can be construed in a much gentler form than in ways they have been understood up until now, yet if Jesus has taken over from Wisdom and stands as Jesus–Sophia, then Sophia's universality has been lost. Rosemary Ruether has pointed out that the 'crucial issue' in John is 'his theological principle that only through Christ is there access to the Father'.[6]

This has had grevious consequences for many of the world's peoples; only today do we see signs that Christians will countenance a parity of faiths. For the last two thousand years an essential part of the domination–subjugation ethos that started with the banishing of female Wisdom has been the notion of the superiority of Christianity over all other religions.

The Christian Fathers and the domination of women and Nature
The concept of alienation from 'the world' to be found in the

Fourth Gospel, and of salvation only for those who take up Christian belief, is, of course, fully resonant with Paul's teachings. Such salvation is to do with the soul after death, and while resurrection eventually is in the body yet, with belief in Jesus as Redeemer as expressed in his life, death and resurrection, religious attitudes moved towards a concentration on such personal salvation and away from the material and the world in which we live. The early Church Fathers also looked closely at the similarities and contrasts between Wisdom and Jesus Christ and took further steps to concentrate Wisdom's new person into His.

We see the acceptance of Christ as Wisdom Incarnate and also his function of relating to sense-bound intelligence, and of conveying the soul – which is pre-existent – further on its path of assimilation to the spiritual divine. The path of the soul is not as it was in the BWS 1:5–6, that is, to offer a home to Wisdom because of righteous acts and thought in this world; rather, its specific purpose is concerned with salvation. Wisdom is incarnate in Jesus the human and mediates between the divine and the material, and because of this incarnation humans are able to regain their path to pre-Fall divine purity. Essentially humans are prone to sin by nature and there is the fact of universal sinfulness.

Other Fathers disputed whether Wisdom was God's word or God's spirit. What was never in dispute was that Wisdom was appropriated into the Trinity. Although the Eastern Church retained to a large extent her title of Sophia, and she was the mediator and performer of God's work in the world, yet emphasis in both East and West turned away from nature and the material, took little interest in observation and measurement of natural laws and seasons, and turned to personal salvation and eventually a hatred of the material world of everyday life, of 'the body', and eventually of women.

The acid rain of the Church Fathers' vituperation falls on women in particular. The relatively liberal Clement of Alexandria called upon women to 'blush for shame when you think on what nature you are'. This nature was clearly outlined by Tertullian who describes Eve, and thus women, as 'the devil's gateway . . . *you* destroyed so easily God's image, man. On account of *your* descent, is death, even the Son of God had to die.'[7] Thus women have to carry guilt for the advent of death into the world, for the death of Jesus and, therefore, though never expressed, for the death of Wisdom in the world.

Augustine, the great saint and founder of theological doctrine, makes it clear that women, alone, stand for carnality – sin – and man, alone, for spirit. In man alone, that is, the male, is the image of God. A woman alone, however, is not in the image of God. For this to happen, she has to be accompanied by her husband. Augustine writes:

The woman together with her husband is the image of God, so that the whole substance may be one image, but when she is referred to separately in her quality as a helpmeet which regards the woman alone then she is not the image of God. But as regards the man alone, he is the image of God as fully and as completely as when the woman too is formed with him in one.

Thus women are not only not in the image of God in their own right, but since men are so, without women, the implication is that women have no place with divinity, or only that which comes to them by the fact of their standing with their husbands. And it is to be noted here that we are also concerned with a definition of female as body and the male as spirit.

Sherry B Ortner in 'Is female to male as nature is to culture?' (1973) has outlined how women came to be seen as closer to nature than men, and how men have appropriated the term 'culture' to themselves, and have determined that culture must rule and control nature. She writes, 'Women are universally devalued because they are seen as closer to nature than men, men being seen as more unequivocally occupying the high ground of culture . . . because culture's job is to control nature, men are accorded the right to control women' (pp. 67–88). This statement has been challenged because of its 'universal nature', many scholars pointing to the sacralisation of women and of nature in early cultures.[8] However I see it as essentially accurate in the context here. Again, Rosemary Ruether (1974) has charted the progress of the devaluation of women and of nature in discussing the misogyny of the Church Fathers. She points out that virginal women are acceptable, but at the price of the male despising all women's physicality. She refers to Augustine's view that there is a natural subordination of female to male as flesh must be subject to spirit in the right ordering of nature (p. 157), and points out that woman is 'peculiarly the symbol of the Fall and sin . . .' in that she represents 'the body principle which revolts against its ruling spirit and draws the reason down to its lower dictates' (p. 157). Ruether discusses woman both as a submissive body in the order of nature and as a 'revolting' body in the disorder of sin. Augustine, says Ruether, can explain women's subjugation as natural because of their 'bodiliness'. The virulence of the Church Fathers against women was expressed later by the medieval theologian Aquinas: 'As regards the individual nature, woman is defective and misbegotten, for the active force in the male leads to the production of a perfect likeness in the masculine sex; while the production of women comes from a defect in the active force.'[9]

That this view of women continued in the Christian church and still has not been eradicated can be seen by a brief glance at some Christian utterances. Saint Bonaventure in his life of Saint Francis comments:

He bade that intimate intercourse with women, holding converse with them, and looking upon them – the which be unto many an

occasion of falling – should be zealously shunned, declaring that by
such things a weak spirit is broken, and a strong one offtimes
weakened. He said that one who held converse with women –
unless he were of an especial uprightness – could as little avoid
contamination there from as he could, in the words of Scripture go
upon hot coals and his feet not be burned. He himself so turned
away his eyes that they might not behold vanity after this sort that
he knew the features of scarce any woman . . . he maintained that
converse with women was a vain toy, except only for confession or
the briefest instruction . . .[10]

In our own era such views have not greatly changed. Women who
aspire to ordination in the Anglican church meet with considerable
misogyny: it is good that these views are at long last being strongly
challenged.

Here are some recent statements:

We maintain that the ministration of women will tend to produce a
lowering of the spiritual tone of Christian worship, such as is not
produced by the ministrations of men before congregations largely
or exclusively female . . . we believe that it would be impossible for
the male members of the average Anglican congregation to be
present at a service at which a woman ministered without
becoming unduly conscious of her sex. (Archbishops' Commission
on Women and the Ministry, 1936.)

The priesthood of Women will be like an ineradicable virus in the
bloodstream of the universal Church which once it is there will
never be got out again. (Bishop of London, Dr Graham Leonard,
General Synod, February, 1987.)

Dr Leonard, in the run-up to a Synod discussion on the ordination
of women priests in late 1989, compared the situation of the
Anglican church with that of Britain facing the French enemy

during the Napoleonic wars: 'We face an invasion here and now. We must declare ourselves so that we may resist it, and it is hoped, be able to repel it' (Graham Leonard, *Independent*, 31 October, 1989). Here the bishop makes his message quite clear. Just as the French were once his country's enemy so are women the church's enemy now. They have to be resisted and, if possible, repelled.

It is of some interest that Leonard raises the memory of the Napoleonic wars in his discourse. Jean-Marie Aubert (1973), following an overview of Patristic misogyny, points out that the church taught that 'women's weakness obliged man to exercise tutelage – as in the Code Napoleon – a subjection to Lord and Master' (p. 105). Women's association with 'carnality' brought them into a despised category because of the tendency to deprecate everything carnal. Not only, says Aubert, did 'women appear as the symbol and seat of sexuality, women were marginalised to the sexual function only . . . women had to accept the burden of the spiritual hatred of the flesh' (pp. 54–55).

The Code Napoleon which takes the superiority of the male to the female as a major rationale, with the consequent loss of social, sexual, economic and political power on the part of the female, is, according to Aubert, based on 'la marginalisation canonique de la femme' (p. 68).

Matilda Joslyn Gage, a nineteenth-century American feminist, saw the Christian Church as the principal cause of Western society's oppression of women, and held that the church was built on this oppression. In her major work *Women, Church and State* (1893) she writes: 'The most stupendous system of organised robbery known has been that of the church towards women, a robbery that has not only taken her self-respect but all rights of person; the fruits of her own industry; the opportunities for education, the exercise of her own independence, her own conscience, her own will' (p. viii).

Matilda Gage traces the development of this 'system' through the misogyny of the Church Fathers, through celibacy which she sees as nourishing such misogyny, to canon law which enshrined the disablement of women in society. She cites the feudal practice of 'marquette', given sanction and encouragement by the church, as the sexual enslavement of female serfs by their feudal lord. Then the excesses of witch crazes, under the aegis of the church, further reinforced the refusal to women of any status of self–respect or social autonomy. She traces these developemnts as being the justification for the situation of women as chattels with no legal defence against the brutality, cheating and domination by their male relatives. She links the Russian proverb 'A hen is not a bird, nor is a woman a human being' with the teachings of Augustine and Aquinas.

Joseph McCabe (1931), in referring to Jerome, Augustine and Justin, speaks of their 'ghastly contempt' for women, and declares that 'to the Fathers, women is the diabolical source of all the unpleasantness of sex'. A purely masculine hierarchy, generally upholding that woman was unclean, was set up (p. 54). McCabe contrasts this Christian view of women, particularly after the establishment of Christianity as the state religion, with an earlier, less 'ferocious' view. Women came to be identified with sex and 'the world [of the fourth century CE] became obsessed by sex'. he describes a situation where women – the 'cause, object and extension of sin' and the 'seat of carnality' – were continually sexually exploited as victims by the very 'images of God' and 'seats of spirituality' that men had assumed themselves to be. He writes of the position of 95 per cent of women from the fifth to the twelfth century as one of 'increasing subjection . . . while from the thirteenth century when the Church completed a despotic power over European life the position of women steadily worsened' (p. 59). It can be no surprise that this situation arose. Augustine's view was that woman is naturally 'inferior' as body in relation to mind, thus 'a woman has no right to dispose of her own body without male permission'. Procreation is the only reason why there is a female body at all – and there is the famous charge of this Father that the male loses control of his 'bodily member' because of a female presence; therefore the woman is totally sinful. The identification of woman with sex, and sex with sin, are key concepts in patristic thought.

Since women 'entice' men from their higher spiritual concerns, they are right to use every method, including physical cruelty, to control her.

Ruether (1974) describes the confusion in patristic thought over sexual character after the resurrection of the body. Augustine was asked that if woman was 'essentially body and had sensual and depraved characteristics of mind', would there then be only male bodies in the Resurrection? Augustine and Jerome both answer that humanity will rise as 'male and female', but that there will be a transformation of the female body so that it is no longer suited to intercourse and child bearing but is fitted now to 'glory rather than to shame' (p. 160).

It is my contention that this Christian demonisation of women, and of nature, was in large part due to the banishment of the female Wisdom. As memories of her faded into almost total forgetfulness, divine insistence of Jesus Christ's human person as a man became more and more forceful, together with denial of any sexuality to him and determination that 'spirituality' had nothing to do with the body. As all recognition of female divinity perished so it became possible for a persecution to arise which set new standards of ferocity, standards which were to be emulated time and again.

The witch crazes
The subjugation of the female because of the notion of her carnality and her association with nature rose to its peak in the witch crazes of Europe which traversed the Middle Ages and the Renaissance. They died down only in the late eighteenth and early nineteenth

centuries, by which time they had also taken root in North America. Led by the church, these persecutions entailed generations of terror for women – and for those men who stood out against the witch hunts. Records show that numerous people, very probably many millions, and mostly women, in every European village, town and city were tortured and executed. The text which inspired the witch hunters in the fifteenth century and later was the infamous *Malleus Maleficarum*, written by two Dominican inquistors, Sprenger and Kramer, between 1487 and 1489.[11] The authors spend time over women's sexuality, pointing to their lust as a major cause of witchcraft and refer to a defect in women's intelligence which makes them more prone than men to abjure the faith. Concerning men, the *Malleus Maleficarum* remarks: 'Blessed be the Most High who has so far preserved the male sex from so great a crime.' And: 'all wickedness is little to the wickedness of a woman . . . what else is a woman but a foe to friendship, an inescapable punishment, a necessary evil, a natural temptation, an evil nature . . . when a woman thinks alone, she things evil.'[12]

It is important to understand that this was a time of great distress, following the Black Death in Europe, with unending wars which attended the change from a feudal to a nationalistic system and a hardness of life which the sixteenth-century philosopher Thomas Hobbes called 'nasty, brutish and short'. Women were designated as the major evil, or evil itself. Andrea Dworkin (1974) comments that although some men did become witches or wizards or made magic, they were never considered to be as evil as women. 'Men were protected from becoming witches not only by virtue of superior intellect and faith but because Jesus Christ . . . died to preserve the male sex from so great a crime; since he was willing to be born and die for us therefore he has granted men this privilege'.[13]

Among the many records of witch trials in Europe, those easily available can be found in the 'Witch Museum' in the island of Jersey. They provide a month-by-month account of the accused and their sentences, covering most of the late sixteenth and seventeenth centuries. Taken at random, October 1625 shows that, under the bailiff Jean Hearault, three witches were hanged and strangled, one executed on the gibbet, two banished forever, and one – Marie Carne – 'Refused to plea, sent to Castle, fate unknown'. In that same month Jeanne Gradon was hanged and strangled. During that year several whole families were executed by various means. Mothers and daughters were sent to the gibbet – and in some cases mothers, daughters, sons and husbands. In a record of those tried in another part of the island during August 1617, Jeanne Guigon, Michelle Jervane, Marie Broquet and Aulne Maine were burned at the stake.

These are a few only of the many hundreds of thousands who suffered, while the various tortures (some of them prolonged) designed to gain confessions are described in detail. The question that has to be asked in this context has to do with a definition of evil. This is not a matter that comes into the realm of theological philosophy. Theodily, for example, concerns itself with the problem of how God, who is all good, can allow evil to exist in the world. This is no such question. The evil I see is in the actions of men who believed themselves to be acting in the interest of the church. These men were prepared to torture with a heinous viciousness and malign objective that can be equalled in history only by those who perpetrated the Holocaust of the Jews in the Second World War, the participants in the Slave Trade and the colonisers who use genocide to acquire land and its valuable contents from indigeneous peoples such as the South American Indians, the First Australians and the Native Americans.

There can be no doubt that the inquisitors and judges who sentenced the so-called witches acted upon what was said in the *Malleus maleficarum*, that is, that there is no evil as great as that of a woman. The evil they themselves perpetrated was accounted by, and to, themselves as good.

The notion of women as deficient, of male as superior, of woman as body and nature and therefore evil, and male as spirit and culture and therefore in a position, and with a duty, to control woman and nature, led to these heights of domination. The *Malleus maleficarum* thundered that 'Jesus Christ died to preserve the male sex from so great a crime [witchcraft]; since He was willing to be born and die for us, therefore he has granted men this privilege'. The conclusion here is that women are excluded from Jesus' plan of salvation. And although a modern, 'rational' response might be to deride this as an abominable historical and theological aberration, Graham Leonard, former Bishop of London, and his clergy following, the 'Cost of Conscience' movement, with its acceptance of labelling women priests as 'viruses' and 'enemies to be repelled' can be viewed as being quite close to the position adopted by the authors of the *Malleus Maleficarum*.

It is the traditional view of the masculinity of Jesus which provides this movement with its philosophy and the justification for its actions. Many Christian readers by this time may be quarrelling with me and declaring that it is not the perception of Jesus as masculine that has caused all the trouble. They may point to other perceptions, notably the transition of Wisdom in the Jewish religion from female to the Book of the Law, the Torah; also to the male dominance and misogyny that became incorporated into the Jewish tradition. I have shown in my paper on 'Antisemitism in Britain' (1991) that it has been easy for such perceptions to be used out of context and to fuel anti-Jewish sentiment. Those who like to think 'the Jews killed the Goddess' are answered by Carol Christ and Judith Plaskow (1979). Other readers may point to the writings of such Jewish philosophers as Philo who lived in the first century CE who was most ambivalent about Wisdom. On the one hand he accepted her as part of God, but on the other declared that she could not be female but must be understood as masculine, because only the masculine is superior. And certainly such readers may bring forward the male dominance and female persecution that has taken place over the millenia throughout the world which has not been influenced by Christianity – from Chinese footbinding to Indian *suttee*, for example, practices which Christians have strongly opposed.

All of this is true and undeniable. Others have attempted overviews of world civilisations to explain how this came about.[14] Nevertheless I write specifically from the point of view of my own century and culture. I am part of, and I speak to, women and men brought up in Western culture, and it is *that* culture I am analysing. Within it there has been an ancient tradition of Wisdom, as female aspect of God, creator, nurturer, teacher, architect, and one who dwells with, and mediates on behalf of, human beings. Within herself she holds memories of more ancient goddesses, and typified independent, autonomous, intellectual and spiritual women, and also delighted in their bodies. It is that divine woman that Western culture, brought about by Christianity, overturned and derided, labelled as deficient and evil, and set against the male, typified by a concept of Jesus Christ, a male person who carries God within himself only. Whatever the living preacher from Galilee may have thought or wished, his heritage has until the present been built up in this way.

Summary

We have seen in the gospels that Jesus associates himself with Wisdom, but does not appear to claim to be Wisdom himself. However this claim is made on his behalf by scholars, reinforced by Paul's conviction that all Wisdom is in Jesus Christ. At this point, Wisdom changes not only gender, but also her character, as creator of nature and teacher of nature's secrets. Attention is diverted from an understanding of the material universe and care for it towards concepts of salvation in the afterlife brought about by belief in

Jesus Christ, his crucifixion and resurrection. This also includes a demand that to obtain such salvation all must share this belief.

Wisdom's attributes and titles are used in the New Testament as descriptions of Jesus, with the result that, as Christianity developed, the concent of a divine female, part of God, or God Herself, became entirely lost. Rather, since nature was devalued in comparison with salvation, and women were associated with nature, a notion of control arose in which men who represented the spiritual were in authority over women and the material world, and were able to exploit both for their perceived needs. Further, women were held to be accountable through the Fall, for evil in the world, and were treated with pitiless savagery.

This state of affairs set the scene for Western civilisation, and has conditioned its society and laws, and the present relationship between women and men in the world.

9. The Mother of God, God The Mother and the Shekinah

Considerable speculation concerning the gender aspects of the three persons of the Trinity comprised a constituent of Christian thought in the early centuries CE. For a long time the Eastern church continued to assent to the female identity of the Holy Spirit. In the West some early theologians and thinkers ascribed feminine aspects to Jesus, or the Father, or the Holy Spirit, but there is a sting in the heart of the arguments. This is made very clear in an early poem from the first century CE.

A cup of milk I was offered
and I drank its sweetness as the delight of the Lord.
The Son is the cup
and he who was milked is the Father
and he who milked him is the Holy Ghost.
His breasts were full
and his milk should not drip out wastefully.
The Holy Ghost opened the Father's raiment and mingled the milk
   from the
Father's two breasts
and gave that mingling to the world, which was unknowing.
Those who drink it are near his right hand.
The Spirit opened the Virgin's womb
and she received the milk.

The Virgin became a mother of great mercy;
she labored, but not in pain, and bore a Son.
No midwife came.
She bore him as if she were a man,
open, with dignity, with kindness.
She loved him, swaddled him and revealed his majesty. (Ode 19,
Odes of Solomon.)[1]

While this poem cannot be ascribed to a mainstream Christian
tradition, yet it is obviously Christian in content, and makes its
point very clearly. The female figure is called the father, giving
milk from his breasts. The virgin, a woman, bore a Son not in pain –
and thus escaped the 'curse of Eve', and openly with dignity 'bore
him as if she were a man'. It is clearly to be understood that to be a
man is better than to be a woman, and a father is superior to a
mother.

Somewhat later Clement of Alexandria repeats a similar theme:

> Milk of the bride
> Given of heaven
> Pressed from sweet breasts, Gifts of thy Wisdom –
> These thy little ones
> Draw for their nourishment . . .
> With spiritual savour
> From breasts of the Word.[2]

Here we are to understand that the Word, *Logos*,[3] also the human
Jesus, is providing, in the milk from his breasts, the gifts of
Wisdom. Wisdom has been totally integrated into him. All that
was Hochma's – the nourishment of the world, her spiritual aspect,
her home base of heaven has been brought into the incarnation, the
bodily presence, of Jesus, who even takes over a female biology yet
is never a female.

Jesus has become the bride and the mother, but does not lose his male character. Ann Loades, who is a Christian feminist theologian, comments on this. 'It seems to be the tradition of the all-sufficient male ... androgynously all competent, embodying female wisdom' (1987, p. 91). It is to be noted that even where divine female imagery is used, it is manipulated to help the cause of male supremacy. Loades makes the point even clearer with a reference to the eleventh-century Christian philosopher Anselm. He asks himself why it is not reasonable to refer to the second and third persons of the Trinity as mother and daughter, since both are truth and wisdom – *veritas et sapienta* (both feminine). He comes to the conclusion that it is more consistent to use the language of Father and 'Son' because 'the first and principal cause of offspring is always in the father' (Loades, 1987, p. 94).

Mainstream Christian theology in the ensuing centuries continued to insist on the superiority of men and the subordination of women. Gratian of Bologna (1140 CE) writes: 'Women should be subject to their men. The natural order for mankind is that women should serve men, and children their parents, for it is just that the lesser should serve the greater.'[4] And this fearful doctrine has not yet, over 800 years later, been expunged from society's consiousness. It is necessary, however, to be very clear that the cause of domination and oppression is not a simple matter of gender. What is in question is the attribution of 'superior' qualities to the male person and the consequent use made, and power exercised, by him. An egalitarian viewpoint based on a concept of 'equal but different' is perhaps one way out of this cul-de-sac.

Mary, the Virgin
That evil is supposed to be inherent in the sexuality of the woman, and the idea that men are both the potential victims and necessary controllers of female sexuality led to exaggerated emphasis on the status of virginity.

Since the Fathers could hardly suggest a genocide of women (although this did actually happen during the witch hunts in later times), they found a solution to their problem in the figure of the Virgin Mary.

The Blessed Virgin in conceiving a son neither lost her virginity nor experienced any venereal pleasure . . . the troublesome weariness that all pregnant women are burdened with she did not experience, who alone, conceived without pleasure . . . she has not only the honour of having given the substance of her flesh to the only begotten god, hers was the task as well of caring for and nourishing the victim and even of placing it near the altar at the appointed hour . . . nor was she merely engaged in witnessing a cruel spectacle, rather she rejoiced utterly that her only begotten being was offered for the salvation of the human race. (Francisco Suarez, died 1617.)[5]

With this picture Suarez sets out fully the content and the ongoing results of the construction of the Virgin Birth and its effects upon women and on society. That Mary did not lose her virginity in becoming pregnant sets virginity against Eve's punishment (Genesis 3). That she *alone* of women did not experience pleasure in conception highlights the misogyny of the writer's tradition. Father Suarez does not consider the substantial majority of women who submit, or are forced to submit, to unwelcome sexual intercourse; who are raped; who in conceiving know they may be likely to die in nine months time; who even in so-called romantic circumstances have seldom within and outside marriage, until the present, been considered as more than a vehicle for the male partner's pleasure. Rather, an idea is imposed that sexual intercourse necessarily means pleasure for women. Women who are thus described – apparently all women – are therefore set apart from the Virgin, not only by the apparent impossibility of parthenogenesis but by their supposed sexual enjoyment. In addition, actual human conception, as well as sexual pleasure, is considered evil. This is set out clearly by Suarez' fellow seventeenth-century cleric, St. Jean Eudes, quoted by Marina Warner in her excellent account of the politics of Mariology, *Alone of All Her Sex* (1979).

It is a subject of humiliation to all the mothers of the children of Adam to know that when they are with child they carry within them an infant, who is the enemy of God, the object of his hatred and malediction and the shrine of the demon (p. 57).

Lest women should presume to lay some of the blame for this state of affairs upon the fathers of their children, the church need only hark back to the fourth-century church Father Jerome for an answer: 'As long as a woman is for birth and children, she is different from man as body is from soul. But when she wishes to serve Christ more than the world, then she will cease to be a woman and will be called a man.'[6] Only then, it would appear, is she a real human being. Mary is blessed because she experienced no pleasure in conception, and because of her virginity she is able to reverse the consequences of the Fall. What did this mean? The comprehensive dimensions of the cult of virginity trailed a corollary of asceticism and misogyny. Men vented their hostility on women, who had no means of repelling unwanted sexual advances or of controlling conception. Their punishment was not only alienation from a society where the male was the norm, but alienation from the divine. A virgin mother who experienced no sexual intercourse and who was submissive to male authority was to be women's role model.

In so far as Mary was chosen to bear the human who was divine, women had to stay apart from her. Once she had given birth however, she could act as a model for mothers. Suarez has her caring and nourishing the victim, placing him for sacrifice and rejoicing in it. Mothers whose sons were and are taken from them to fight in wars across the world have been able to take this aspect of Mary as consolation for their loss and to learn from her what is expected of them.[7]

Virgin birth which came about by submission carries this theme further. Mary submits to caring for her son, being rejected by him, and rejoicing in his sacrifice, a path presented to women who had no other alternative than to pass along it.

The church's view of Mary's submission to impregnation by the Holy Spirit enshrined two separate but interconnected themes which were used against women. The first is to do with the overthrowing of the consequences of the Fall, the regeneration of sinful humankind, and in particular the reversal of the sins of disobedience by Eve. The second spiritualises virginity and takes it out of the realm of the body or matter, which were both considered evil. Since no woman can emulate the Virgin Mother, however, each woman has to be identified with 'sinful' Eve and be responsible for death entering the world.

Showing any pleasure in sexual activity – even in the 'lawful' area of marriage, until recently branded woman in Christian society as defiled and degraded. (Other types of sexual acitivity or orientation of course still attract abuse and often persecution.)

The emphasis on virginity as 'spiritual' and divorced from the body made women's view of themselves split into further divisions. It is difficult to believe one's body is evil; if we are required to do so, then we take on self-hatred, and thus reinforce the view of patriarchal society. We internalise its hatred of us.

Thus the paradox appeared of the submissive virgin, who in the fifth century CE was named Theotokos, mother of God, and was lauded and worshipped as such. A later doctrine described her immaculate assumption to heaven. Then she is translated into becoming the recipient of Wisdom and Goddess titles, and venerated over a long period in vast areas in ways not unlike those previously used in the worship of the mother goddesses. But there is always a difference. Mary is set apart from the ancient goddesses by her virginity. Although Anat, for example, is described as a virgin – *betulah* – the Hebrew word which, together with its synonym *almah*, were translated into Greek as *parthenos*, virgin, such words in the Semitic languages merely indicated an unmarried woman during her nubile period. The Virgin Anat renewed her virginity by bathing in a stream each year, indicating the renewal of life in spring time and even the renewal of life after death. The 'virgin who conceived and bore a child' in the Book of Isaiah was not necessarily *virgo intacta*, simply a young unmarried woman.

A possible Canaanite background for Mary has been proposed by the Australian scholar E C B MacLaurin (1980). He has traced her lineage from at least Hittite Anat, and compares Mariolatry during the fifth and subsequent early centuries of our era with Isis worship. Others draw similar conclusions about Mary's relationship with pagan goddesses. Ean Begg (1985) has surveyed the continuous cult of the Black Virgin and has pursued a strong case for identifying these mysterious statues and icons with former local female divinities. One must realise the essential differences however. Anat, for example is part of the vegetation cycle and reflects Nature, or indeed is Nature, and encourages humans to identify with such cycles of Nature. Mary's virginity, however, sets her *apart* from Nature and from human nature. It is the death and resurrection of her son that is the key point of Christian doctrine. She is set far away from the human or natural condition, as shown by Elinor Gadon (1989): 'The image of the Mother Goddess with her child represented her sexuality and procreative power, whereas that of the Virgin and child stood for her celibacy and the will of God. She was merely the agent through which he acted' (p. 192).

Yet although Mary as Virgin appears to deny the ancient

goddesses, she cannot extinguish them. This paradox becomes more potent when one considers the content of the paeans of praise for Mary. Wisdom, so long forgotten and obscured, suddenly returns in her new form. She is recalled in the 'Litany of the Blessed Virgin', which contains a number of Wisdom titles and derivatives. The Virgin is called 'Mirror of Justice, Seat of Wisdom'. She is the 'health of the sick' and 'comforter of the afflicted'. She is the 'mother of good counsel'. Alongside such titles others echo those of Ishtar: 'Gate of Heaven', 'Morning Star'. She is apostrophised as Queen of Heaven as well as Virgin and Mother.

But Mary is nowhere God the Mother. Her most fervent adorers may go no further than 'Mother of our creator, Mother of Christ'. While she is praised and lauded, her virginity takes on all those characteristics for which she is given homage. The more Mary is worshipped, the further she is removed by her worshippers from participation in the natural world.

Her followers may sometimes believe that she works miracles on their behalf – at Fatima or Lourdes, for example. But however much power such popular cults may ascribe to her, what has been called 'the problem of the immaculate womb' has set a seal of disgust relating to women's sexuality and has laid guilt on all women with the exception of those dedicated to virginity – and even they must be declared 'becoming a man' in order to enter heaven on equal terms with men.[8]

As far as her Wisdom titles are concerned, Mary cannot resemble Hochma to any great extent. Her functions are not to co-architect and create, or to sustain and teach the world, but to comfort and to intercede with the deity on the suppliant's behalf. She is not the 'spirit of God dwelling in a good soul', and even though she was revered as 'Queen of Heaven', yet women on earth remained the repository of evil and could identify with her only as a suffering mother. It has been noted that where female images are used, such as in the description of the sweetness of breast milk, and where bodily functions are described, they are converted to the unnatural. Breast milk comes from the *father*, Mary is *intacta* after the birth of her child, having conceived *without* impregnation by a man. The world of the everyday in such thinking is not holy, not the realm of the divine, not to be looked to for inspiration and education. Rather it is degraded, and women, who are classed as being more in touch with, and representative of, the world of nature, degraded alongside it. In the case of the Virgin Mary the manner in which the feminine was introduced fuelled more misogyny rather than less, since she was both virgin and mother, an impossibility for the ordinary woman. This gave no opening for any redress. She was the submissive virgin; submissive virgins in this world, however, would be made pregnant – and would no longer be virgins. And women's hope in the next world depended on their losing their female characteristics and becoming like a man. In Mary, the 'Seat of Wisdom', the Wisdom of the past, Hochma, even divided Sophia, was forgotten and buried.

The Jewish experience

So far I have dwelt at some length on my perception of Christianity's persecution of consciousness of divinity in the female – whether in heaven or on earth – with all the destructive effects that such persecution brings. Other monotheistic faiths which perceive God in the masculine gender and serve him with male priests and hierarchy are also guilty of misogyny, resulting in poisonous effects on individuals and on society. Judaism, Islam, and other religions have been, and sometimes still are, guilty of cruelty to women, and certainly of regarding them as less important than men. I now want to look at the Jewish experience as regards the denial of the divine female.[9]

The Hebrew bible writers and their successors, the editors and final collators of the bible, certainly attempted to banish female divinity. They also instituted commandments which appear to us to be misogynistic. The so-called 'purity' laws regarding menstruation and childbirth in the Hebrew bible, for example, have an anti-woman character, as do other commandments. And it is particularly distressing to read the polemics against goddesses and records of their destruction. Later there are many examples of rabbinic misogyny, and interpretations of Jewish law in the community that put women at a disadvantage.

Normative Jewish tradition has certainly given man a higher status than woman, no matter how often she is declared to be 'Queen of the Home' and to have domestic power. It has been pointed out in fact that no matter what job women or men are doing, the latter will have a superior standing in the community.[10]

Women's sexuality has certainly been seen to be restricted to heterosexuality and marriage which together, with the corollaries of childbearing and rearing, are traditonally held to be their destinies. Yet even within these constrictions some aspects of former beliefs and practice have filtered through, and the sacredness of heterosexuality (though not of any other form of sex) has been a ground of belief and, to some extent, practice.

Yet given that within marriage women's sexual life is not considered evil or sinful – indeed it is considered to be a matter of joy – there is still a catch. The sexuality is in the control of the male and the subject of male–regulated laws. Women in the Jewish tradition have no power of saying 'no' if they do not feel like having intercourse, at a time when the obligation based on rabbinic law says they have to do so.

Sex outside marriage is considered sinful, and if with persons of one's own sex, or non-Jewish or both, positively evil. There is much in Jewish tradition that speaks in double tongue, on the one hand lauding the 'Queen of the Home', while on the other making sure she is controlled by male tradition. The Jewish religion has never labelled women as evil, however, and unlike Christianity does not count them as the source of sin or death. Consequently women have not suffered the type of hostility to them like that displayed by male Christians to Christian women.

Wisdom, the Torah and the Shekinah

I want now to see the reflections of the divine female Hochma as she filtered into androcentric Jewish life. I suggest that in the life of traditional Judaism as it has come down to us, and which I have experienced, Hochma is there, hidden in disguise; she was not, however, until very recently available to women at all.

I have already discussed the way in which the problem of female Wisdom was solved by the thinkers in Judaism at the end of the biblical period. The problem centred around two issues. Not only was Wisdom female but she appeared to be separate from God, and this challenged the monotheism that was so important in the religion. By making the Books of the Law most holy, in which all Wisdom was to be found, the solution seemed to have been found. Enoch's book described how the Lady Wisdom retired to heaven, and the seeker after her followed her and came back to earth with a written text of commands, punishments and rewards. These became the Torah and replaced the earlier universal nature-centred Wisdom.

Yet this written text has never remained only within the pages of a book, however sacred. Any visitor to a synagogue today will see that the heart of the service is a drama. From a recess, what appears to be a figure with richly embroidered clothing is lifted out; it is then seen not to be an image or statue – that would be strictly forbidden. But it wears a silver crown, and from its skirts two carved cylinders of wood protrude. It is lifted into the arms of the celebrant and carried in procession. Then its garment is removed, and it is seen to be the Scroll of the Law – the *sefer Torah* which is then unrolled to the part which provides the reading for the day. When this is completed, the ceremony takes place in reverse; the Scroll is again dressed in its rich garments, and with great deference placed out of sight. When I was a child, sitting in the gallery of an Orthodox synagogue, I always felt embarrassed that men – for it was only men, who were separate from the women – should be carrying in their arms an object which seemed to me to be a half life–size woman, or a girl like myself, and dressing and undressing it, and that this should be the most sacred part of the service. I see now that, like so many childish perceptions, this one was quite accurate. The Scroll of the Law, the Torah – loved, venerated, the object of the most sacred attention, is the Lady Wisdom. The very words, even letters, are holy. Yet, in this religion, where God may not be given an image and is totally separate from humanity, the Law is presented not just as a book or even as a scroll in itself; it is arranged to resemble a female figure, one that can be carried and cradled in one's arms and where the ceremony of undressing and dressing must indeed evoke echoes, no matter how repressed, of the sexual act. Such sexual overtones are certainly present in a Jewish understanding of the relationship of God and Israel and God and the Sacred Presence of God – the Shekinah.

I am happy that today in the Reform synagogues women may do the same as the men, and that girls may take part in the ritual and the service on equal terms with men and boys.

Because the Shekinah has been of such immense importance in Jewish life, and because until the present time her most important aspect was totally hidden from the majority of Jewish women, I need to spend some time with Her.

We have already looked at *baetyls* (see p. 127) and found that they were connected to the Hebrew word *Bethel*, denoting the house of God, where God might dwell; and in early times might indicate the actual living presence of God within a certain place. The Shekinah contains the Hebrew word *shakan*, meaning 'to dwell', and was held to indicate God's indwelling glory. In the mainstream religion conveyed to the ordinary worshippers, the

Shekinah was an alternative expression for God, and was often used when God was said to be in a certain place, particularly when 'dwelling' among the children of Israel, for example.

There is always, even in the most bland of texts, a suggestion of the mystical and the numinous. In Jewish tradition the Shekinah was often used as a description of the mystical community of Israel in relation to God. It was sometimes referred to as God's Holy spirit (*ruach–ha kodesh*), or even as the essence of God. The Shekinah's glory could appear as light, could rest on selected people (for example, Moses) and accompanied the Israelites in their exile, mourning with them and comforting them. It was said that when the ills of the world are repaired in the last days the Shekinah and God will be reunited.[11]

An aspect of the Shekinah that was never discussed when women were present was that not only is the Hebrew word feminine in gender but that for a particular sect of men within Judaism the Shekinah actually *was* female, and was understood to be, like Wisdom, not only the alter ego of God, a personage in Her own right, but even God Herself. This sect is the Kabbalists. Today the Kabbalah which they study is available and open to any who wish to give it their attention. But for many centuries it was held in tight security, first by Jewish and later by some Christian scholars; it flourished at various periods during the course of the centuries with new waves of interest and speculation coming from Jews in Spain and later from those in Eastern Europe. The Kabbalah is a system of interpretation of the traditional Hebrew texts, together with much mystical and magical speculation about the nature of the creation, the universe, humankind and God. It has been called a 'Jewish Theosophy'. A central thesis is the concept of the Tree of Life, which is expressed in ten emanations called Sephiroth. Together they form a unity of creation. They are shown as pairs of female and male, thus it is said, reflecting the 'image of God' in

Genesis 1:27 – male and female he created them. Enveloping all in her glory is the divine female Shekinah.

Modern scholars have no difficulty in asserting that the Shekinah is a female part of God, and go even further. Gershom Scholem in *The Kabbalah and its Symbolism* (1969), writes, 'she becomes an aspect of God that is a quasi independent feminine element' (p. 105), and declared 'The necessary discovery of the female element with God . . . regarded with the utmost misgiving by non–Kabbalistic sources, was a mystical conception of the feminine principle . . . [it] achieved enormous popularity . . . showing that the Kabbalah had uncovered one of the primordial impulses still latent in Judaism' (p. 105). This latent impulse in Judaism is the understanding of the female element, or female nature of God, or the existence of a divine female presence. Kabbalists used a great deal of sexual language to describe the Shekinah, which made it possible for them both to venerate her but also to see her as controllable by the male.

Today Jewish women for the first time are able to study material concerning the Shekinah. In doing so, many feel their lives transformed. That Judaism has always had, and has never lost, such a divine female, that she has been with women in their distress, that because she is female she is so much more easily accessible to women, that she recalls the ancient tradition of female deities, all this has transformed the religion of Judaism for many women. They can discard the sexist barnacles and relate to the Shekinah as One-in-Herself.

For me it is clear that much of Wisdom's character and essence became part of the Shekinah. Both are concerned in creation, both are the Tree of Life (Proverbs 3:18), both are the presence of God, expressed in light and glory. The light of the Shekinah was seen as an intermediary between God and the world, as was Wisdom's light. There is much material concerning the Shekinah's ascent and descent from heaven to earth, her enthronement in heaven, and even her wings, all reflecting descriptions of Wisdom. Above all, her place as the enveloping radiance of the Tree of Life, encompassing the whole of creation, identifies her as the early Hochma.

In that mystical Judaism, available to men only, and even among men only a certain elite, there were plenty of sexist notions about the Shekinah, very similar to those we met earlier relating to Wisdom. Men have to be married to her, have intimate association with her, possess her. In some texts God and the Shekinah are married. When on the tree of life we look at the different branches or emanations, the *sephiroth*, male and female, we find that Hochma is there certainly, but that she is there as male. Because she is the active principle of knowledge, intelligence and action, she has to be turned into a male form. The accompanying female is Binah–perception, understood to be passive and receptive. Many Jungians today would no doubt go along with this. For me, however, it is sexist, and detracts from Wisdom–Hochma–Sophia of the BWS, where knowledge of all kinds was hers.

There are connections and echoes which link the Shekinah, Mary, Wisdom and the Word (*Logos*). While in the past it has been impossible to identify the first three named as God Herself, today many women are able to do so. Others identify *Logos* as Sophia.

Conclusion

It is difficult to overestimate the significance of this alternative way of perceiving the 'image of God'. It is a question of fundamental re-appraisal by both women and men of their most profound concepts of gender. We have been conditioned by, let us say, the previous sixty-five generations to believe that God manifested himself as a male, either on earth as Jesus, or more abstractly as Father, Lord, King, and so on. This not only has given men, as we have seen, an undue appreciation of themselves as superior beings, set against women and the whole of Nature; it has also bred within women an agony of conflict between what they truly know about themselves and what society tells them to believe.

When in 1977 the London Matriarchy Study Group produced its first publication of *Goddess Shrew* – by chance it received some small attention in a national newspaper – the response was overwhelming. Over five hundred women wrote in one week, asking for a copy. They wrote: 'You have put me in touch with my past. I always knew I was not inferior, but I could never find the words to says so'; and 'I always believed that I was dirty – that menstrual blood made me unclean, yet somehow I couldn't really see why. Now I know it's a lie'. Other women's letters referred to disgust and loathing of their bodies, and their sense of sin and self-abasement. They gave accounts of how they had been brought up to ignore their sexual feelings, and how often in adolescent rebellion they had emphasised these feelings in their behaviour and clothing, yet had still retained a strong sense of guilt.

Many women mentioned the word guilt, in relation to their desire to have some private space in the home for themselves, or time to themselves. The list could be much greater. Basic to all the accounts was an expression of relief. It was summed up by one writer who said 'It was like breathing oxygen'. Restoring to women their own identity as part of the divine and as equal in divinity with men can truly be understood to be the 'breath of life'.

The naming of God as female, or at least having the female named as an aspect of God, has enormous consequences, not least in our attitude to the world itself.

10. The Decline of Wisdom and Decline of Nature

What do the forest bear?
Soil water and pure air
Soil water and pure air
Sustain the earth and all she bears.

(Song of the Chipko women, quoted by Vandana Shiva in *Staying Alive: women, ecology and development*, 1988).

In the ancient world, Wisdom goddesses were venerated as creators and teachers. They were identified with the earth itself and the course of nature. They were the source of blessings and well–being; they were spiritual guides, and could be understood to be the cosmic forces that are the essential structure of the universe. At the same time, they could mediate between the earthly and the spiritual and always called upon human beings to understand that their best course was to seek wisdom. In practice this meant a view of nature as universal guide and source of wisdom.

This widely-held religious system was eventually extinguished by a volcanic uprush of history whose lava and dead ash enveloped all ideas of wisdom goddesses and of the deity of nature. Rather, the notion took root that the earth and this world were of little importance compared with the condition of the individual human being's soul after death. This blended in with a comparable idea that nature itself was inferior to a spiritual dimension. Yet the riches to nature were noted and, since no deity resided in them, no veneration appeared to be needed. The ancient identification between nature and the female was distorted to a pattern where both were assumed to be degraded.

The results of the banishment of a female divine principle have extended from misogyny and oppression of women to domination and exploitation of nature and of the earth's resources. Many thinkers have made the comparison between Women and Nature in this respect, most notably Susan Griffin.[1]

Who is Nature?

We have seen that in the religions of the Ancient Near East, and in much of the Hellenistic cultures, there was general acceptance of Nature as giver and sustainer of life. Personified as a variety of goddesses, a common theme of Nature was that she was depicted as female. Certainly various male deities, for example, Baal-Hadad of the Hittites, personified aspects of weather or elements within nature; but Nature as a totality was female: as the cosmic producer, nurturer, teacher and often saviour.

Nature is self-renewing but may be helped to renew itself by humans, who will benefit from so doing. Nature, in the form of one goddess or another, teaches humans the arts of agriculture, medicine, etc., and in so doing exhibits the two major characteristics of Wisdom, the order of the world and cosmic order, and she teaches such order to humans. Implicit in this is the need for human beings to participate in the rules and laws of Nature, to learn from her, to understand her and to put into practice such rules and laws of harmony and order that can be learned.

The term 'Nature' is subject to many intepretations. She is 'all-parent', Mother–Father, heavenly, abundant, untamed, all taming, an ever–splendid light, all ruling. She is immortal, first born and 'ever still the same'. She is 'to all things common and in all things known'. She is both mother and father, yet without a father.

She is all wife and great father, Providence, immortal, divine architect, who gives 'plenteous seasons and sufficient wealth'.

A modern writer, Carolyn Merchant (1982) introduces Dame Nature in contrast to art and artificially created things. Personified as female, her force is actualised by the course of and laws of Nature (p. xix). Merchant uses the term 'organic' to contrast her to the mechanical, and describes Nature as a living organism. Merchant's theme is the 'Death of Nature' which comes about when the cosmos ceases to be viewed as organic or as a nurturing mother but rather as a machine to be exploited.

She writes: 'Central to the organic theory was the identification of nature, especially the earth, with a nurturing mother: a kindly beneficent female who provided for the needs of mankind [sic] in an ordered planned universe. But another opposing image of nature was also prevalent: wild and uncontrollable . . . that could render violence, storms, droughts and general chaos' (p. 3). She claims that 'both were identified with the female' sex and states that, as the image of the nurturing mother disappeared, the idea of nature as disorder was countered by the concept of power over nature. She suggests such ideas started in the Greek and early Christian period, but that it was in the seventeenth century that the notions of mastery and domination were translated into the actual destruction of Nature.

Merchant charts the various stages of the journey, from a sacred nature to total tyranny and exploitation. She quotes Bacon: 'We can, if need be, ransack the whole globe, penetrate into the bowels of the earth, descend to the bottom of the deep, travel to the farthest regions of this world to acquire wealth, to increase our knowledge or even only to please our eye and fancy' (p. 249). In this statement Bacon has reversed but still retained a concept of Nature as all bountiful; for him, Nature contains all wealth and knowledge, even the aesthetics of beauty and pleasure; only he sees that all this is at the mercy of whoever wants to ransack it, as of right. One is reminded of the BWS 8:9–15. There the Sage's eulogy of Wisdom is in respect of the many benefits, temporal and aesthetic, that will accrue to him through possession of her (see pp. 56–58). By the seventeenth century 'man' was in a position to put such ideas into practice, without acknowledgement of Wisdom-Nature's sacrality, indeed without mercy, compassion or prayer.

Biblical authority for such ideas is claimed through both Genesis creation stories in the first two chapters of the bible. The one believed to be from an older source makes it clear that while Adam was created from the dust of the ground like other living creatures (Genesis 2:7) yet other living creatures are not fit companions for him and a woman is produced from his body (Genesis 21–23). Consequently the woman had no autonomy in creation, less so than 'every beast of the field or bird of the air'. And Adam in this story exercises his power over all creatures by naming them, including naming Woman.

By contrast, in the version of creation in Genesis 1:26–28 dominion is given to the human being, created male and female in the image of God. Even so, it is still dominion over, rather than participation with, Nature. The concept of equality is reinforced by the continuation of this narrative in Genesis 3:20 where Adam although still naming, or renaming the woman, calls her Eve, or the Mother of all living. In this last phrase there are definite echoes of Mother Nature, and the biological connection is made between her and living beings. She resembles Mother Earth in this respect, and here it is appropriate to suggest a similar echo in the story where Adam the man is formed from *adamah*, the ground, a Hebrew feminine word which carries the thought that the 'mother of all living' was the source of Adam's creation, as well as that of the rest of the living world.[2]

The echo dies away. Genesis 3:17–19 has the ground as 'cursed' and offers scope for interpretation that death came to the world because of the sin of the first couple.

St Augustine's view was that with the sin of Adam 'all nature was changed for the worse'.[3] From the Fall onwards it was not nature and this world that mattered, but the expiation of inborn sin through belief and dependence on God's grace. The world to come supplanted this one as source of the good and the proper and the right. Humankind lived in the shadow of the Fall, tainted by sin, Elaine Pagels (1988) suggests that: 'Augustine . . . denies the existence of nature per se for he cannot think of the natural world except as a reflection of human desire and will' (p. 134). She makes the point that his voice was only one in a developing religion and that others dissented on a major scale. But in the end it was Augustine who prevailed, and with him there came the doctrine of original sin identified with the fault of women and sexuality. And there was more to come.

There is a well-known paper by Lynn White Jnr, entitled 'The historical roots of our ecological crisis' (1967). Having described pagan attitudes to nature, he says 'Christianity made it possible to exploit Nature in a mood of indifference to natural objects' (p. 1205). Further, he points out, 'For nearly two millenia Christian missionaries have been chopping down sacred groves which are idolatrous because they assume spirit in nature' (p. 1206). Christian 'arrogance towards nature' (p. 1207) is based on 'man's effective monopoly of the spirit world' (p. 1205).

Many efforts have been made to give a satisfactory answer to Lynn White. It has been pointed out that the Hebrew bible sees Nature as part of God's creation and there are commandments which order human beings to treat it wisely. While the New Testament was a gospel of salvation, placed firmly in the world to come, yet Jesus himself was very aware of the beauty of the earth in this world and was constantly bringing in references to it and its products. Both these indications of a gentler approach, however, have in no way restrained man from ruthlessly exploiting all the earth's products, including the labour power of its subject inhabitants.

It is important to note that while the general outcome of the Augustinian view helped rulers of the world to disregard this world's needs, there has been strong undercurrents of mysticism in Judaism and Christianity that saw God as immanent in the universe as well as transcendent, and saw Nature as the expression of God's handywork and thus to be praised and adored.

The mystical relationship of some of the rabbis with the Shekinah, the immanent presence of God, was contained entirely within extremely narrow male confines. They lived in persecuted Jewish communities, with no power in wider society. But it should be noted that this relationship did in fact exist, and can perhaps be called upon in different circumstances to provide wider and more harmonious ways of living on our planet. This is also true of those Christian religious philosophers and mystics who have envisioned Nature and the universe as one with God, and have called upon humankind to understand this, respect it and work within it.

The treatment meted out by his superiors to Teilhard de Chardin, the leading exponent of such views in the twentieth century, is saddening although it runs true to form. Teilhard de Chardin, a modern mystic, scientist and a Jesuit, was able to envision a reconciliation between God and Nature, heaven and earth.[4] He was able to find enough scope in his Christian faith for a view of a synthesis between the transcendence of God and His immanence in Nature. It must be stressed that this is original to de Chardin. That even by the mid-twentieth century such views still could not be published during the author's lifetime says much about the continuous domination of mainstream theology which has informed much of Christian thinking up to the present time. It was only because of the devotion of those around Teilhard de Chardin and those who worked with him that after his death his works can now be read in their entirety.

There still may be time for a remedy. What that remedy is is the essence of the new, 'green' thinking that has recognised the total exploitation of Nature which has led to the possibility, if not probability, of planetary catastrophe, at least as far as humans are concerned. As many feminists are pointing out, however, 'green thinking' by itself is not enough.

Eco-feminism

Recent books on eco-feminism address the disaster that confronts the human race. There is general agreement that the cause of this disaster is the domination of Nature by patriarchy and that there is some hope of reprieve, provided that humans change their attitudes and practice.

What is eco-feminism? Its theology is best described by Rosemary Radford Ruether, in her essay 'Toward an ecological–feminist theory of Nature', in Judith Plant, *Healing the Wounds* (1989).[5]

'An ecological-feminist theology of nature must rethink the whole western theological tradition of the hierarchical chain of being and chain of command. The theology must question the hierarchy of human over non-human nature as a relationship of ontological and moral value . . . it must unmask the structures of social domination, male over female, owner over worker, that mediate this domination . . . finally it must question the model of hierarchy that starts with non-material spirit [God] as the source of the chain of being and continue down to non-spiritual 'matter' as the bottom of the chain of being and the most inferior, valueless, and dominated point in the chain of command.' Ruether further makes the point that non-human Nature has been disrooted by human development. 'There is virtually no place on the planet where one can go to find "nature untouched by human hands"' (p. 149). Because of this, because Nature has been so marred by humans, the 'remaking of our relation with nature and with each other is an historical project and struggle of re-creation' (p. 149). She emphasises that no relationship of 'mind' and 'nature' can be achieved or evolve without first recognising the 'interconnection of social domination and the domination of nature', and then setting about changing this mind-set and practice. To do this one must 'disrupt the linear concept or order' and endeavour to fit human ecology into non-human ecology in a way that maximises the welfare of the whole (p. 149).[6]

Vandana Shiva in *Staying Alive: women, ecology and development* (1988) specifically addresses the effect on women in 'developing' countries, in particular India, of the violation of nature implicit in the concept of 'development' as portrayed by the First World. She says there needs to be an appreciation of the needs of ecology together with an appreciation of the 'feminine principle', and introduces an analysis of development which she terms 'maldevelopment' and such 'maldevelopment' as the 'death of the feminine principle' (pp. 3–5). She defines maldevelopment as 'the violation of the integrity, of organic interconnected and interdependent systems that sets in motion a process of exploitation, inequality, injustice and violence' (pp. 5–6). She also describes the desecration of the natural world of the 'undeveloped' countries and the effect this has on women's lives.

She speaks of the Goddess of the forest, Aranyi, who is the 'primary source of life and fertility', where the 'diversity harmony and self-sustaining nature of the forest formed the organisational principles guilding Indian civilisation' (p. 54). Such harmony was disregarded and the ecology of the forest destroyed by the 'masculinist' forestry of the colonial powers, leading to the destruction of the trees and the land. As a result there was increasing hardship for women, whose lot was to go ever further in search of fuel. Such 'development' Shiva categorises as life-destroying. She describes the work of the Chipko women who risked their lives to save trees from being cut down, and who link their struggles against the exploitation of the forest with a spirituality of wholeness. The song they sing, quoted at the beginning of this chapter, links with her vision of the 'feminine principle'. She sees Terra Mater – the earth – as our mother, where she declares that Nature is *Prakriti*, the creator and source of wealth, and that rural women, peasants and tribals who live in and derive sustenance from nature have a systematic and deep knowledge of Nature's processes of reproducing wealth. Here I see a strong similarity with Wisdom's place as creator and source of nature.

Vandana Shiva says that what the understanding and practice of the feminine principle will achieve is an overturning of the view that Nature and women are worthless and passive 'and perhaps finally dispensable'. The elements of nature that the dominant view has treated as 'waste' are the very ones that will sustain us. Women's work, including her reproductive work and women's survival expertise, must come back on to the centre stage in human history. The work and example of Third World women should be recognised as 'laying the foundations for the recovery of the feminine principle in nature and society and through it the recovery of the earth sustainer and provider' (p. 224).

Vandana Shiva insists that the 'scientific', masculinist attitude to development of the Third World countries is a destroyer of wealth, not a developer. Based on the Western hierarchical principle, without knowledge of, or interest in, the older feminine principle, it is totally counterproductive. Even the 'green revolution' which was hailed as a breakthrough in the 1960s and 1970s has 'converted a recycling self renewing food system into a production line'. This impoverishes the land as well as the people, resulting in 'desertification and death of soil on the one hand and the deprivation, devaluation and death of women on the other' (p. 120). Through their long years of survival and work in the forests and on the land, women have an understanding of the eco-system and how to work within it which has been utterly overlooked and despised, not because there was anything wrong with the feminine principle, simply because women themselves were unrecognised and invisible.

The central theme of the essays in Judith Plant (ed.) *Healing the Wounds* is to explore eco-feminism from many points of view, and to suggest ways in which a central theme can be brought into being. For example, Susan Griffin's description of the split that affects women's psyches (and men's) leads to her passionate cry for a remedy. This has two forms. 'We are connected not only by the fact of our dependency on this biosphere and our participation in one field of matter and energy, in which no boundary exists between my skin and the air and you but also by what we know and what we feel. Our own knowledge, if we can once again possess it, is as vast as existence' (p. 17). Again, I hear a cry to recover our own Wisdom and the Wisdom that has been described in the BWS.

In their contributions to the same book, other writers take the matter further. Ynestra King connects misogyny with hatred of nature and calls for male ecologists to deal with their own misogyny and 'nature hating in their own lives' (p. 42). Quoting this, Sharon Dubiago stresses that male–biased ecology is not real ecology. Ecologists have to understand that the exclusion of feminism forms their thinking and practice and that this means an unequal and traditional hierarchical system that has to fail, just as previous systems have failed. In the same mode Starhawk describes eco-feminism as a spiritual movement where a sense of the sacredness of the earth embodies a concept of the immanence of the divine, which shifts our values so that 'each being has a value that cannot be rated, diminished or ranked, that does not have to be earned or granted' (p. 177). This immanence also changes our sense of power, from the dominant notion of power–over to the participatory one of power–within. This is the 'inherent ability of each of us to become what we are meant to be – as a seed has within it the inherent power to root, grow, flower and fruit. Power–from–within is not limited and there is no scarcity of it in the universe.' Starhawk suggests that a change from power–over to power–from–within us is connected with earth–based spirituality. 'Each of us is part of the creative being who is the universe herself' (p. 184). 'Practice of this concept can change the structures of war and domination, and in so changing them we become agents of transformation and bring a new world to birth' (p. 184).

Inherent in these new concepts is a drive towards recognising women, who, no less than men, establish the norm of culture and standards in society, with all the changes that this perception must make to society. Writers are harking back to the Female Principle and the Goddess Terra Mater, and Rosemary Ruether in *Healing the Wounds* speaks of a perception that 'spirit and matter are but the inside and outside of the same thing' (p. 145). She writes of the 'Goddess who is primal matrix'. This fits in with concepts in the ancient world where world harmony and cosmic order were believed to be implicit in Nature, which in varying communities was itself held to be either an aspect of the divine or divine in herself. Indeed 'herself' is the correct pronoun. Nature was, and is now, understood to be female.

Anne Primavesi in *From Apocalypse to Genesis* (1991) has, from the viewpoint of a Christian eco-feminist, examined the sorry story of Christianity's interaction with the plunder of the resources of the earth. She has linked this to traditional views about the Fall and women's place in it, but reverses the thinking. She reviews the story of the Fall, in the light of today's appreciation of ecological needs. She points out that the Garden is full of food for human beings and that this is offered them; that there is a relationship between them and God in which they are part of a divine and earthly union. She calls on us all to be in touch with the divine earth with the food it bears, and with the sacredness of creation. While in no way discounting the evils that have occurred through the hierarchy of male power and its destruction of nature and of women, she sees a chance that we may move away from the destruction to a full maturity of understanding and co-operation.

Summary

The writers referred to in this chapter are among many who use a critique of patriarchal power over nature to demonstrate not only how such power is malign but also how threadbare. As this book goes to press, reports are being received of the break-up of the Soviet Union, and in particular how comprehensively polluted and wasted are the formerly rich lands and rivers of its many varying terrains. Here is a paradigm of the whole. For it was the philosophy of the Soviet leaders to bend Nature to man's will, and to use the wealth within the environment for the enhancement of industry and of 'man'. To the Soviet ideologists, the task was to learn how to grasp from Nature all that could be extracted. Their stated aim was to relieve poverty and to provide everyone with the means of satisfying their needs. The results have been a catastrophe, both for the land and for the people. Huge lakes have dried up, enormous areas of ground have been despoiled, and people today are desperately hungry and impoverished.

This has been a modern exposition of the thought of Bacon, that Nature can be tortured to provide the requirements that men think they need and want. Apart from any moral judgment, it has been found not to work.

It is ironic that, on paper at least, declarations were made that Socialist principles demanded equality between women and men. In practice, as Hilda Scott has pointed out (1974), women's problems in Socialist Eastern Europe were always put to the bottom of any agenda and seldom reached. They were thought to be far less important than other industrial, social, political or economic matters.

Today, in the West, there is some attention being paid to the fact that the rich world of Nature is gradually dying on our planet, and such phrases as 'the greening of the earth' suggest action and concern. Eco-feminists are declaring that for such action to be at all successful, both more and less is needed.

A relationship needs to be re-established with the earth, in which men take a humbler part than they have done up until now, and where women's voices and everyday experiences are heard and taken into account. A veneration of the earth and her ways is needed.

The problem is spiritual as well as practical; political as well as religious.

Nothing less than a total reversal of the exploitative attitude to Nature and to women has any chance of re-setting the balance so that the world itself can continue to exist.

11. Wisdom, the Bible and the Present

> I learned what is secret and what is manifest, for Wisdom, the fashioner of all things, taught me. (BWS 7:21–22)

In the context of my own culture, I have explored the long-lived figures of the ancient goddesses who are hidden in its background. The goddesses are located from the beginning, in the texts and sources of the bible and extra biblical material related to it.

The bible, far from being one seamless cloth of history and revelation, is in fact a patchwork with many threads, colours, weaves, pictures and patterns which have been woven together and created into a dazzling, magical web that deceives while it instructs.

The glowing accounts of divinity and directions as to human behaviour and salvation, usually believed to be unique to Judaism, Christianity and, in another culture, to Islam, are actually part of a heritage dating from further back in time. And these accounts of divinity and directions remain spiritual signposts for millions of people today, just as they have done for millenia.

If we change the metaphor we can understand that the full flowering of this spiritual landscape has been poisoned, similar to the way that plant biologists today have created systemic insecticides. Such chemicals are inserted in the seed and grow throughout the life of the plant at every stage, from green leaf, bud, to flower, fruit and harvest, retaining their toxicity to intruders, and assisting the creation of what appears to be a magnificent specimen of its kind. Eventually, however, it seems that many such plants, which are beautiful, strong, easy to cultivate and to harvest, and attractive to acquire, build up a store of venom in the humans and animals which consume them that is eventually life-threatening and full of pain.

The metaphor holds a further truth. Increasing numbers of people are adopting a 'green' outlook in an urge to care for the earth and its creatures, including themselves. One of the major tenets of this philosophy is to reduce chemical methods of agriculture and return to more organic systems. 'Greens' look to Nature and seek to understand her ways of creating and to put these methods to use in a spirit of participation and harmony. And while they are doing this in the physical world, many also seek to make similar changes in the world of ideas and the spirit.

Returning to the bible, we can see it as a magnificent garden of brilliant plants, some flowering, some fruiting, some in seed, or in bud, shaded by trees of age-old, luxurious growth. Yet in the very soil which gives it life the poison has been inserted, and this creeps through every essence within, eventually entering and permeating our consciousness and perception of the world.

The poison is that of misogyny, the hatred of women, half of the human race. It is the task of humans living now, and for those who will live in the future, to free the garden from this toxin, and then determine which of the flowers, which of the trees, what fruits, what shades shall act as nourishment.

I have tried to identify one path in this process in seeking out Wisdom and, as I hope and believe, being guided by her lamp.

In re-evaluating the bible, it seems that we find Wisdom to be our friend, and as we uncover the pieces that tell of our female heritage, we also come to see how she came to be so obscured. In understanding the toxin that has poisoned us, we find the antidote. In finding the antidote, in our understanding of female Wisdom, we start to be healed. Who is healed? Not only those who have made this journey, who have identified the sickness and the remedy. The remedy heals all who listen and will hear. Does not Wisdom cry, even to those who are 'without sense' (Proverbs 9:4–5) 'Come eat of my bread, and drink of the wine I have mixed, and walk in the way of insight'?

As we come to perceive the divine female Wisdom, very difficult questions arise. One of these was put to me by a woman who cried out: 'What have you done to God?'[1] She felt that God, the God of her faith and her background culture, had been banished and demoted, and she found this intolerable. Others ask why all the emphasis is on the female. Why, they ask, cannot there be a female –male balance and harmony? If we are to talk of goddesses, then what about gods? And what is the position of men in this new approach? Are we asking for a world without men? Of a world where women are dominant? No, no and again no.

Here I would like to quote from an unpublished paper I wrote some time ago in which I addressed this question.[2] I turned to the place of the god and, through him, the male person in ancient religions. I pointed out that many writers speak of sacrifice as an integral part of 'dark religions' (where the word 'dark' is pejorative) and that undoubtedly their revulsion is at the idea of human sacrifice and specifically the supposed sacrifice of the Divine King in seasonal ritual; that whatever the case in antiquity human sacrifice is repulsive to us now.

But we must see, I said, that the voluntary death of the Divine King, often called the Corn King,[3] to give life to the crops could be understood in many ways. One was that in a society which was more harmonious, more in touch with nature than our own, the disparity between women's and men's part in the life and death process could be better understood. I wrote:

I see that it was women who then, as now, conceived, carried, gave birth to and nurtured children. Women have always known and still do that sexual intercourse may inevitably lead to pregnancy, birth and death. In ancient times, a high proportion of women in a community would die within the year and a day of the Divine King's reign. All fertile women in such a community would be in danger of such a death, would be aware of this, every time they joined in sex with a man. Esther Harding in *Women's Mysteries*, (1971), talks about the different parts that women and men play in procreation and states that it takes but a small part of man's time and energy; but from the woman it demands the sacrifice of the whole of her life – at least temporarily. Harding believes that in every act of sexual intercourse the woman implicitly accepts her role as partaker in the cyle of life. Starhawk (1979) goes further. In *The Spiral Dance* she writes: 'Women were never sacrificed in witchcraft. Women shed their own blood monthly and risk death in service to the life force with every pregnancy and birth. For this reason their bodies were considered sacred and held inviolate' (p. 32).

I believe, therefore, that the ritual of the Corn's King's voluntary death intimated that men as well as women understood that the man, too, had to give in order to get. That he should not live unscathed, taking pleasure whilst dealing out death; that women should not be the only victims of the power of life.

I pointed out that the Corn King as a male symbol brought men to equal spiritual stature with women. He was showing, on behalf of all men, that while women, as representatives of the Goddess, were no more than human, men, by sharing women's fate, were no less than human. The Corn King showed and assumed a balance in the community between female and male.

But I was now asking for this understanding to be expressed in a different way. 'In considering the sacrifice of the Divine King, the assumption of death with the assurance of re-birth, I suggest to all of us, women and men labouring in the slavery of patriarchy that we can choose to go into a death. For men, it is the death of the use of their power against women, and for women the extinction and overcoming of the old subservience and guilt. Let us voluntarily, women and men, enter into these deaths.'[4]

I don't think I would change that conclusion now. I see all sorts of men's groups arising that attempt to help men rid themselves of patriarchal conditioning – the brutalisation of boys in the interest of 'manliness', the denial of emotional expression, the lack of nurturing of their ability to care for others – and I am happy that this is taking place. I am, however, suspicious of the 'wild men' groups and the 'brotherhood groups' that have recently become popular and which seem to be without any appreciation of men's political position in relation to their power over women. Without a clearing of the undergrowth of this oppressive power, I doubt whether the harmony and wholeness we are seeking can be achieved.

One much acclaimed recent writer on this theme is Riane Eisler (1987). In her exposition of women's and men's relationships throughout human history she sets out her vision of a move towards a partnership between the two, rather than the present domination of men and subordination of women. She writes of a transformation from androcracy[5] into such partnership – a move away, she says, from the millenia of recorded history when the human spirit has been imprisoned by the fetters of androcracy. One of the most evocative images of this transformation for her is the caterpillar metamorphosed into the butterfly (p. 198). On reading Riane Eisler, the discomfort I feel is not to do with her analysis. Rather, it is that I do not believe the change can be as 'natural' as she suggests. I believe that men must stand, and some now have brought themselves to stand, at the bar of history. They are not there to be judged or condemned; they are not there to plead guilty or not guilty. But they should remember the soul's Negative Confession to Ma'at (see p. 85). Have they caused any to weep? Have they falsified the balance between themselves and the women in their lives and community? Can they realise that, even if their own lives are exemplary, women are likely to hold men responsible for the abuses of the past and the present? Can they join with women to look at this abuse and say 'Yes, this is how it was and this is how it is?' If men can do this, it is in such companionship, such partnership, where men can accept the reality of women's hurt and start to change themselves, that healing can take place. I understand that for men this is a very hard and painful task. They have to relinquish their sovereignty and accept everyday humanity on a par with that of women, neither more nor less.

We return to the figure of Hochma–Sophia. In all the lessons we may learn from her, for me, two are outstanding. The first that she was 'there' at all; the female at the beginning, companion and delight of God, perhaps God herself or God's spirit. Men may contemplate her in these aspects and follow her call to seek her out and be guided by her. They need to avoid seeking to possess her for themselves and use her to aggrandise and enrich themselves, but rather to find 'the companionship with her that has no bitterness' (BWS 8:16). The second that women, understanding Wisdom's divine presence, may be encouraged to love themselves and grow. Not only can she be understood as divine, but she, the 'fashioner of all things' was the source of all knowledge and the inspiration of the intellect as well as the soul. She can 'do all things'. She may point her lamp as a beacon for women to follow in her path. But while she is 'mother of all good things' she does not impose motherhood on women – women are free to make their own choices. She is autonomous, and she relates to all who wish to be with her on her own terms.

Women and men alike may draw strength from Wisdom. Those of us nurtured in Judaism, or in Christianity, or in backgrounds which have moved away from these religions but which are nevertheless influenced by their history, may understand that, contrary to all we have been led to believe, female divinity has been continuously present.

In kinship with Wisdom there is immortality, and in friendship with her pure delight.

Notes

Preface

1 Claudia Camp, *Wisdom and the Feminine in the Book of Proverbs*, 1985, p. 36.

Chapter 1

1 See the Book of Proverbs. She is there throughout, for example Proverbs 8:22–30; 3:18–19; 3:13; 7:4. In the Book of Wisdom of Solomon, see particularly 7:12; 7:22; 8:1; 8:9–15. In Job, see whole chapters 28 and 38. In Ecclesiasticus (the Book of Sirach), see 24:1–6, 28–34. Also look at the Books of Baruch and Enoch.

2 *Jewish Encyclopaedia*, Vol. VIII, 1904, p. 548.

3 See II Kings 23:6.

4 This is numbered No. XXXVI in the collection by Thomas Taylor, original English edition 1792, reprinted 1981; and No. 27 in that by Apostolos Athanassakis, *The Orphic Hymns: text, translations, and notes*, 1977.

The Orphic Hymns are a group of praises to various deities, ascribed to Orpheus, the Greek 'sweet singer'. They derive from many sources. Thomas Taylor, an eighteenth-century classicist and poet, known as 'The English Platonist', provided a set of translations which have recently been reprinted in facsimile (1981). The Hymns have been the subjects of translation and commentary by Apostolos Athanassakis, 1977, op. cit., and by the contemporary

English poet Kathleen Raine, in *Thomas Taylor the Platonist*, 1969. The Hymn to Nature (*Physis*) is No. IX in Taylor's collection and No. 10 elsewhere.

See also the works of Marija Gimbutas listed in the Bibliography, a pre-eminent authority on Goddess cultures of Old Europe. Her works explore the role of Goddess as Nature, giver and taker of life, and renewer of existence and of Herself. She has made profound explorations and interpretations of the symbols of ancient Goddess figures and carvings and has opened up an entirely new field which she terms 'archaeomythology'.

5 See Elisabeth Schussler Fiorenza, *Bread Not Stone: the challenge of feminist biblical interpretation*, 1984, pp. xxi-xiii.

6 Maarten J. Vermaseren, *Cybele and Attis: the myth and the cult*, 1977, p. 9.

7 Ibid.

8 Ibid.

9 See Note 4 above.

Chapter 2

1 Wisdom literature in the Hebrew bible is generally held to include the Books of Proverbs, Job, Ecclesiastes and a number of Psalms. To these should be added, from the Apocrypha and other inter-testamental literature, the Book of Wisdom of Solomon, the Book of Ecclesiasticus (Sirach), the book of Baruch and the book of Enoch.

2 Carol Meyers in *Discovering Eve: ancient Israelite women in context*, 1988, makes the point that 'to translate Adam as "man" in the creation stories is to imply a priority for male existence', but that it actually indicates 'human life'. Adam is made from *Adamah*, which is ground or earth. This in Meyers' view is a piece of magnificent Hebrew word play. She translates the verse of Genesis 2:7 as 'The God Yahweh formed an *earthling* of clods from the *earth* . . . and the *earthling* became a living being,' pp. 81–2. (Italics in the original.)

Mary Phil Korsak, in Anne Primavesi, *From Apocalypse to Genesis: ecology, feminism and Christianity*, 1991, in the same mode, in her new translation of the Book of Genesis, uses the word 'groundling' for Adam, who was formed from the 'ground'. See also chapter 10 Note 2 of this book.

3 Harmut Gese 'Wisdom literature in the Persian Period', in W. D. Davies and L. Finkelstein (eds) *The Cambridge History of Judaism, Vol. 1, 'The Persian Period'*.

4 The fifth-century BCE Athenian philosopher Plato embodied much of his thinking in his published *Dialogues* of his wise contemporary Socrates. In these he records conversations of Socrates with a number of his students, one of whom is Euthyphro. The key question in the Euthyphro dialogue of Socrates asks: 'Does God love the good because it is Good, or is it good because it is loved by God?' Or 'Does God love the holy because it is Holy, or is it holy because it is loved by God?' The implication of the first part of each question is that the Good and the Holy are intrinsic in themselves and independent of God. The relevance of these questions to the nature of Wisdom is apparent. (There are many translations of Plato. A good source is the Loeb Classical Library.)

5 Robert B. Y. Scott 'Wisdom in Creation: the "Amon" of Prov. 8–30', in *Vetus Testmentum*, No. 10, pp. 213–33.

6 The suggestion that in order to relate to Wisdom the male human being has to enjoy sexual intimacies with her is conveyed in Proverbs 4:8; 7:4; and Book of Wisdom of Solomon 8:2, 8, 9, 18. For a more comprehensive outline of this theme, see Gerhard von Rad, *Wisdom in Israel*, 1972, pp. 166–70.

7 Ecclesiasticus, or the Wisdom of Jesus the Son of Sirach, known as Ben-Sirach.

8 See, for example, the *Jewish Encylopaedia*, 1906, Vol. XII, pp. 196–7.

9 The Book of Enoch LXXII and LXXVIII deals with the courses of the stars and the other heavenly luminaries. See Robert H. Charles, translator of the *Book of Enoch*, 1917, pp. 95–106. The

'perversion of Nature and the Heavenly Bodies owing to the Sins of Men' is set out in LXXX. The 'heavenly tablets' are introduced in LXXXI, ibid pp. 106–07.

Chapter 3

1 See the Preface p. 10.

2 William J. Deane (1886) in *The Book of Wisdom: Translation and Commentary* was an early commentator on the Book of Wisdom of Solomon (BWS) to make this suggestion, now enlarged by David Winston in *The Wisdom of Solomon: translation, introduction and commentary*, 1979 and Dieter Georgi *Frau Weisheit oder das Recht aus Freiheit als Schoepferische Kraft*, 1988.

3 John H Hayes, *An Introduction to the Study of the Old Testament*, 1979, p. 322.

4 Joseph Reider in *The Book of Wisdom: Commentary*, 1957, discusses the problem of Wisdom as fashioner or contriver, pointing out that it might be implied that Wisdom is the creator of all things. His opinion is that it is God who is the contriver, Wisdom the intermediary. David Winston compares the description with the Stoic 'artistically working fire' of Nature. James Reese in *The Book of Wisdom*, 1983, comments on the ambiguity that makes the text suggest that God and the Lady Wisdom are identical. The difficulty that commentators seem to experience derives, it seems, from their preconceived notion that the Lady Wisdom and God must *not* be identical, so some way out of the difficulty of what the text is actually saying has to be found.

5 The beginning and end and middle of times may well remind the reader of the inscription to Isis on her temple at Sais, Egypt: 'I am all that was, is, or ever will be'; and the text from Exodus when God tells Moses His name is 'I am', the Hebrew giving the tenses of the verb 'to be'. As I have pointed out in 'The Goddess in Judaism: a historical perspective', in Alix Pirani (ed.) *The Absent Mother: Rediscovering the Goddess in Judaism and Christianity*, 1991, Moses, if

he existed, and at the time usually associated with him (c. 1300 BCE) might have been familiar with the Isis text and transmitted it to the name of Jaweh.

6 While it is usually believed that intellectual enquiry was confined to men, it has in fact been shown that the Hellenistic world gave women much space for intellectual endeavours. (See, for example, Margaret Alic, *Hypatia's Heritage*, 1986 and Sandra Henry and Emily Taitz *Written Out of History: our Jewish foremothers*, 1983, amongst others.) Miriam of Alexandria, working in the first century CE, was a noted scientist who invented, amongst much else, a method of distillation of chemicals. This was accomplished in a vessel called 'Maria's bath' (*Balnia Mariae*), which has come down to us nearly two thousand years later as a useful cooking device, the 'Bain Marie'. Women concerned with the sciences continued to flourish, a most distinguished member being Hypatia, librarian of the great library at Alexandria. She, a foremost mathematician, was lynched in the fourth century CE, and her library destroyed.

7 Joseph Reider, 1957, op. cit., p. 103.

8 Erwin R. Goodenough, *By Light, Light: the mystic gospel of Hellenistic Judaism*, 1935.

9 There is a fascinating controversy concerning the text of John 1:9 (b). The RSV translates it as: 'The true light that enlightens every man was coming into the world.' The Greek literally reads: 'He was the true light, which lights all human beings, coming into the world.' Some readings have it as the light comes into the world, others that the human being coming into the world contains the true light. The difference is phenomenal and the subject of much speculation: if the human being contains the true light, them there is no division between creator and created; if, however, the 'true light' is Jesus Christ, he contains it only in himself.

10 Acute controversy which raged in fourth-century Christendom centred on the exact relationship of the Son to the Father. It

involved the nature of Jesus Christ, his divinity and his humanity. Was Jesus 'like' the Father, or was he 'of the same substance' as the Father? The Greek words for each resemble each other, the difference being of one letter only. (*Homoiousios*, meaning 'like' and *Homoousios*, meaning 'of the same substance'. Those, following the scholar Arius who disagreed with the majority view, kept a minority view alive for many centuries.

11 Philo *De Ebrietate*, 30. Quoted in David Winston, 1979, op. cit, p. 170.

12 Wisdom is given twenty-one characteristics. Various scholars have commented on this number: seven time three. Both these numbers, prime and of themselves only, have had great mystical significance. A typical interpretation from a Jewish source is quoted by David Winston, ibid p. 179. 'Moses was in a one to seven relationship with the angels, since they mention the name after three words, and he after twenty-one words.' Of the number seven, Philo writes, 'Such is the holiness inherent by nature in the numbers within the decade . . . [it] is of such a nature as neither to engender nor be engendered. It is on this account that other philosophers compare this number to the motherless and virgin Nike . . . the sole thing that neither moves nor is moved, it the senior Rule and Commander, of whom it may properly be said that seven is his image.' *De Opificio Mundi*, pp. 89–90 in Winston, 1981, p. 85.

It is noteworthy that Philo is not averse to perceiving the 'motherless and virgin Nike' (also identified with Aphrodite) as of a similar order to God, the 'senior ruler and commander'.

Philo refers to the Creator as 'he who invented numbers, measures and equality in them' (Proverbs 2: 50–1, Winston, ibid, p. 98), and in speaking of the creation of the world is ahead of many later thinkers in describing it as spherical (Proverbs 2:56, Winston, ibid, p. 118). Philo's work on numerology and creation builds up into an elaborate edifice which most modern scholars discount, but it is worth noting since such speculation would not be foreign to the author of the BWS.

13 Joseph Reider, 1957, op. cit., p. 114–15.

14 James Reese, 1983, op. cit., p. 86.

15 David Winston, 1979, op. cit., p. 180.

16 Joseph Reider, 1957, op. cit., p. 155.

17 The Hymn to Eleusinian Demeter addresses her as *monogones*, with many children and power over mortals. Apostolos Athanassakis, in *The Orphic Hymns: text, translations, and notes*, 1977, translates the word as 'only daughter'; Thomas Taylor, in *The Hymns of Orpheus*, 1792, is nearer the original when he writes (of the same line) 'Only begotten, much producing queen'. This word, *monogones*, starts the hymn to Pallas Athene, translated by Thomas Taylor again as only begotten, and by Apostolos Athanassakis as 'revered'! Taylor also translates it in the same way in the Hymn to Persephone (Proserpine), while Athanassakis addresses her as 'sole offspring' of Demeter – but Demeter is not mentioned in the original Greek. We can only conclude that Athanassakis is fully aware of the particular power of the word *monogones* and is avoiding its implications.

18 Ernest G. Clarke, *The Wisdom of Solomon (Commentary)*, 1973, p. 54.

19 James Reese, 1983, op. cit., p. 86.

20 Ernest Clarke, 1973, op. cit., p. 54.

21 David Winston, 1979, op. cit., p. 181.

22 William Deane, 1881, op. cit., p. .

23 Joseph Reider, 1957, op. cit., p. 116.

24 Ibid.

25 Ernest Clarke, 1973, op. cit., p. 181.

26 David Winston, 1979, op. cit., p. 181.

27 Starhawk, in *Dreaming the Dark*, 1982, pp. 1–14, outlines her vision of 'power-from-within', replacing the traditional notion of 'power-over'. She writes: 'We are of the world, and of each other,

and the power within us is great, if not an invincible power. Though we can be hurt, we can heal; though each one of us can be destroyed, within us is the power of renewal.' The ideas she sets out have been taken up strongly by feminists, in many different areas.

28 William J. Deane, 1881, op. cit.

29 Ernest Clarke, 1973, op. cit., p. 55.

30 Ibid.

31 Arthur T. S. Goodrich, *The Book of Wisdom: Commentary*, 1913, p. 196.

32 See the account of the Shekinah in chapter 7.

33 The body as defilement, and the source of sin and degradation has been the theme of countless meditations and texts. Peter Brown in *The Body and Society: men, women and sexual renunciation in early Christianity*, 1989, has surveyed this subject in depth, and Uta Ranke-Heinemann in *Eunuchs for Heaven: The Catholic Church and Sexuality*, 1991, has also commented on the subject and its effects on women and society generally. The latter book, it seems, has had an adverse affect on her career, not because it is not accurate, but possibly because it is.

34 See 'Orphic Hymn to Nature' in chapter 4, p. 67–8. Night is addressed as the parent of gods and humans.

35 The fourth Gospel (John) concentrates on Jesus as the 'true light', and the 'Light of the World' (8:12), and makes a strong point that darkness was negative and evil (John 1:4). This is in contrast to the vision of Genesis where evening and morning together, that is, night and day, make up a whole day (Genesis 1:5, 8, 13, 18, 23, 24). It is noteworthy that where God divides the light from the darkness (Genesis 1:18) he saw that 'it', that is, the whole process, 'was good'. The definition of dark with evil and harm was not part of this scheme.

36 Comparisons have been made between the spirit of god, Hebrew *ruach*, with Wisdom. The image of huge wings stretching across the world is also duplicated in the Hebrew vision of

cherubim guarding the Ark of the Covenant, and the Shekinah, usually portrayed with wings, surrounding it and also covering the world with God's glory. The creative figures with wings guarding and protecting the world is also replicated in Egyptian iconography, particularly the goddesses Isis and Ma'at, while the complex Ancient Near Eastern figure of Lilith, whose longevity stretches from 3000 BCE until almost the present day, is most often portrayed with wings and birds' feet. Although her name was usually translated as relating to night, it is now known that its Sumerian meaning is 'female spirit', 'breath', or 'wind'. Compare the Latin, *anima*, the Greek, *pneuma* and Hebrew, *ruach*. See A. P. Long in Alix Pirani, 1991, op. cit., pp. 36–7.

Chapter 4

1 Orphic Hymn: to the 'Mother of the Gods'. Translated by A. P. Long and J. D. Winter, 1991.

2 Orphic Hymn to 'Aphrodite'. Transalted by Kathleen Raine and G. M. Harper, in *Thomas Taylor the Platonist*, 1969.

3 See Note 5, chapter 1.

4 Edwin R. Goodenough spent a lifetime researching alternative forms of Judaism in the centuries just before and just after the birth of Christianity. His twelve-volume opus, *Jewish Symbols in the Graeco-Roman Period*, was published in full in New York between 1953 and 1965. His discoveries, particularly those concerning a Jewish veneration for the 'Female Principle' in God, and a similarity between unorthodox but nevertheless accepted Jewish ritual with what was previously deemed pagan, brought him into disrepute with his contemporaries. However, Samuel Sandmel and other contemporary and distinguished Jewish scholars have since suggested that while Goodenough's theories about an alternative form of Judaism in the first centuries before our era cannot be satisfactorily substantiated, yet there is much in them that cannot

be discounted. See Samuel Sandmel, *Philo of Alexandria: An Introduction*, 1979, pp. 140–7.

5 Edwin Goodenough, *By Light, Light: the mystic gospel of Hellenistic Judaism*, 1935, pp. 13, 15 and 19.

6 See Georg Fohrer, *Introduction to the Old Testament*, 1968, pp. 404–08 for a summary of scholastic opinion on this subject.

7 The mythology and iconography of goddesses associated with lions is enormous. A recent summary is given by Ruth Hestrin in 'Understanding Asherah: exploring Semitic iconography', in *BAR*, Vol. XVII, No. 5, 1991. Among many other deities, Asherah and Ishtar are particularly to be seen with lions or lionesses.

8 Edwin Goodenough, 1935, op. cit., p. 11.

9 On Wisdom's attitudes to night and darkness, see Note 36, chapter 3.

10 The quotations are from Lucius Apuleius, *The Golden Ass*, 'Metamorphoses', 1:3 and 1:8. (See Luther Martin, 1987, pp. 27–8. For the full text in English, see Lucius Apuleius, *The Golden Ass*, translated by Robert Graves, 1950.)

11 Ibid.

12 Plotinus, *Enneades*, Vol. IX, No. 4, verse 40 (third century CE), quoted in Martin, 1987, op. cit., p. 28.

13 These and other recipes are to be found in the collection by Walter A. Jayne, *The Healing Gods of Ancient Civilisation*, 1925.

14 Lawrence Durdin-Robertson, *The Goddesses of Chaldea, Syria and Egypt*, 1975, pp. 288 *et seq*.

15 Philo: *De Migratione Abrahami*, verses 178–81, quoted in Winston, 1981, p. 113.

16 Carl Jung suggests how 'synchronicity' works in his exploration of the subject in an eponymous book published in 1955. At any time in our lives, the various happenings at all levels of consciousness within us and in the world itself can be pinpointed and are related at that instant to each other.

17 Heraclitus, *Fragment 4*, quoted in Francis M. Cornford, *From Religion to Philosophy*, 1980, p. 186.

18 The Orhpic Hymn to 'Rhea', addressed as Mother of the Gods and Men, shows her both in frenzy and in harmony. At first:

> 'Mother of Jove, whose mighty arm can wield
> Th'avenging bolt and shake the dreadful shield.
> Drum-beating, frantic of a splendid mien . . .'

she changes into: 'Goddess . . . pleased with wanderings, blessed and divine. With peace attended on our labours shine'. (Translations by Thomas Taylor, *The Hymns of Orpheus*, original English edition 1792, reprinted by the Philosophical Research Society, Inc, 1981.)

19 Ibid.

Chapter 5

1 Lucius Apuleius, *The Golden Ass*, translated by Robert Graves, 1950, p. 271.

2 The many names of Isis are recorded by Lawrence Durdin-Robertson, in *The Goddess of Chaldea, Syria and Egypt*, 1975, p. 284 *et seq*, where many details of her position in history and mythology can be found.

3 Lucius Apuleius, 1950, op. cit, p. 272.

4 Ibid, p. 273.

5 The aretalogy of Isis can be found in full in Joan C. Engelsman, *The Feminine Dimension of the Divine*, 1979. The lines quoted here are translated from the Greek by A. P. Long, 1991.

6 Lawrence Durdin-Robertson, 1975, op. cit., pp 324–5. Also quoted in Asphodel P. Long 'The Goddess in Judaism: a historical perspective', in Alix Pirani (ed.) *The Absent Mother: Rediscovering the Goddess in Judaism and Christianity*, 1991, p. 52.

7 See Note 2 above.

8 We are reminded, too, that such a practice of the liberal and scientific arts and the profession of wise women-midwife existed throughout the ages. That women in Egypt held a premier place in the professions for many centuries is attested by their records; see also chapter 3, Note 6.

9 Matriarchy Study Group, *Goddess Shrew*, Matriarchy Study Group, 1976, p. 7. This magazine, one of a series named 'Shrew' and produced by different groups within the Women's Liberation Movement in Britain in the 1970s, brought an immediate response from hundreds of women. It was among the first records of 'Goddess research' to appear in the UK.

10 *The Nag Hammadi Library in English*, edited by James M. Robinson, 1977 and 1988, contains an English translation of all the material so far published from the desert finds of 1945. Each text or 'tractate' is introduced by its particular editor who comments on specific points, and an outline of its contents is provided.

In 1961 a group of scholars from diverse disciplines and a number of countries met in Messina in Italy to pool their researches concerning the texts. The results were published as the *Final Document of the Messina Colloquium*. I intend to follow the terms suggested within it. According to this, the word 'Gnosticism' describes a certain group of Christian-type systems of the second-century CE, while 'Gnosis', with dates that span 200 BCE to 200 CE approximately, is a knowledge of the divine mysteries, reserved for the elite. Such Gnosis has been thought of as a total religious system, incorporating material from both Western and Eastern sources and spanning a vast area.

Difficulties in dating and discovering sources, as well as controversy over understanding texts and their meanings, continue. The varied material has opened up large areas of dispute; at the same time, many groups not specifically associated with scholastic research have taken up different strands of Gnosis or Gnosticism to suit their own beliefs. The Messina Colloquium called it a 'minefield', and I think this is an accurate description.

11 James M. Robinson (ed.), 1977, op. cit., pp. 98–117.

12 'The Thunder, Perfect Mind', VI, 2, in James M. Robinson, (ed.) 1977, op. cit., pp. 271–7.

13 'Trimorphic Protennoia', in James M. Robinson, (ed.), 1977, op. cit., pp. 461–70. First or primal thought is three-formed, according to this title.

14 Ibid.

15 Androgyny, a combination of male and female, puts the male element (from Greek *andros*, a man) first, followed by woman, *gyne*. I see no reason why we should not reverse this word, using gynandry, to mean the same thing. I suggested (*Politics of Matriarchy*, 1978, p. 28) that this gynandry assumes the adulthood of humankind with equality and harmony between the sexes.

16 See descriptions of Anat in chapter 6. An excellent portrait of her is to be found by Umberto Cassuto in *The Goddess Anath*, 1971.

17 See chapter 7. This subject has been much discussed in the new climate of thought concerning the role of women in antiquity. See, for example, Merlin Stone, *The Paradise Papers*, 1976.

18 'The Apocryphon of John', in James M. Robinson (ed.), 1977, op. cit., pp. 98–116.

19 Ibid, pp. 103–04.

Chapter 6

1 For information, illustrations and an analysis of material that associates the menstrual cycle with early mathematics and art, see Alexander Marshack, *The Roots of Civilization*, 1971. Margaret Murray, in *Genesis of Religion*, 1963, has suggested reasons for women's need to learn computation and mathematical organisation.

2 While it is common to assume that goodesses in early societies were either divinities to do with the earth and 'fertility', or the moon and menstruation, Lucy Goodison, 1990, Janet McCrickard, 1990 and Patricia Monaghan, 1981, in *Moving Heaven and Earth,*

Eclipse of the Sun: an investigation into sun and moon myths, and *Women in Myth and Legend*, respectively, have all shown that there is substantial evidence for sun goddesses in societies throughout the world.

3 See N. K. Sanders, (translator) *The Epic of Gilgamesh*, 1960.

4 See N. K. Sanders, *Poems of Heaven and Hell from Ancient Mesopotamia*, 1971; also James B. Pritchard, *The Ancient Near East*, Vols 1 and 2, 1958 and D. Winton Thomas (ed.), *Documents from Old Testament Times*, 1961.

5 See Aubrey Johnson, *Sacral Kingship in Ancient Israel*, 1967, and A. P. Long, 'The Goddess in Judaism: a historical perspective', in Alix Priani, *The Absent Mother: discovering the Goddess in Judaism and Christianity*, 1991. Biblical references such as Isaiah 27:1, Psalm 74:13 and Psalm 89:10 are taken to refer to Jahweh's victory over the sea monster, which has strong similarities with the Epic of Creation, Enuma Elish.

6 This story and that of Gudea will be found in Thorkild Jacobsen, *The Harps that Once . . .*, 1987, which contains a treasury of Sumerian poetry translated into English.

7 See Samuel H. Hooke, *Middle Eastern Mythology*, 1963, p. 115.

8 See Samuel N. Kramer in Diane Wolkstein and Samuel N. Kramer *Inanna, Queen of Heaven and Earth*, 1983, p. 53 *et seq*.

9 Ibid.

10 Eva Meyerowitz, *And Yet Women Once Reigned Supreme*, 1977, has shown that in nineteenth-century West Africa, for example, the goddess of the earth, Dugbo, was also the goddess of justice. Similarly, the Kono people in Africa believed that their behaviour affected the fertility of the soil, so they tried to maintain Dugbo's favour by good conduct in order to ensure good harvests.

11 The translations used are from those presented (with the original language transcribed into Roman letters) by Godfrey R. Driver, *Canaanite Myths and Legends*, 1956–71.

12 The Ugaritic Athirat of Ras Shamra is also translated as

Asherah, then Ashtart/Astart. She is the Creatress of the Gods and Lady of the Sea (see Helmer Ringgren 'Religions of the Ancient Near East', in *Ancient Near East*, Vol. 1, 1958, p. 140). James Pritchard, in *The Ancient Near East*, Vol. 1, 1958, pp. 97–102, refers to her as Lady Asherah of the sea.

In an enlarged doctoral thesis, Walter A. Maier III, in *Asera: extrabiblical evidence*, 1986, it is suggested that Atirat is the same as Asherah throughout. Commenting on Atirat's relationship with El, as he yields to her demand for a house for Baal, Maier writes: 'The success of Atirat points to her power and prestige as the senior wife of El and the Creatress of the Gods' (p. 35) – a position also assigned to Asherah. He shows a relationship, too, with the similarly named Asertu, a Hittite goddess who is obviously in a power struggle with her husband El-kunirsa, 'Creator of the earth'. Maier writes: 'In the text, Asertu . . . asks the Storm God to sleep with her, threatening him with physical and verbal harassment if he refuses. The Storm God, in turn, reveals Asertu's desire to El-kunirsa, who then tells the storm god to yield to her advances and also to humble her. Listening to El-kunirsa the Storm God sleeps with Asertu, and humiliates her by telling her he slew her sons' (p. 34).

In this text we see a vestige of the time when the Mother Goddess chose her own mates and was not subordinate to her husband. We also see how she has to be humbled. In the present rendering, Maier (among others) points out that Atirat-Asera is also the goddess Qodsu (holiness), and she has the appellation 'Qde' in the Ugaritic texts (p. 42). These link with the 'holy ones', Qodeshem and the goddess Qodsha, described in the Hebrew religion. See p. 133 of this book.

13 A good introduction to Hittite mythology and an account of the myths can be found in Oliver Gurney, *Some Aspects of Hittite Religion*, 1976. Another useful source is Samuel N. Kramer, *Mythologies of the Ancient World*, 1961.

14 This is a huge subject, pursued with enthusiasm throughout this century by scholars and spiritual seekers alike. James Frazer's famous twelve-volume compendium, *The Golden Bough*, which has been continuously reprinted in abridged form after its original publication in 1896, provides a starting place for a journey of exploration into this subject, although for many years various academic disciplines dismissed his work as unscholarly. Many modern books dealing with Celtic and Arthurian legends raise the theme, as does a recent film entitled 'The Fisher King'. Certainly in the world of the Ancient Near East, the health and strength of the sovereign of the land were linked to its fertility and prosperity.

Chapter 7

1 The goddess Ashtaroth, often translated as 'abomination', combines in the Hebrew the name 'Asherah' and the word *boseth*, meaning shameful.

2 Peter Ackroyd 'Goddesses, Women and Jezebel', in A. Cameron and A. Kuhrt, 1983, p. 256.

3 Joseph Plessis in *Etude sur les Textes Concernant Ishtar-Astarte*, 1921, gives a comprehensive overview of the worship of Ishtar-Astarte. Similar material with later additions is provided by Mathias Delcor in *Le Culte de la Reine du Ciel*, 1982.

4 Quoted in Mathias Delcor 'Le culte de la Reine du Ciel', 1982, p. 109. Translated from the French by A. P. Long, 1992.

5 Diane Wolkstein, a storyteller and folklorist, and Samuel N. Kramer, 1983, a distinguished authority on Sumer, worked together to produce a new translation and commentary on the ancient myth of Inanna's descent to the Underworld, entitled *Inanna, Queen of Heaven and Earth*. This has been widely taken up by feminists and others interested both to learn the myths and to renew them in the light of today's problems.

6 See Hymn to Ishtar, in James Pritchard, *The Ancient Near East*, Vol. 1, 1958, p. 232.

7 Robert Briffault, *The Mothers*, Vol. 2, 1927, pp. 433–5.

8 Mathias Delcor, 1982, op. cit., pp. 104–05.

9 Ibid.

10 Ibid, p. 106.

11 W. R. Smith, *The Religion of the Semites*, originally published in 1889, reprinted 1972, p. 225.

12 Ibid.

13 Mathias Delcor, 1982, op. cit., p. 112.

14 That divinity is present in stones, or that stones themselves can retain its presence, is not only a concept reaching back to antiquity but is also present today. Numerous people visit the ancient megaliths of Britain, Brittany, Malta and elsewhere, not only to view historical remains but also to experience their numinous qualities. In ancient Israel, huge pillars named *masseboth* stood at sacred shrines, and were also installed by Solomon at the entrance to the temple. Mathias Delcor's survey of the worship of the Queen of Heaven makes the connection between her presence in the stone and the cult of the baetylus very clear.

15 Ibid.

16 Ibid, p. 111.

17 Ze'ev Meshel, 'Did Jahweh have a Consort?', in *BAR*, Vol. 5, No. 2, 1979, pp. 24–36. Also, Z. Zevit, 'The Khirbet El-Qom inscription mentioning a goddess', in BASOR, No. 255, 1984, pp. 39–47; and William Dever, 'Asherah, consort of Jahweh. New evidence from Kuntillet Ajrud', *BASOR*, No. 255, 1984, pp. 21–37.

18 Z. Zevit, 1984, op. cit., pp. 44–5.

19 Raphael Patai in *The Hebrew Goddess*, 1990 gives a full account of these goddesses.

20 The Hebrew bible has many references to the worship of 'an Asherah' or 'Asherahs'. For example, I Kings 16:33, II Kings 21:3, II Chronicles 33:3, Isaiah 27:9, Deuteronomy 16:21. In most cases, they are in the context of a wooden image. Raphael Patai, ibid, has analysed the references, pointing out that the Asherahs were

artifacts made by human hands, not natural trees, and that they are both cut down and broken into pieces (p. 296). The Asherah in the AV is often referred to as a 'grove', and is worshipped in 'high places' (see, for example, I Kings 15:13, II Kings 17:16, II Kings 23 *passim*). A grove is a grouping of trees, and it is interesting that the earlier translators of the bible used this word instead of the name of the goddess. In fact, the argument concerning the actual meaning of Asherah still continues. A recent scholar, Mark Smith, in *The Early History of God: Jahweh and the other deities in ancient Israel*, 1990, is reluctant to accept her as an Israelite goddess, or the consort of Jahweh. Rather, he sees the memory of the Canaanite goddess Asherah being assimilated into the early Hebrew religion, not as a deity but as a cultic symbol, which later was to be destroyed, in the interests of a total monotheism (pp. 90–103). It is important to emphasise that the AV, which is still the most widely read bible in Protestant circles in Britain, has, by the use of the word 'grove', completely obscured any knowledge that a goddess Asherah might ever have existed. Reference, for example, to the widely used Cruden's Concordance to the Old and New Testaments and the Apocrypha, 1791 (and numerous modern reprints), will yield no mention of Asherah. To find her, it is necessary to look up the word 'grove'.

21 See, for example, Judges 6:25–30, II Kings 18:4, II Kings 23:6, 14, II Chronicles 34:4, 7, Jeremiah 17:2, Micah 5: 13–14.

22 See Note 20.

23 In the 1980s, there was a cult of the 'natural' in Europe and the United States. Wearing apparel, household textiles and equipment were expected to be made out of what were thought of as 'natural' materials, such as wool, cotton, silk, wood, etc. There appeared to be a swing away from merchandise made from synthetic fibres or plastics which were thought to be 'unnatural'. Such chemically produced materials had as their base waste products from oil or coal. I suggest that making use of these instead of destroying them

or leaving them to pollute the atmosphere could be said to be performing a useful ecological function. Further, such materials themselves are 'natural' in the sense that ultimately they too are derived from products of the earth. In fact it can be argued that the real culprit in the fashion eco-stakes is not the synthetic fibre as such but the yarns produced from a base of wood, and for which whole forests are regularly cut down. These are used for the manufacture of rayons, viscose, modal, etc. There appears to be no outcry against their use. Another anomaly in the 'natural fashion' craze was insistence on 'faded' jeans. This meant the use, in preference to modern dyestuffs, of natural indigo, which is a major cause of dermatitis to the people who handle this substance. That these people are usually underpaid and probably Third World women made no impact on cult consciousness. I believe a much more critical approach to our increasing awareness of the need for a change in our use of world resources and energy is needed.

24 See biblical references in Note 20.

Chapter 8

1 Matilda Gage's book, *Women, Church and State*, first published in 1893, mounts a strong feminist attack on the Church's history from earliest times to the (then) present in its attitude towards, and treatment of, women. She points out that even where the Church itself was not the actual perpetrator of crimes against women, its attitudes, rules and laws still to a large extent condoned them.

2 Rosemary Ruether in *Faith and Fratricide: the theological roots of anti-semitism*, 1974, was among the first to acknowledge Christian anti-Judaism, its base in the New Testament and the dreadful results that ensued on a long-term basis. Her analysis and calls for understanding and change have made a major contribution to healing the wounds and thus making possible co-operation between Jews and Christians.

3 Sophia worship is growing among various Christian congregations in the United States and has been condemned by the Church authorities. See, for example, 'The brewing storm over Sophia Worship', in *Good News The Bi-Monthly Magazine for United Methodists*, July/August, 1990, pp. 10–16.

4 There are a number of possible interpretations of the Hebrew word *kana*, which is translated (RSV) as 'created'. The AV gives 'possessed' but more modern scholarship indicates that *kana* has a wide range of meanings, based on creation. It can mean 'engender' or 'give birth to', both forms of creation. There is a great deal of dispute on this subject.

5 Rudolph Bultmann, *Primitive Christianity*, translated by R. H. Fuller, 1983, Hans Conzelmann 'The Mother of Wisdom: the future of our religious past', in J. M. Robinson and H. Koester (eds) *Trajectories in Early Christianity*, Wilfred Knox 'The Divine Wisdom', in *JTS*, No. 38, 1937, and Howard Lee Kee in 'Myth and Miracle: Isis, Wisdom and the Logos of John', in A. Olson, *Myth, Symbol and Reality*, 1980 are among the many who have found similarities between the prologue to the Fourth Gospel and the texts concerning Isis and Wisdom.

6 Rosemary Ruether, 1968, op. cit., p. 112.

7 The texts and sources of the opinions of the Fathers about women can most easily be found in the Ante-Nicene Christian Library and in Rosemary Ruether (ed.), *Religion and Sexism*, 1974, pp. 150–83.

8 Peggy Sanday, in *Female Power and Male Dominance*, 1981, spells this out in some detail.

9 Aquinas. *Summa Theologica* IV, i, quoted in Julia o'Faolain and Lauro Martines, *Not in God's Image: women in history from the Greeks to the Victorians*, 1973, p. 193.

10 Quoted by Marina Warner in *Alone of All Her Sex; the myth and cult of the Virgin Mary*, 1979, pp. 39, 43 and 220.

11 The *Malleus Maleficarum*, 'The Hammer of the Witches', is

described in detail and with commentary in Russell Robbins, *The Encyclopaedia of Witchcraft and Demonology*, 1964. This encyclopaedia gives some idea of what it calls 'fantastic sacrifice of logic and commonsense' (p. 338). For example, *femina* (woman) is said to be derived from *fe* (faith) and *minus* (less).

12 Quoted in Andrea Dworkin, *Woman Hating*, 1974, pp. 130–2.

13 Ibid.

14 Since the early 1970s, feminist scholars have been reviewing history to reclaim the hidden stories of the female and of women. Some have undertaken the huge task of looking at the stretch of time from earliest societies until the present. Among the many I recall the work of E. Gould Davies, *The First Sex*, 1975. Evelyn Reed, *Women's Evolution*, 1975 and *Sexism and Science*, 1978, Elisabeth Fisher, *Women's Creation: sexual evolution and the shaping of society*, 1980, and Elise Boulding, *The Underside of History: a view of women through time*, 1976, were among the pioneers of this work. Nearly two decades later they are in danger of being overlooked and forgotten. While today's feminists might carp at some of the details, it is never to be forgotten that they were our pioneering foremothers in this work; indeed, they suffered for their temerity.

Chapter 9

1 See Willis Barnstone, *The Other Bible*, 1984, pp. 279–80.

2 Quoted in Ann Loades, *Searching for Lost Coins: explorations in Christianity and feminism*, 1987, pp. 91–2.

3 *Logos*, Greek for 'word', was used in the pre-Christian Hellenistic world to express order and reason in the universe. It was sometimes, though not always, thought to be of divine origin. Philo personified *Logos* to some extent as a mediator between God and the world, in contrast to, or occasionally indistinguishable from, Wisdom. In the New Testament, the author of the Prologue to the Fourth Gospel takes this concept much further, applying it to Jesus Christ as a full person in the world. He defines Jesus as the

Logos ('the 'Word'), and the Gospel starts with the verse: 'In the beginning was the Word and the Word was with God and the Word was God' (John 1:1). Theologians of the early Christian centuries frequently referred to Jesus as 'the Word'.

The Motherhood of Jesus Christ, so movingly portrayed by the fourteenth-century Dame Julian of Norwich, is a source of inspiration to many Christian feminists. Yet again, she writes totally within a tradition that insists on the masculinity of God, even if God is to be a mother. The second person of the Trinity is 'our Mother in nature in our substantial creation in whom we are founded and rooted, and he is our Mother of mercy in taking our sensuality. And so our Mother is working on us in various ways . . . for in our Mother Christ we profit an increase.' (Quoted in Ann Loades, 1987, op. cit., p. 39.) Dame Julian writes of Christ's passion which she would wish to share and which she describes in detail. There can be no doubt that Julian's concept of Christ as Mother ascribes motherhood to *him*, again emphasising the 'all-competence of the male' (Loades, 1987, op. cit.). See also Julian of Norwich, *Showings*, translated and with an Introduction by Edmund Colledge and James Walsh, Paulist Press, New York, 1978, p. 180.

4 Quoted in Marina Warner, *Alone of All Her Sex: the myth and cult of the Virgin*, 1979, p. 39.

5 Quoted in Marina Warner, 1979, op. cit., p. 73.

6 Jerome. Commentary on Epistles to the Ephesians. III.5 Quoted in Marina Warner, 1979, op. cit., p. 73.

7 Mothers have struggled against this senseless waste of lives, but their herstory has hardly been acknowledged. During the First World War, countless women met and organised against the war; today Mothers for Peace are petitioning the United Nations against continued strife in Yogoslavia. Throughout the world women have refused and are refusing the model cast for them by Mary's sacrifice.

8 A nun who takes a vow of chastity is perceived to be a spiritual bride of Christ.

9 This is difficult for me because I am a Jew with a background of Orthodox Judaism. This was sloughed off, first in the interests of a left-wing universalism and then, disillusioned with this, into a commitment to that other universalism, feminism, and finally, still holding to the latter, driven back to an assertion of my Jewish heritage and ancestors by the anti-semitism in both my previous allegiances.

The difficulty has many aspects. The one that faces me with the sharpest menace has to do with the anti-semitism I have experienced in my own life, from earliest childhood to the present time. The contemporary form presents itself most appositely in phrases used indiscriminately by feminists who turn to goddess culture for inspiration and re-empowerment. So often, one of the first remarks made is: 'The Jews killed the goddess'. The deicide charge that has rumbled on through the centuries changes its form over the years but still holds all the old animosity, fear and, I believe, hatred.

The non-Jewish feminist scholar Carol P. Christ has attempted to explain this phenomenon and to suggest ways to negating it in her excellent essay, 'On not blaming the Jews for the death of the Goddess', 1987, pp. 83–102. She starts by saying that 'while feminist scholars have attempted to correct . . . history of religion in the Ancient Near East and Mediterranean for androcentric bias, their work has sometimes repeated or unconsciously reinforced the anti-Judaic biases that . . . we have inherited.' She points out that if Jesus Christ is to be received as a universal saviour then other religions will be portrayed negatively. But the Jews stand in a special relationship. They refused to recognise Jesus as Messiah and were the first to do so, and 'Christians have always attacked the Jews for this denial'. Another factor is also operative:

Those of us who grew up thinking of the Bible as a source of revelation about the nature of God and truth, and who have now discovered the goddesses, who were suppressed in the histories of biblical religions cannot fail to be outraged . . . many feminist writers have stronger feelings about the suppression of the Goddess within other traditions such as those of Greece or of Sumer. Unfortunately such feelings can easily be attached to traditions of anti-Judaism, which are readily available. (p. 84). See also Judith Plaskow, 'Blaming Jews for inventing patriarchy', *Lilith*, 7, 1980, pp. 12–14; and Annette Daum, 'Blaming Jews for the death of the Goddess', *Lilith*, 7, 1980, pp. 12–17.

This encapsulates for me my difficulty in criticising the Jewish establishment religion in a non-Jewish context. So often such fault-finding has the effect of apparently colluding in the anti-semitism of the general atmosphere around me. Susannah Heschel (*On Being a Jewish Feminist*, 1983) and Judith Plaskow (*Standing Again at Sinai*, 1990) are among those Jewish feminists who have described this situation in detail.

10 See Rikkie Burman, 'The Jewish woman as breadwinner', in *Oral History Journal*, 1982.

11 Scholarly appreciation of the Shekinah is to be found in Gershom Scholem, *The Kabbalah and its Symbolism*, 1969 and *Kabbalah*, 1974. For feminist viewpoints and the relationship of Jewish women to the Shekinah, see Alix Pirani (ed.), *The Absent Mother: rediscovering the Goddess in Judaism and Christianity*, 1991.

Chapter 10

1 Susan Griffin, *Women and Nature*, 1978.

2 The echo in the word *adamah* is faint, an echo suggesting that she might be an earth goddess, or Mother Nature herself. The word merely tells us that 'Adam', a human being, was created from female *adamah*. It is of some interest that the root of both words

means the colour red, and there are other sources which speak of 'red earth', as most fertile. Red is a sacred colour associated with blood, the symbol of life. (See also chapter 2, Note 2 and A. P. Long 'Red is for Life', in *Menstrual Taboos*, 1978, pp. 1–10.)

Echoes of Adamah are heard again when God appears to Moses by the burning bush (Exodus 3; 3–5) on 'holy ground' (Hebrew *Admat-Kodesh*). It is usually accepted that Moses is told to take off his shoes for that reason. I am indebted to Alix Pirani for the information that the verse may reasonably mean that it is Moses who tells God to do this. I also see that *Admat-Kodesh* combines the names of two goddesses – Adamah and Kodesh – and both may be associated with the earth.

3 St. Augustine challenged the doctrine proposed, among others, by the British monk Pelagius that human beings are born free of sin into a world that is basically just and good. Augustine denied that there is free will and freedom to choose, or that human beings other than Christians may enter heaven. One may rephrase Pelagius to suggest that human beings are born at home in a world that is not evil and does not reject them but offers them scope for growth. The world that receives them is this world of Nature, of which they are a part. None of this was allowed to enter Augustinian theology which came to dominate Christianity.

4 For in-depth surveys and analysis of Chardin's work, see Ursula King's studies: *Towards a New Mysticism: Teilhard de Chardin and Eastern Religions*, 1980, and *The Spirit of One Earth: Reflections on Teilhard de Chardin and Global Spirituality*, 1989.

5 Rosemary Ruether, 'Toward an ecological-feminist theory of nature' in Judith Plant (ed.) *Healing the Wounds: the promise of eco-feminism*, 1989.

6 Three recent studies, Vandana Shiva, in *Staying Alive: women, ecology and development*, 1988, Judith Plant (ed.) *Healing the Wounds: the promise of eco-feminism*, 1989, and Anne Primavesi (ed.) *From Apocalyse to Genesis: ecology, feminism and Christianity*, bring forward,

respectively, Indian women's experience, Western feminist theory and a revolutionary Christian viewpoint, as ingredients of an eco-feminist solution to the disaster confronting Nature.

Chapter 11

1 She had read my contribution 'The Goddess in Judaism, a historical perspective', in Alix Pirani, *The Absent Mother: Restoring the Goddess to Judaism and Christianity*, 1991.

2 'Paganism, Feminism and Sacrifice', 1978. (Unpublished.)

3 In many ancient societies there are myths and legends that suppose that a man volunteers each year to represent the growing corn on which the life of the community depends. He becomes the lover-spouse of the priestess-queen, and is treated royally by her, and by his subjects. After a year and a day, he is sacrificed and his body and blood spread upon the earth, to ensure next year's fertility of the soil. The spirit of the corn is embodied in him, and since the corn must be cut down, so must he be. Many folksongs, still current, hark back to this theme, notably 'John Barleycorn' and 'The bonny lad is young but he's growing'. It is interesting that the first named sets out the process of turning the corn into the 'water of life', which in the Gaelic is the word from which 'whisky' is derived. At the end, after enduring all these batterings and grindings, John Barleycorn in his new form is 'the best man of all'. Reaching back nearly four thousand years, a similar description is given in the Ras Shamra texts (see pp. 111–14) of the death and rebirth of the storm god, Baal.

4 'Paganism, Feminism and Sacrifice', 1978, op. cit.

5 Androcracy literally means 'rule by men', and is commonly used to denote the idea of male supremacy in all walks of life.

Bibliography

Abbreviations

ANEP   The Ancient Near East in Pictures Relating to the Old Testament

ANEP   Ancient Near Eastern Texts Relating to the Old Testament

BA   Biblical Archaeologist

BAR   Biblical Archaeological Review

BASOR   Bulletin of the American Schools of Oriental Research

BIB.   Biblica

CBQ   Catholic Biblical Quarterly

EPRO   Etudes Préliminaires aux Religions Orientales dans l'Empire Romaine

HUCA   Hebrew Union College Annual

IDB   Interpreters' Dictionary of the Bible

IEJ   Israel Exploration Journal

JAAR   Journal of the American Academy of Religion

JBL   Journal of Biblical Literature

JES   Journal of Economics and Society

JFSR   Journal of Feminist Studies in Religion

JJS   Journal of Jewish Studies

JQR   Jewish Quarterly Review

JRAS   Journal of the Royal Asiatic Society

228   In a Chariot Drawn by Lions

JTS   Journal of Theological Studies
MRRN   Matriarchy Research and Reclaim Network
NT   Novum Testamentum
OR (NS)   Orientalia (New Series)
SJT   Scottish Journal of Theology
ZAW   Zeitschrift fur alttestamentliche Wissenschaften

Abelson, Joshua, *The Immanence of God in Rabbinical Literature*, Macmillan, London, 1912.

Ackroyd, Peter R., 'Goddesses, women and Jezebel', in A. Cameron, and A. Kuhrt (eds) *Images of Woman in Antiquity*, Croom Helm, London, 1983.

Albright, William F., 'Goddess of life and wisdom', *Hebraica* No. 36, 1920, pp. 258–394.
   From the Stone Age to Christianity, John Hopkins, Baltimore, 1940 (reprinted 1957).
   'Some Canaanite–Phoenician sources of Hebrew wisdom' *Vetus Testamentum Supplement* No. 3, 1955, pp. 1–15.
   Yahweh and the Gods of Canaan, Doubleday, Garden City, New York, 1968.

Anderson, Bernhard W. (ed.), *Creation in the Old Testament*, Fortress Press, Philadelphia, SPCK, London, 1984.

Amadiume Ifi, *Afrikan Matriarchal Foundations: the Igbo case*, Karnak House, London, 1987.

Apuleius, Lucius, translated by Robert Graves, *The Golden Ass*, Penguin, Harmondsworth, 1950.

Armstrong, Karen, *The Gospel According to Woman*, Elm Tree Books, London, 1986.

Arthur, Rose H. *The Wisdom Goddess: feminine motifs in eight Nag Hammadi documents*, University Press of America, Lanham, Maryland, 1984.

Ashe, Geoffrey, *The Virgin*, Routledge & Kegan Paul, London, 1976.

Athanassakis, Apostolos, *The Orphic Hymns: text, translations, and notes*, Scholars Press, Atlanta GA., 1977.

Atkinson, Clarissa W., Buchanan, Constance H., and Miles, Margaret R., *Immaculate and Powerful: the female in sacred image and social reality*, Beacon Press, Boston, 1985.

Aubert, Jean-Marie, *La Femme: anti-féminisme et Christianité* Cerf/ Desclee, Paris, 1975.

Bach, Alice (ed.) 'Ad Feminam' *Union Seminary Quarterly Review*, New York, 1989.

Bakan, David, *And They Took Themselves Wives*, Harper & Row, New York, 1979.

Barnstone, Willis, *The Other Bible*, Harper & Row, San Francisco, 1984.

Barrett, Charles K., *The New Testament Background: selected documents*, SPCK, London, 1956.

Beck, Pirhiya, 'The drawings from Horvat Teiman (Kuntillet Ajrud)', Tel Aviv 9, 1982, pp. 3–68.

Begg, Ean, *The Cult of the Black Virgin*, Arkana, London, 1985.

Beltz, Walter, *God and the Gods: Myths of the Bible*, Penguin, Harmondsworth, 1983.

Berger, Pamela, *The Goddess Obscured: transformation of the grain protectress from goddess to saint*, Beacon Press, Boston, 1985.

Bernal, Martin, *Black Athena: The Afro-Asiatic roots of classical civilisation, Vols 1 and 2*, Free Association Books, London, 1987 and 1991.

Betz, Hans Dieter (ed.) *The Greek magical Papyri in Translation, including the Demotic Spells*, Chicago University Press, Chicago, 1986.

Biale, Rachel, *Women and Jewish Law*, Schocken, New York, 1984.

Bleeker, C.J., 'I, Isis', in *Scottish Journal of Theology*, Vol. 38, No. 4, 1983.

de Boer, Peter, A.H., 'Wisdom in Israel and the Ancient Near East', in: *Vetus Testamentum Supplement* No. 3, 1955.

Bonanno, Anthony (ed.) *Archaeology and Fertility Cult in the Ancient Mediterranean*, B. R. Gruner Publishing, Amsterdam (for University of Malta), 1986.

Bonnard, Pierre E., 'De la Sagesse personnifiée dans l'Ancien Testament a la Sagesse en personne dans le Nouveau' in Martin Gilbert (ed.) *La Sagesse de l'Ancien Testament*, editions J Daculot S.A., Leuven University Press, Gembloux, Belgium, 1979, pp. 117–49.

Borresen, Kari R., *Subordination and Equivalence: nature and the role of women according to Augustine and Thomas Aquinas*, Paris/Oslo, 1968.

Bostrom, Gustav, *Proverbiastudien; die Weisheit und das fremole Weib*, in Spring pp. 1–9, C.W.K. Gleenup, Lund, Sweden, 1935.

Boulding, Elise, *The Underside of History: a view of women through time*, Westview Press, Boulder, COL, 1976.

Boyce, Mary, *A History of Zoroastrianism* Vols. 1 and 2, Brill, Leiden/Köln, 1975; 1982.

Brenner, Athalya, *The Israelite Woman: social role and literary type in biblical narrative*, Almond, Sheffield, 1984.

Bridenthal, Renate and Koontz, Claudia (eds), *Becoming Visible: women in European history*, Houghton Mifflin, Boston, 1977.

Briffault, Robert, *The Mothers*, Vols 1, 2 and 3, Allen & Unwin, London, 1927, (abridged edition 1959).

Bril, J., *Lilith, ou, La Mère Obscure*, Payor, Paris, 1981.

Brooten, Bernadette J., *Women Leaders in the Ancient Synagogue*, Scholars Press, Chico, 1982.

Brown, Peter, *The Body and Society: men, women and sexual renunciation in early Christianity*, Faber & Faber, London and Boston, 1989.

Brown, Raymond E., *The Semitic Background of the Term 'Mystery' in the New Testament*, Fortress Press, Philadelphia, 1968.

Brown, R.E., *Mary in the New Testament*, Geoffrey Chapman, London, 1978.

Brown, Steven G., *The Serpent Charms of Ugarit*, Brandeis University, (PhD. thesis), 1974.

Buckley, Jorunn J., *Female Fault and Fulfilment in Gnosticism*, University of North Carolina Press, Chapel Hill and London, 1986.

Bulgakov, Sergei, N., *The Wisdom of God*, Williams and Norgate, London, 1937.

Bultmann, Rudolf C., *Gnosis*, A. and C. Black, London, 1952. *Primitive Christianity* translated by R.H. Fuller, Thames & Hudson, London, 1983.

Burman, Rikkie, 'The Jewish woman as breadwinner', Oral History Journal Vo. 10, No. 2, autumn 1982, pp. 27–37.

Burney, Charles F., *The Aramaic Origin of the Fourth Gospel*, Clarendon Press, Oxford, 1922.

Cady, Susan, Ronan, Marion, and Taussig, Hal, *Sophia: the future of feminist spirituality* Harper & Row, San Francisco, 1986.

Cameron, Avril and Kuhrt, Amelie (eds), *Images of Women in Antiquity*, Croom Helm, London, 1983.

Camp, Claudia V., *Wisdom and the Feminine in the Book of Proverbs*, Almond, Sheffield, 1985.

Campbell, Joseph, *The Mythic Image*, Princeton University Press, Princeton, NJ, 1974.

Campbell, Joseph (ed.), 'Spirit and Nature', papers from the *Eranos yearbooks*, Princeton University Press, (Bollingen Series XXX) Princeton, 1982.

Cassuto, Umberto, *The Goddess Anath*, Hebrew University press, Jerusalem, 1971.

Cerfaux, Lucien, 'Influence des Mystères sur le Judaisme Alexandrien avant Philon', *Museon* XXXVII, Paris, 1924, pp. 36–48.

Charles, Robert, H, (translator), *The Book of Enoch* (I Enoch), SPCK, London, 1917.

Charlesworth, James H. (ed.), *Odes of Solomon (Old Testament Pseudepigripha and Modern Research)*, Scholars Press, Missoula, 1977.

Christ, Carol P., *The Laughter of Aphrodite*, Harper & Row, San Francisco, 1987.

Christ, Carol P. and Plaskow, Judith (eds), *Womanspirit Rising: a feminist reader on religion*, Harper & Row, San Francisco, 1979.

Clarke, Ernest G., *The Wisdom of Solomon (commentary)*, Cambridge University Press, Cambridge, 1973.

Clemen, Charles C., *Primitive Christianity and its Non-Jewish Sources*, T. and T. Clark, Edinburgh, 1912.

Cles-Reden, Sibylle, *The Realm of the Great Goddess*, Thames & Hudson, London, 1961.

Collingwood, Robin G, *The Idea of Nature*, Clarendon Press, Oxford, 1965.

Colonna, Maria Theresa, 'Lilith or the Black Moon', in *Journal of Analytical Psychology*, London, October, 1980.

Conybeare, Frederick C., *Myth, Magic and Morals*, Watts, London, 1909.

Conzelmann, Hans, 'The Mother of Wisdom, the future of our religious past' in J. M. Robinson, (ed.) 1971.

Cook, Stanley A., *The Religion of Ancient Palestine in the Light of Archaeology*, British Academy, London, 1930.

Cornford, Francis M, *From Religion to Philosophy*, Harvester Press, Sussex, reprinted 1980.

Cowley, Arthur E, *Aramaic Papyri of the Fifth Century BC*, Clarendon Press, Oxford, 1923.

Craig, James A, *Assyrian and Babylonian Religious Texts*, Vols 1 and 2, Leipzig, 1895.

Craigie, P.C., 'Deborah and Anat: a study of poetic imagery', *ZAW, No. 90*, 1978, pp. 374–81.

Crawford, Osbert G.S., *The Eye Goddess*, Phoenix House, London, 1957.

Crenshaw, James L., *Old Testament Wisdom: an introduction*, SCM Press, London, 1932.

Crenshaw, James L. (ed.), *Studies in Ancient Israelite Wisdom*, Ktav, New York, 1974.

Cross, Frank L. (ed.), *Studia Patristica*, Vol. IV, part II, Akademie-Verlag, Berlin, 1961.

Cross, Frank M and Talmon, S., *Canaanite Myth and Hebrew Epic*, Harvard University Press, 1973.

Cruden, Alexander P., *A complete Concordance to the Old and New Testaments*, Warne & Co, London and New York, 1737.

Cullman, Oscar, *Christ and Time*, SCM Press, London, 1951.

Cumont, Franz, *Oriental Religions in Roman Paganism*, Open Court Publishing Co, Chicago, 1911.
Astrology and Religion among the Greeks and Romans, Dover Publications, New York, 1960. First published 1912.

Daly, Mary, *Beyond God the Father*, Beacon Press, Boston, 1973.
Gyn/Ecology, The Women's Press, London, 1979.

Davies, William D. and Finkelstein, Louis (eds), *The Cambridge History of Judaism: Vol 1, the Persian Period*, Cambridge University Press, Cambridge, 1984.

Davis, Elizabeth Gould, *The First Sex*, Penguin Books, London, 1975.

Day, John, *Asherah in the Hebrew Bible and Northern Semitic Literature*, JBL, Vol. 105, No. 3, 1986, pp. 395–408.

d'Eaubonne, Françoise, *Le Féminisme: feminism and ecology*, A. Moreau, Paris, 1972.

Deane, William, J., *The Book of Wisdom: Translation and Commentary*, Oxford University Press, Oxford, 1881.

Delaney, Carol, 'Seeds of honour, fields of shame' in David Gilmore, 1987, pp. 35–48.

Delcor, Mathias, 'Les cultes etrangers en Israel au moment de la reforme de Josiah (2 Kings:23)', in *Festchrift M.H. Cazelles Melanges Bibliques et Orientaux*, Kevelter: Burzon und Bercker, Neukirchen-Vluyn, 1981.
'Le culte de la Reine du Ciel', in W. C. Delsman, *et al.* (eds), *Von*

Canaan bis Kerala, pp. 101–22, Kevelter: Burzon und Bercker, Neukirchen-Vluyn, 1982.

Denning-Bolle, Sara J, 'Wisdom and dialogue in the Ancient Near East', Numen (fasc. 2, December 1978), pp. 214–34.

Dever, William G., 'Asherah, Consort of Jahweh? New evidence from Kuntillet Ajrud', *BASOR* No. 255, 1984, pp. 21–37.

'Recent Archaeological confirmation of the cult of Asherah in Ancient Israel: *Hebrew Studies*, No. 23, 1982, pp. 37–43.

'Women's popular religion, suppressed in the Bible, now revealed by archaeology', *BAR*, March/April, 1991.

Dexter, Miriam R., *Whence the Goddesses: a source book*, Pergamon Press, Oxford, 1990.

Driver, Godfrey R., *Aramaic Documents of the 5th Century BC*, Oxford University Press, Oxford, 1954.

Canaanite Myths and Legends, T. and T. Clark, Edinburgh, 1956–71.

Dunn, James D.G., *Unity and Diversity in the New Testament*, SCM Press, London, 1977.

Christology in the Making, SCM Press, London, 1980.

Durdin-Robertson, Lawrence, *The Goddesses of Chaldea, Syria, and Egypt*, Cesara Publications, Eire, 1975.

Juno Covella, Cesara Publications, Eire, 1982.

Dworkin, Andrea, *Woman-Hating*, Dutton, New York, 1974.

Easlea, Brian, *Science and Sexual Oppression: patriarchy's confrontation with women and nature*, Weidenfeld & Nicholson, London, 1981.

Eisler, Riane, *The Chalice and the Blade: our history, our future*, Harper & Row, San Francisco, 1987.

Eliade, Mircea, *Myth and Reality*, Harper & Row, New York, 1963.

The Quest, University of Chicago Press, Chicago, 1969.

(translated by W. R. Trask) *A History of Religious Ideas Vol. 1, From The Stone Age to the Eleusinian Mysteries*, University of Chicago Press, Chicago, 1978.

Emerton, J. A. 'New light on Israelite religion: the implications of the inscriptions from Kuntillet Ajrud', *ZAW* No. 94, 1982, pp. 2–20.

Engels, Friedrich, *The Origin of the Family, Private Property and the State*, Foreign Languages Publishing House, Moscow, 1961. (Reprint.)

Engelsman, Joan C., *The Feminine Dimension of the Divine*, Westminster Press, Philadelphia, 1979.

Epstein, Isidore, *The Babylonian Talmud*, Soncino Press, London, 1978.

Evans, Arthur J., *The Earlier Religion of Greece in the Light of Cretan Discoveries*, Macmillan, London, 1931.

Fantar, Mhamed, *Eschatologie Phenicienne Punique*, Institut national d'archaeologie et d'arts, Tunis, 1970.

Farrar, Frederick, 'Book of Wisdom of Solomon: commentary' in H. Wace, (ed.), *Apocrypha*, New York, 1888.

Farrington, Benjamin, *Science in Antiquity*, Home University Library, Oxford, 1936. (reprinted, Oxford University Press 1968).
Science and Politics in the Ancient World, Unwin (University Books), London, 1939.

Fawcett, Thomas, *Hebrew Myth and Christian Gospel*, SCM Press, London, 1973.

Fisher, Elizabeth, *Women's Creation: sexual evolution and the shaping of society*, Wildwood House, London, 1980.

Fiorenza, Elizabeth S., 'Wisdom mythology and the Christological hymns of the New Testament', in R.L. Wilken, University of Notre Dame Press, 1975.
In Memory of Her, Crossroad, New York, 1983.
Bread, Not Stone: the challenge of feminist biblical interpretation, Beacon Press, Boston, 1984.

Fiorenza, Francis S., 'The influence of feminist theory on my theological work', *Journal of Feminist Studies in Religion* Vol. 7, No. 1, spring 1991, pp. 95–128.

Fitzmyer, Joseph A., *Essays on the Semitic Background of the New Testament*, G. Chapman, London, 1971.

Flusser, David, 'The Great Goddess of Samaria', *IEJ*, 1975, pp. 17–20.

Foerster, Werner, *Gnosis: A Selection of Gnostic Texts*, two vols, Clarendon Press, Oxford, 1972–4.

Fohrer, Georg, *Introduction to the Old Testament*, SPCK, London, 1968.

Fontaine, Carol R., 'A heifer from thy stable: on goddesses and the status of women in the Ancient Near East', in A Bach, 1989, pp. 67–91.

Frankfort, Henri and Frankfort H. A., *et al*, *The Intellectual Adventure of Ancient Man*, University of Chicago Press, Chicago, 1946.

Frazer, James G., *The Golden Bough: a study in magic and religion*, Macmillan, London, 1896, definitive edition 1907–1975 (12 Vols).

Freedman, David N., *et al* (eds), *New Directions in Biblical Archaeology* Doubleday, New York, 1969.

French, Marilyn., *Beyond Power: women, men and morals*, Jonathan Cape, London, 1985.

Freudenthal, Jakob, 'Refutation of Margolioueth on Hebrew Language for the Book of Wisdom of Solomon', JQR Vol. III, 1891, p. 722 ff.

Friedmann, Richard E., *Who Wrote the Bible*? Jonathan Cape, London, 1988.

Fuller, Reginald H., *Foundation of New Testament Christology*, Lutterworth, London, 1965.

Gadon, Elinor W., *The Once and Future Goddess*, Harper & Row, San Francisco, 1989.

Gage, Matilda J., *Woman, Church and State*, Persephone Press, Watertown MA, 1980.

Gammie, John G., et al. (eds), 'Israelite Wisdom: essays in honour of S. Terrien', in *Wisdom Colloquium*, Scholars Press, New York, (for Union Theological Seminary), 1978.

Garstang, John and Strong, H.A., *The Syrian Goddess* (translation, with introduction and notes, of Lucian, *De Dea Syria*), Constable, London, 1913.

Gasparro, Giulia Sfameni, 'I culti Orientali in Sicilia', in *EPRO* No. 31, Leiden, 1973.

'Gnostica et Hermetica', *Saggi Sullo Gnosticismoe soll'Ermetico*, Edizione dell Ateneo, Rome, 1982.

Soteriology and Mystic Aspects in the Cult of Cybele and Attis, Brill, Leiden, 1985.

Gaster, Theodore, H., *The Holy and the Profane*, W. Sloane Associates, New York, 1955.

Thespis: ritual, myth and drama in the Ancient Near East, Doubleday, New York, 1961.

Myth, Legend and Custom in the Old Testament, Vols. 1 and 2, Harper & Row, New York, 1975.

Georgi, Dieter, Frau Weisheit oder das Recht aus Freiheit als schoepferische Kraft in Siegele-Wenschkewitz, L. (ed.), 1988.

Gese, Hartmut, Wisdom Literature in the Persian Period in W.D. Davies and Z. Finkelstein, 1984, pp. 189–218.

Gilbert, Martin (ed.), *La Sagesse de l'Ancien Testament*, editions J. Daculot SA, Leuven University Press, Gembloux, Belgium, 1979.

Gilmore, David D (ed.), *Honour and Shame and the Unity of the Mediterranean*, American Anthropological Association, Special Publication No. 22, Washington DC, 1987.

Gimbutas, Marija, *Goddess and Gods of Old Europe*, Thames & Hudson, London, 1982.

The Language of the Goddess, Harper & Row, San Francisco, 1989.

Gimbutas, Marija and Marler, Joan (eds), *The Civilisation of the Goddess: The World of Old Europe*, Harper & Row, San Francisco, 1991.

Goddess Shrew, Matriarchy Study Group, London, 1976.

Goldenberg, Naomi, *Changing of the Gods*, Beacon Press, Boston, 1979.

Goldstein, David, *Jewish Folklore and Legend*, Paul Hamlyn, London, 1980.

Goodenough, Erwin R., *By Light, Light: the mystic gosepl of Hellenistic Judaism*, Yale University Press, New Haven, 1935.

Jewish Symbols in the Graeco-Roman Period, 12 vols, Bollingen Foundation, New York, 1953–65.

Goodison, Lucy, *Moving Heaven and Earth: sexuality, spirituality and social change*, The Women's Press, London, 1990.

Goodrick, Arthur T.S., *The Book of Wisdom: commentary*, Rivingtons, London, 1913.

Gordon, Cyrus H., *Before the Bible: the common background of Greek and Hebrew civilisation*, Collins, London, 1962.

Graves, Robert, *The White Goddess*, Faber & Faber, London, 1948.

The Greek Myths, Penguin Books, London, 1955.

Graves, Robert and Patai, Raphael, *Hebrew Myths: the Book of Genesis*, Greenwich House, New York, 1983.

Gray, John, *The Legacy of Canaan*, Brill, Leiden, 1957.

Archaeology and the Old Testament World, Nelson, London, 1962.

The Canaanites, Thames & Hudson, London, 1964.

Gray, William, 'Wisdom Christology in the New Testament: its Scope and relevance', *Theology*, Vol. LXXXIX, November, 1986, pp. 448–59.

Greenfield, Jonas C., 'The Seven Pillars of Wisdom: a mistranslation' *Jewish Quarterly Review*, Vol. LXXVI, 1985, pp. 13–20.

Gregg, John A.F., *The Wisdom of Solomon*, Cambridge University Press, Cambridge, 1909.

Griffin, Susan, *Woman and Nature*, Harper & Row, New York, 1978.

Griffiths, John G. (ed.), *Plutarch's de Iside et Osiride: introduction, translation, and commentary*, University of Wales Press, Cardiff, 1970.

Gross, Rita M., (ed.), *Beyond Androcentrism: new essays on women and religion*, Scholars Press, Missoula, 1977.

Gurney, Oliver R., *The Hittites*, Penguin Books, Hammondsworth, 1952.

Some Aspects of Hittite Religion, Oxford University Press, London, 1976.

Guthrie, William K.C., *Orpheus and the Greek Religion*, Methuen, London, 1937.

The Greeks and their Gods, Beacon Press, Boston Mass., 1951.

A History of Greek Philosophy, Vols. 1 and 2, Cambridge University Press, Cambridge, 1962.

Hadley, Judith M., 'The Khirbet el Qom inscription', *Vetus Testamentum*, Vol. *XXXVII, No. 1, 1987, pp. 50–62.*

'Two Pithoi from Kuntillet Ajrud', *Vetus Testamentum*, Vol. XXXVII, No. 2, 1987, pp. 208–11.

Hallo, William W. and Simpson, William K., *The Ancient Near East*, Harcourt Brace Jovanovitch, New York, 1971.

Hanson, Paul D., *The Dawn of Apocalyptic*, Fortress Press, Philadelphia, 1975.

Harden, Donald, *The Phoenicians*, Thames & Hudson, London, 1962.

Harding, Esther, *Women's Mysteries*, Rider & Co., London, 1971.

Harrison, Jane E., *Prolegomena to the Study of Greek Religion*, Cambridge University Press, Cambridge, 1908.

Ancient Art and Ritual, Oxford University press, Oxford, 1911.

Themis: a study of the social origins of Greek religion, Cambridge University Press, Cambridge, 1912.

Epilegomena to the Study of Greek Religion, Cambridge University Press, Cambridge, 1921.

Hayes, John H., *An Introduction to the Study of the Old Testament*, SCM Press, London, 1979.

Hays, Hoffmann R., *In the Beginning*, Putnam, New York, 1963.

Healey, Joseph G., 'The Kition Tariffs', *BASOR*, No. 216, 1974, pp. 53–60.

Heidel, Alexander, *The Babylonian Genesis: the story of the Creation*, University of Chicago Press, Chicago, 1942.

Hengel, Martin. *Judaism and Hellenism*, Vols 1 and 2, SCM Press, London, 1974.

Henry, Sandra and Taitz, Emily, *Written out of History: our Jewish foremothers*, Biblio Press, New York, 1983.

Hermisson, Hans-Jurgen, *Observations on the Creation Theology in Wisdom*, in Gammie John G., *et al.*, 1978, pp. 43–57.

Heschel, Susannah, *On Being a Jewish Feminist*, Schocken, New York, 1983.

Hestrin, Ruth, 'Understanding Asherah: exploring Semitic iconography', *BAR*, Vol. XVII, No. 5, 1991, pp. 50–9.

Heyob, Sharon, *The Cult of Isis among Women in the Graeco-Roman World*, Brill, Leiden, 1975.

Hill, David, *Greek Words and Hebrew Meanings*, Cambridge University Press, Cambridge, 1967.

Hooke, Samuel H., *Babylonian and Assyrian Religion*, Hutchinson University Library, London, 1953.

Middle Eastern Mythology, Penguin, Harmondsworth, 1963.

Hooke, Samuel H. (ed.), *Myth, Ritual and Kingship*, Clarendon Press, Oxford, 1953.

Hooykaas, Reyer, *Religion and the Rise of Modern Science*, Scottish Academic Press, Edinburgh, 1973.

Humbert, Paul, *Recherche sur les Sources Egyptiennes de la Literature Sapientale d'Israel*, Memoires de l'université de Neuchatel, Vol. 7, 1929.

Hvidberg-Hansen, F. O., *La Deesse T.N.T.: une etude sur la religion Canaaneo-Punique*, 2 Vols., G.E.C. Gad's Forlag, Copenhagen, 1979.

Uni-Ashtarte and Tanit-Juno Caelestis: two Phoenician goddesses, reconsidered in Bonanno, 1986, pp. 170–95.

Hyatt, James (ed.), *The Bible in Modern Scholarship*, Carey Kingsgate Press, London, 1966.

Irwin, William A., 'Where shall wisdom be found?', *JBL* No. 80, 1961, pp. 133–42.

Jacobsen, Thorkild, 'Mesopotamia', in Henri Frankfort and Hennetta A. Frankfort, *et al*, 1946, pp. 125–219.

   The Treasures of Darkness: a history of Mesopotamian religion, Yale University Press, New Haven, 1976.

   The Harps that Once . . ., Yale University Press, New Haven, 1987.

Jaeger, H., *The Patristic Conception of Wisdom in the Light of Biblical and Rabbinical Research*, in F.L. Cross, 1961.

James, Edwin O., *Myth and Ritual in the Anceint Near East*, Thames and Hudson, London, 1958.

   The Cult of the Mother Goddess, Thames and Hudson, London, 1959.

Janssens, Yvonne, 'Trimorphic Protennoia and the Gospel of John I – Sayings', in *SJT* Vol. 38, No. 4, Edinburgh, 1983.

Jastrow, Morris, *Aspects of Religious Beliefs and Practice in Babylonia and Assyria*, Putnam, New York, 1911.

Jayne, Walter A., *The Healing Gods of Ancient Civilisation*, Yale University Press, New Haven, 1925.

(Pope) John Paul II, 'Redemptorio Mater: the Blessed Virgin Mary in the life of the pilgrim church', *The Tablet*, 28 March, 1987, London, pp. 355–9.

Johnson, Aubrey R., *Sacral Kingship in Ancient Israel*, University of Wales, Cardiff, 1967.

Johnson, Buffie, *Lady of the Beasts*, Harper & Row, San Francisco, 1988.

Jonas, Hans, *The Gnostic Religion*, Beacon Press, Boston, 1958.

Jones, C.H., *The Earth Goddess*, London, 1938.

Jonge, Marinus de, and Safrai, Shmuel (eds), *Studies in the Jewish Background of the New Testament*, Van Gorcum, Assen, 1969.

Jung, Carl G., *Synchronicity*, Routledge & Kegan Paul, London, 1955. (first published Zurich 1952.)

Kabbani, Rani, *Letter to Christendom*, Virago, London, 1989.

Kapelrud, Arvid, S., *The Ras Shamra Discoveries and the Old Testament*, Blackwell, Oxford, 1965.

Kasemann, Ernst, *New Testament Questions of Today*, Fortress Howe, Philadelphia, 1969.

Kee, Howard, 'Myth and miracle: Isis, Wisdom and the Logos of John', in A.M. Olson (ed.), 1980, pp. 145–64.

Keller, Mara, 'The Eleusinian Mysteries of Demeter and Persephone', *Journal of Feminist Studies in Religion*, Vol. 4, No. 1, Spring 1988, pp. 27–54.

Kelly, J., *Early Christian Doctrines*, London, A & C Black, 1958.

Kenyon, Kathleen M., *Amorites and Canaanites*, Oxford University Press, Oxford, 1966.

   The Bible and Recent Archaeology, Collonade, London, 1978.

Kerenyi, Karl, *Goddess of Sun and Moon*, Spring Publications, Dallas, 1979.

King, L. W., *Babylonian Religion*, K. Paul, Trench, Trubner & Co., London, 1899.

King, Ursula, *Women and Spirituality: voices of protest and promise*, Macmillan, London, 1989.

Kirk, Geoffrey S., and Raven, John E., *The Presocratic Philosophers*, Cambridge University Press, Cambridge, 1957.

Knox, Wilfrid L., 'The Divine Wisdom', *JTS*, No. 38, 1937, pp. 230–7.

   Some Hellenistic Elements in Primitive Christianity, Humphrey Milford, London, 1944.

Koester, Helmut, *History, Culture and the Religion of the Hellenistic Age*, Fortress Press, Philadelphia, 1982.

Koltuv, Barbara B., *The Book of Lilith*, Nicholas-Hays, York Beach, Maine, 1986.

Kraeling, Emil G.H., (ed.), *The Brooklyn Musuem Aramaic Papyri*, Yale University Press, New Haven, 1953.

Kraemer, Ross S. (ed.)., *Maenads, Martyrs, Matrons, Monastics: a sourcebook on women's religions in the Graeco-Roman world*, Fortress Press, Philadelphia, 1988.

Kramer, Samuel N., *History Begins at Sumer*, Thames & Hudson, London, 1958.

Kramer, Samuel N. (ed.), *Mythologies of the Ancient World*, Doubleday, New York, 1961.

Kummel, Werner, G., *Introduction to the New Testament*, SCM Press, London, 1977.

Laffey, Alice B., *Wives, Harlots and Concubines: the Old Testament in feminist perspective*, SPCK, London, 1990.

Lambert, Wilfrid, G., *Babylonian Wisdom Literature*, Clarendon press, Oxford, 1960.

Lambert, W. G., 'A new look at the Babylonian background of Genesis', *JTS*, Vol. XVI, 1965, pp. 287–300.

Lambert, W. G. and Parker, Simon B., *Enuma Elish*, Oxford University Press, Oxford, 1966.

Landes, George M., 'Creation Tradition in Prov.8:22–31 and Genesis 1', in Howard N. Bream, Ralph D. Helm, and Carey Moore, (eds), *Festschrift Jacob M. Myers, A Light Unto My Path*, Temple University Press, Philadelphia, pp. 279–93.

Lang, Bernhard, *Wisdom and the Book of Proverbs – an Israelite Goddess Redefined*, Pilgrim Press, New York, 1986.

Larcher, C., *Etudes sur le Livre de la Sagesse*, J. Gibalde et cie, Paris, 1979.

Le Livre de la Sagesse, ou la Sagesse de Solomon, J. Gibalde et cie, Paris, 1982.

Lemaire, Andre, 'Who or what was Jahweh's Asherah?' *BAR*, No. 10, 1984, pp. 42–51.

Leon, Harry, J., *The Jews of Ancient Rome*, Jewish Publication Society of America, Philadelphia, 1960.

Lerner, Gerda, *The Creation of Patriarchy*, Oxford University Press, Oxford, 1986.

Levy, Gertrude R., *The Gate of Horn*, Faber & Faber, London, 1946.

Lewis, Alan E., *The Motherhood of God*, St. Andrews Press, St. Andrews, 1987.

Lindars, Barnabas, *The Gospel of John*, Oliphants, London, 1972.

Lipinski, Edward, 'The Goddess Atirat in Ancient Arabia, in Babylonia and in Ugarit', *Orientalia Lovaniensia Periodica*, No. 3, 1972, pp. 101–19.

Loades, Ann, *Searching for Lost Coins: explorations in Christianity and feminism*, SPCK, London, 1987.

Lods, Adolphe, Israel from its Beginning to the Middle of the 8th Century (translation by Samuel H. Hooke), Routledge & Kegan Paul, London, 1932.

Logan, A. H. B. and Wedderburn, A. J. M. (eds), *The New Testament and Gnosis: festschrift for R. McL. Wilson*, (T. and T. Clark, Edinburgh, 1983.

Long, Asphodel P., 'Feminism and spirituality', *Women's Studies International Forum*, Vol. 5, No. 1, 1982. pp. 103–8.

'Healing goddesses', *Panakeia* No. 1, 1983, pp. 14–19.

'Canaanite goddesses', *Arachne*, No. 5, 1986, pp. 1–5.

'Goddesses of wisdom', *Arachne*, No. 6, 1987, pp. 4–8.

'Orphic Hymns', *Arachne*, No. 9, 1989, pp. 15–18.

'The Goddess in Judaism: a historical perspective, in Pirani, 1991.

'Anti-Judaism in Britain', *Journal of Feminist Studies in Religion*, Vol. 7, No. 2, 1991, pp. 125–133.

'Old Testament: covenant against the goddess' *Goddess Shrew*, 1976, pp. 8–9.

'Red is for life', in *Menstrual Taboos*, Matriarchy Study Group, London, 1978a, pp. 1–10.

'The politics of sexuality', in *Politics of Matriarchy*, Matriarchy Study Group, London, 1978(b), pp. 21–28.

Longenecker, Richard N., *The Christology of Early Jewish Christianity*, SCM Press, London, 1970.

Lubac, Henri de, *The Eternal Feminine: a study on the text of Teilhard de Chardin*, translated by Réné Hagne, Collins, London, 1971.

Luckenbill, Daniel D., *Ancient Records of Assyria and Babylonia*, Vols. 1 and 2, Chicago University Press, Chicago, 1926 and 1927.

Maccoby, Hyam, *Revolution in Judaea: Jesus and Jewish resistance*, Orbach and Chambers, London, 1973.

The Sacred Executioner: human sacrifice and the legacy of guilt, Thames & Hudson, London, 1982.

Mack, Burton L., 'Wisdom myth and mythology', *Interpretation*, No. XXIV, 1970, pp. 46–60.

Logos und Sophia, Vandenhoeck and Ruprecht, Gottingen, 1973.

MacLaurin, E. C. B., 'The Canaanite background of the doctrine of the Virgin Mary', *Religious Traditions* (University of Sydney) Vol. 3, No. 2, 1980, pp. 1–11.

MacMillan, Glen E., 'Wisdom, Logos, Christology and Gnostic Speculation', Ph.D. thesis, St. Andrews University, St. Andrews, 1969.

Macrae, George W., 'The Jewish background of the Gnostic Sophia myth', *NT*, No. 12, 1970, pp. 86–101.

Maier, Walter A. III, *Asherah: extrabiblical evidence*, Scholars Press, Atlanta, 1986.

Marcus, R., On biblical hypostases of wisdom', *HUCA*, No. 23, 1950/51, pp. 157–71.

Margolioueth, David S., 'Was the Book of Wisdom of Solomon written in Hebrew?', *JRAS*, 1890, pp. 263–97.

Marshack, Alexander, *The Roots of Civilization*, McGraw-Hill, New York, 1971.

Martin, Luther H., *Hellenistic Religions*, Oxford University Press, New York and Oxford, 1987.

Marzal, A., *Gleanings from the Wisdom of Mari*, Biblical Institute Press, Rome, 1976.

Matriarchy Research and Reclaim Network, *Arachne: a journal of matriarchal studies*, MRRN, London, 1983 to the present.

Matthews, Caitlin, *Sophia, Goddess of Wisdom: the divine feminine from black goddess to world soul*, Mandala, London, 1991.

McCabe, Joseph, 'How Christianity treated women', in S. D. Schmalhausen, and V. F. Calverton, 1931, pp. 49–68.

McCrickard, Janet, *Eclipse of the Sun: an investigation into sun and moon myths*, Gothic Image Publications, Glastonbury, 1990.

McKane, William, Proverbs: a new approach, SCM, London, 1970.

Mellaart, James, Earliest Civilisations of the Near East, Thames & Hudson, London, 1965.

Menard Jacques–E. (ed.) *Les textes de Nag Hammadi, Collogue du Centre d'Histoire des Religions*, Strasbourg, 23–25 October, 1974, Brill, Leiden, 1975.

Merchant, Carolyn, *The Death of nature: women, ecology and the scientific revolution*, Harper & Son, New York, 1982.

Meshel, Ze'ev, *Kuntillet Ajrud: an Israelite religious centre from the time of the Judean monarchy*, Museum catalogue 175, Israel Museum, Jerusalem, 1978.
'Did Jahweh have a consort?', *BAR* Vol. 5, No. 2, 1979, pp. 24–36.

Metzger, Bruce, M., *An Introduction to the Apocrypha*, Oxford University Press, London and New York, 1957.

Meyers, Carol, 'The roots of restriction', *BA*, September 1978, pp. 91–103.
'Procreation, Production and Protection: male/female balance in early Israel', *JAAR*, No. 51, 1983, pp. 569–93.
Discovering Eve: ancient Israelite women in context, Oxford University Press, Oxford, 1988.

Meyerowitz, Eva, *And Yet Women Once Reigned Supreme*, Pamphlet Press, Hassocks, Sussex, 1987.

Miegge, Giovanni, *The Virgin Mary*, Westminster Press, Philadelphia, 1955.

Miles, Rosalind, *The Women's History of the World*, Michael Joseph, London, 1988.

Milik, Jozef, 'Les Papyrus Araméens d'Hermoupolis et les cultes Syro-Pheniciens en Egypte Perse', *BIB*, No. 48, 1967, pp. 546–621.

Mollenkott, Virginia R., *The Divine Feminine: the biblical imagery of God as female*, Crossroad, New York, 1983.

Momigliano, Arnoldo, *Alien Wisdom: the limits of Hellenisation*, Cambridge University press, Cambridge, 1975.

Monaghan, Patricia, *Women in Myth and Legend*, Junction Books, London, 1981.

Montefiore, Hugh (ed.), *Man and Nature*, Collins, London, 1975.

Moore, George, F., 'Ashteroth Karnaim, Gen. XIV.5', *JBL*, Vol. XVI, 1897, pp. 155–65.

Morgan, Donn F., *Wisdom in the Old Testament Tradition*, Blackwell, Oxford, 1981.

Mulack, Christa, *Die Weiblichkeit Gottes*, Kreuz Verlag, Stuttgart, 1983.

Murphy, Roland E., 'Wisdom – Theses and Hypotheses', in Gammie *et al.*, 1978, pp. 35–41.

Murray, Margaret A., *The Witch-Cult in Western Europe*, Clarendon Press, Oxford, 1921.

The Genesis of Religion, Routledge & Kegan Paul, London, 1963.

Murray, Robert, *Symbols of Church and Kingdom*, Cambridge University Press, Cambridge, 1975.

Neugroschel, Joachim, *Great Works of Jewish Fantasy and the Occult*, Overlook Press, Woodstock NY, 1987.

Neusner, Jacob, *Christianity, Judaism and other Graeco-Roman Cults*, Brill, Leiden, 1975.

The Study of Ancient Judaism, two Vols. Ktav, New York, 1981.

Judaism in the Beginning of Christianity, SPCK, London, 1984.

Neusner, Jacob (ed.), *Religions in Antiquity, Supplement to Numen* 14, Brill, Leiden, 1968.

Nilsson, Martin P., *A History of Greek Religion*, Clarendon Press, Oxford, 1925.

Norwich, Julian of, *Showings* (translated and with an Introduction by Edmund Colledge and James Walsh), Paulist Press, New York.

Noth, Martin, *The History of Israel*, A & C Black, London, 1958.

Noth, M. and Thomas, D. W. (eds), 'Wisdom in Israel and the Ancient Near East', *Vetus Testamentum Supplement*, No. 3, 1955.

Ochs, Carol, *Behind the Sex of God*, Beacon Press, Boston, 1977.

Ochshorn, Judith, *The Female Experience and the Nature of the Divine*, Indiana University Press, Bloomington, IA, 1981.

O'Connor, M., 'Poetic inscriptions from Khirbet-el-Qom', *Vetus Testamentum*, Vol. XXXVII, No. 2, pp. 244f, 1987.

Oden, Robert A., 'The persistence of the Canaanite religion', *BA*, Vol. 39, 1976, pp. 31–36.

Studies in Lucian's 'De Dea Syria', Scholars Press, Missoula GA, 1976.

Oesterley, William, D. E., *The Books of the Apocrypha: their origin, teaching and content*, R. Scott, London, 1914.

The Book of Proverbs, Methuen, London, 1929.

Oesterley, William, D. E. and Robinson, Theodore, *Hebrew Religion: its origin and development*, SPCK, London, 1930.

O'Faolain, Julia and Martines, Lauro, *Not in God's Image: women in history from the Greeks to the Victorians*, Harper & Row, New York, 1973.

Olson, Alan M. (ed.), *Myth, Symbol and Reality*, University of Notre Dame Press, Notre Dame and London, 1980.

Olson, Carl, *The Book of the Goddess Past and Present*, Crossroad, New York, 1985.

Olyan, Saul M., *Asherah and the Cult of Jahweh in Israel*, Scholars Press, Atlanta, 1988.

Oppenheimer, Aharon, *The Am Ha'aretz: A study in the Sochial History of the Jewish People in the Hellenistic Roman Period*, Brill, Leiden, 1977.

Ortner, Sherry B., 'Is female to male as nature is to culture?' in M. Z. Rosaldo, and L. Lamphere, 1974, pp. 67–87.

Ortner, Sherry B. and Whitehead, Harriet (eds), *Sexual Meanings: the cultural construction of gender and sexuality*, Cambridge University Press, Cambridge, 1981.

Otto, Rudolf, *The Idea of the Holy*, Oxford University Press, 1923.

Otzen, Benedikt, 'Old Testament Wisdom and Dualistic Thinking in Late Judaism', *Vetus Testamentum Supplement*, No. 28, 1974, pp. 146–57.

Otzen, Benedict, Gottlieb, Hans and Jeppesen, Knud, *Myths in the Old Testament*, SCM Press, London, 1980.

Pagels, Elaine H., 'What became of God the Mother?', in *Signs*, Vol. 2, No. 2, Winter 1976.

The Gnostic Gospels, Random House, New York, 1979.

Adam, Even and the Serpent, Random House, New York, 1988.

Paget, Robert F., *In the Footsteps of Orpheus*, Hale, London, 1967.

Patai, Raphael, *The Hebrew Goddess*, third, enlarged edition, Wayne State University Press, Detroit, 1990.

Peckham, J. B., 'Notes on a fifth century inscription from Kition', in *OR (NS)*, No. 37, 1968.

Pedler, Kit, *The Quest for Gaia*, Souvenir Press, London, 1979.

Pembroke, Simon C., 'The last of the matriarchs', *JES History of the Orient*, No. 8, 1965, pp. 217–47.

Women in Charge: ancient Greek and tradition and matriarchy, J. Warburg and Courtauld Institute, London, 1967.

Perdue, Leo G., *Wisdom and Cult*, Scholars Press, Missoula GA, 1977.

Pfeiffer, Robert H., 'The dual origins of Hebrew monotheism', *JBL* Vol. XLVI, 1927, pp. 193–203.

History of New Testament Times, with an Introduction to the Apocrypha, Harper & Row, New York, 1949.

Phipps, William E., *Was Jesus Married?*, Harper & Row, New York, 1970.

Pirani, Alix (ed.), *The Absent Mother: Rediscovering the Goddess in Judaism and Christianity*, HarperCollins, London, 1991.

Plant, Judith (ed.), *Healing the Wounds: the promise of eco-feminism*, Merlin Press, London, 1989.

Plaskow, Judith, *Standing Again at Sinai*, Haper & Row, San Francisco, 1990.

Plaskow, Judith and Christ, Carol (eds), *Weaving the Visions: new patterns in feminist spirituality*, Harper & Row, San Francisco, 1989.

Plessis, Joseph, *Etude sur les Textes Concernant Ishtar-Astarté*, Paris, 1921.

Pomeroy, Sarah B., *Goddess, Whores, Wives and Slaves: women in classical antiquity*, Schocken Books, New York, 1975.

Porten, Bezalel, *Archives from Elephantine*, University of California Press, Berkeley and Los Angeles, 1968.

Porten, B. and Greenfield, J. C., 'The Aramaic papyri from Hermopolis', *ZAW*, No. 80, 1968, pp. 219–34.

Porter, Frank C., 'The pre-existence of the soul in the Book of Wisdom and in the Rabbinical writings', in *Festchrift William Rainey Harper*, University of Chicago Press, Chicago, 1908, pp. 208, ff.

Preston, James J. (ed.), *Mother Worship: theme and variations*, University of North Carolina Press, Chapel Hill, 1982.

Primavesi, Anne, *From Apocalypse to Genesis: ecology, feminism and Christianity*, Burns and Oates, Tunbridge Wells, 1991.

Pritchard, James B., 'Palestinian figurines, in relation to certain goddesses known through literature', *American Oriental Society*, New Haven, 1943.

'The Ancient Near East, Vols 1 and 2, Princeton University Press, 1958.

Przyluski, Jean, *The Great Mother Goddess in India and Iran*, London, 1934.

Quardt, G., *Orphei Hymni*, Weidemann, Dublin and Zurich, 1973.

Quere-Jaulmes, F., *La Femme: les grandes textes des pères de l'eglise*, Paris, 1968.

Quispel, Gilles, 'Gnosticism and the New Testament', in J. P. Hyatt, (ed.), 1966, pp. 252–93.

'Jewish Gnosis and Mandean Gnosticism', in Jacques Menard, 1975, pp. 82–94.

Quispel, Gilles and Scholem, Gershom, *Jewish and Gnostic Man*, Spring Publication, Dallas, 1972.

von Rad, Gerhard, *Wisdom in Israel*, SCM Press, London, 1972.

Raine, Kathleen and Harper, G. M. (eds), *Thomas Taylor the Platonist*, Routledge & Kegan Paul, London, 1969.

Ranke-Heinemann, Uta, *Eunuchs for Heaven: the Catholic church and sexuality*, Andre Deutsch, London, 1991.

Rankin, Oliver S., *The Origins of the Festival of Hanukah*, T. and T. Clark, Edinburgh, 1930.

Israel's Wisdom Literature, T. and T. Clark, Edinburgh, 1936.

Reed, Evelyn, *Women's Evolution*, Pathfinder Press, New York, 1975.

Sexism and Science, Pathfinder Press, New York, 1978.

Reed, W. L., *The Asherah in the Old Testament*, Texas Christian University, Fort Worth, 1949.

'Asherah', *IDB* Vol. 1, pp. 250–52.

Reese, James M., 'Plan and structure in the Book of Wisdom', *CBQ*, No. 27, 1965, pp. 391–99.

Hellenistic Influence: Book of Wisdom and its consequences, Biblical Institute Press, Rome, 1970.

The Book of Wisdom, Michael Glazier, Wilmington, USA, 1983.

Reider, Joseph, *The Book of Wisdom: commentary*, Harper & Row, New York, 1957.

Ringgren, Helmer, (translated by John Sturdy), *Religions of the Ancient Near East*, SPCK, London, 1973.

Word and Wisdom, Lund University Press, Lund, 1974.

Robbins, Russell H., *The Encyclopaedia of Witchcraft and Demonology*, Peter Nevill, London, 1964.

Robinson, James M., (ed.), *The Future of Our Religious Past*, SCM Press, London, 1971.

The Nag Hammadi Library in English, Brill, Leiden, 1977. (reprinted and revised, Harper and Row, San Francisco 1988.)

Robinson, James M. and Koester, H., *Trajectories in Early Christianity*, Philadelphia, 1971.

Rohrlich-Leavitt, Ruby, *Women in Egalitarian Societies*, in Bridenthal R. and Kroontz, C. (eds), 1977.

Rohrlich-Leavitt, Ruby and Baruch, Elaine H. (eds), *Women Cross-Culturally: change and challenge*, Aldine, Chicago, 1975.

van Roon, A., 'The Relation between Christ and the Wisdom of God according to Paul', *NT* No. XVI, fasc. 3, July 1974, pp. 207–39.

Rosaldo, Michelle and Lamphere, Louise (eds), *Women, Culture and Society*, Stanford University Press, Palo Alto, 1974.

Rose, Herbert, J., *Ancient Greek Religion*, Hutchinson, London, 1948.

Rosenberg, David (translator) and Bloom, Harold (interpreter) *The Book of J.*, Faber & Faber, London, 1991.

Roswitha (tr. St. John, Christopher) the Plays of Roswitha, Medieval Library, London, 1923.

Rowland, Christopher, *The Open Heaven: a study of apocalyptic in Judaism and early Christianity*, SPCK, London, 1982.

Christian Origins, SPCK, London, 1985.

Rudolph, Kurt, *Gnosis: the nature and history of an ancient religion*, T. and T. Clark, Edinburgh, 1984.

Ruether, Rosemary R., *Faith and Fratricide: the theological roots of anti-semitism*, Crossroad, New York, 1974.

Misogynism and Virginal Feminism in the Fathers of the Church, in Rosemary R. Ruether (ed.), 1974, pp. 150–83.

Sexism and God-Talk SCM Press, London, 1983.

Womanguides, Beacon Press, Boston, 1985.

Ruether, Rosemary R., (ed.), *Religion and Sexism*, Simon & Schuster, New York, 1974.

Ruether, Rosemary R., 'Toward an ecological-feminist theory of nature', in J. Plant, 1989.

Ruether, Rosemary R. and McLaughlin, Eleanor (eds), *Female Leadership in the Jewish and Christian Traditions*, Simon and Schuster, New York, 1979.

Russell, David, S., *Between the Testaments*, SCM Press, London, 1960.

The Jews from Alexander to Herod, Oxford University Press, Oxford, 1967.

Safari, Shmuel, Stern, M. *et al* (eds) *The Jewish People in the First Century*, two vols, Van Gorcum, Assen, 1974.

Salles-Dabadie, Jean-Marie, A., *Recherches sur Simon le Mage*, Gabalda et cie, Paris, 1969.

Sandars, Nancy K., translator, *The Epic of Gilgamesh*, London, 1960. *Poems of Heaven and Hell from Ancient Mesopotamia*, Penguin Books, London, 1971.

Sanday, Peggy R., *Female Power and Male Dominance*, Cambridge University press, Cambridge, 1981.

Sanders, Edward P., *Jesus and Judaism*, SCM Press, London, 1985.

Sanders, Edward P., (ed.), *Jewish and Christian Self-Definition: aspects of Judaism in the Graeco-Roman period, Vol. 2*, SCM Press, London, 1981.

Sandmel, Samuel, *Philo's Place in Judaism*, Oxford University Press, New York, 1971.

Judaism and Christian Beginnings, Oxford University Press, New York and Oxford, 1978.

Philo of Alexandria; an introduction, Oxford University Press, New York and Oxford, 1979.

Schenke, W., *Die Hochma (Sophia) in der Judischen Hypostasen Spekulation*, Kristiana, 1913.

Schmalhausen, Samuel D. and Calverton, V. F., *Women's Coming of Age*, Horace Liveright, New York, 1931.

Scholem, Gershom, *Major Trends in Jewish Mysticism*, Jerusalem, 1941.

Jewish Gnosticism, Merkabah Mysticism and Talmudic Tradition, The Jewish Theological Seminary of America, New York, 1960.

The Kabbalah and its Symbolism, Schocken, New York, 1969.

Kabbalah, Keter, Jerusalem, 1974.

Schurer, Emil (ed. Glatzer, Nahum), *A History of the Jewish People in the Time of Jesus*, Schocken, New York, 1961. (First published 1886–90.)

Scott, Hilda, *Does Socialism Liberate Women? Experiences from Eastern Europe*, Beacon Press, Boston, 1974.

Scott, Robert B. Y., 'Solomon and the Beginnings of Wisdom', in *Vetus Testamentum Supplement*, No. 3, 1960.

'Wisdom in Creation: the "Amon" of Prov. 8–30', *Vetus Testamentum*, No. 10, pp. 213–23.

Segal, J. B., 'The Jewish attitude towards women', *JJS*, autumn 1979, pp. 120–37.

Selzman, Charles, *Women in Antiquity*, Pan Books, London, 1956.

Shiva, Vandana, *Staying Alive: women, ecology and development*, Zed Books, London, 1988.

Showerman, Grant, 'The Great Mother', in *The University of Wisconsin (Madison) Bulletin*, No. 43, 1901.

Siegele-Wenschkewitz, Leonore (ed.), *Verdrangte Vergangenheit, die uns Bedrangt*, Frankfurt, 1988.

Sjöö, Monica and Mor, Barbara, *The Great Cosmic Mother: rediscovering the religion of the earth*, Harper & Row, San Francisco, 1987.

Skehan, Patrick W., 'The Literary Relationship between the Book of Wisdom of Solomon and the Proto-Canonical Books of the Old Testament', *Catholic University of Washington Journal of Theology* No. 54, 1938.

Skehan, P. W., 'Borrowings from the Psalms in the Book of Wisdom', *CBQ* No. X, 1948 pp. 394–97.

Smallwood, E. Mary, *The Jews under Roman Rule: from Pompey to Diocletian*, Brill, Leiden, 1976.

Smith, George, *The Chaldean Account of Genesis*, Low, Marston, Searle and Rivington, London, 1876.

Smith, Mark S., *The Early History of God: Jahweh and the other deities in ancient Israel*, Harper & Row, San Francisco, 1990.

Smith, Morton, *Palestinian Parties and Politics that Shaped the Old Testament*, University Press, Columbia University Press, New York and London, 1971.

Jesus the Magician, Gollancz, London, 1978.

Smith, W. Robertson, 'Sacrifice', in *Encyclopaedia Britannica*, Vol. XXI, 9th edition, 1886, pp. 132–40.

The Religion of the Semites, A. & C. Black, Edinburgh, 1889. (Reprinted, Schocken, New York, 1972.)

Speiser, Ephraim, A., 'The Hebrew Origin of the first part of the Book of Wisdom', in *JQR*, No. 14, 1924, pp. 455 ff.

Speiser, Ephraim, A., Finkelstein, J. J. and Greenberg, M (eds), *Collected Writings*, University of Pennsylvania Press, Philadelphia, 1967.

Simon, Maurice (ed), *The Zohar*, Soncino Press, London, 1984.

Spretnak, Charlene (ed.), *The Politics of Women's Spirituality*, Anchor/Doubleday, New York, 1982.

Starhawk, *The Spiral Dance*, Harper & Row, San Francisco, 1979.
Dreaming the Dark, Beacon Press, Boston, 1982.
Truth or Dare, Harper & Row, San Francisco, 1987.

Stone, Merlin, *The Paradise Papers*, Virago, London, 1976.
Ancient Mirrors of Womanhood, Vols 1 and 2, New Sibylline Books, New York, 1979.

Stone, Michael E., *Jewish Writings of the Second Temple Period*, Van Gorcum, Assen.

Suggs, M. J., *Wisdom Christology and Law in Matthew's Gospel*, Harvard University Press, Cambridge MA, 1970.

Swidler, Leonard, *Biblical Affirmations of Woman*, Westminster Press, Philadelphia, 1979.

Tanner, Nancy, 'Matrifocality in Indonesia and Africa and among Black Americans', in M. Rosaldo, and L. Lamphere, 1974 pp. 29–156.

Tarn, William, W., Griffith, Guy T. ed., *Hellenistic Civilisation*, E. Arnold & Co., London, 1927.

Taylor, Thomas, *The Hymns of Orpheus*, The Philosophical Research Society, Inc., Los Angeles, 1981. (Facsimile reprint of original English edition 1792.)

Tcherikover, Victor, *Hellenistic Civilisation and the Jews*, Atheneum, New York, 1970. (Reprint.)

Techert, Marguerite, 'La notion de la sagesse', *Archiv fur Geschichte Philosophie und Soziologie*, No XXXIX, Berlin, 1930, pp. 9ff.

Teubal, Savina J., *Sarah the Priestess*, Swallow Press, Chicago, 1984.
Hagar the Egyptian, Harper & Row, San Francisco, 1990.

Thomas, D. Winton (ed.), *Wisdom in Israel and the Ancient Near East*, Brill, Leiden, 1960.
Documents from old Testament Times, Harper & Row, New York, 1961.

Thompson, R. Campbell, *Semitic Magic: its origins and development*, Ktav, New York, 1971.

Thompson, William I., *The Time Falling Bodies Take to Light*, Rider Hutchinson, London, 1981.

Thomson, George, *The Prehistoric Aegean*, Lawrence & Wishart, London, 1979. (First published 1949.)

Thureau-Dangin, François, *Rituels Accadiens*, Paris, 1921.

Trachtenberg, Joshua, *Jewish Magic and Superstition*, Behrman's Jewish Book House, New York, 1939.

Trible, Phyllis, 'Wisdom builds a poem: the architecture of Proverbs 1: 20–33', *JBL*, No. 94, 1975, pp. 509–18.
God and the Rhetoric of Sexuality, Fortress Press, Philadelphia, 1978.

Vermaseren, Maarten J., *Cybele and Attis: The myth and the cult*, Thames & Hudson, London, 1977.

Vermes, Geza, *Jesus the Jew: A Historian's Reading of the Gospels*, Collins, London, 1973.

Jesus and the World of Judaism, SCM, London, 1986.

Wagner, Gwenther, *Pauline Baptism and the Pagan Mysteries* Oliver and Boyd, Edinburgh, 1967.

Walker, Barbara, *The Women's Encyclopaedia of Myths and Secrets*, Harper & Row, San Francisco, 1983.

Warner, Marina, *Alone of All Her Sex: the myth and cult of the Virgin Mary*, Weidenfeld & Nicholson, London, 1976.

Watts, Alan, *Myth and Ritual in Christiantiy*, Thames & Hudson, London, 1954.

Weigle, Marta, *Spiders and Spinsters: women and mythology*, University of New Mexico Press, Albuquerque, 1982.

West, Martin, L., *The Orphic Poems*, Clarendon Press, Oxford, 1984.

Westermann, Claus, *Creation*, SPCK, London, 1974.

White, Lynn Jnr., 'The historical roots of our ecological crisis', in *Science*, Vol. 155, No. 3767, 10 March 1967.

Whiting, Pat, 'Women in Ancient Egypt and fertility control', *Goddess Shrew*, (Matriarchy Study Group), 1976, pp. 6–7.

Whybray, Roger N., *Wisdom in Proverbs*, SCM Press, London, 1965.

Wilken, Robert L. (ed.), *Aspects of Wisdom in Judaism and Early Christianity*, University of Notre Dame Press, Notre Dame and London, 1975.

Wilson, Ian, *Jesus: The Evidence*, Weidenfeld & Nicholson, London, 1984.

Wilson, Robert, McLachlan, *The Gnostic Problem*, A. R. Mowbray & Co, London, 1958.

Gnosis and the New Testament, Oxford, 1968.

Wilson, Robert McLachlan (ed.) *Gnosis*, Vols 1 and 2, Clarendon Press, Oxford, 1972 and 1974.

Winston, David, *The Wisdom of Solomon: translation, introduction and commentary*, Doubleday, Garden City, NY, 1979.

Winston, David and Dillen, John, 'Two treatises on Philo of Alexandria', *Brown Judaic Studies*, No. 25, Scholars Press, Chico, CA, 1983.

Witt, Reginald, E., *Isis in the Graeco-Roman World*, Thames & Hudson, London, 1971.

Wolfson, Harry A., *Philo: foundation of religious philsophy in Judaism*, Harvard University Press, Cambridge Mass, 1947.

Wolkstein, Diane and Kramer, Samuel N., *Inanna, Queen of Heaven and Earth*, Harper & Row, New York, 1983.

Wood, James, D., *Wisdom Literature: an introduction*, Duckworth, London, 1967.

Yadin, Yiguel *et al.* 'Symbols and deities at Zingirli, Carthage and Hazor', in *J. Sanders, (ed.) Festschrift Nelson Glueck: Near Eastern Archaeology*, Doubleday, Garden City, NY, 1970.

Yamauchi, Edwin M. *Gnostic Ethics and Mandaean Origins*, Oxford University Press, 1970.

Zevit, Z., 'The Khirbet El-Qom inscription mentioning a goddess', *BASOR* No. 255, 1984, pp. 39–47.

Zimmerli, Walter, 'Concerning the structure of Old Testament Wisdom', in James L. Crenshaw, (ed.) 1981, pp. 175–207.

Zuntz, Gunther, 'Persephone: three essays on religion and magic', in *Magna Graecia*, Oxford University Press, Oxford, 1971.

Index

Ackroyd, Peter, 119, 216
Acts, Book of, 149
Adam, 22, 28, 88, 184, 185, 202, 203, 224
adamah, 184, 202, 224–5
Admat-Kodesh, 225
African cultures, Black goddesses in, 8
after life, and Great Mother, 75
agion (holy), 48, 49
Albright, William F, 103–4
Alexander the Great, 63, 66
Alexandria, 37–8, 43, 66, 74, 205
Alic, Margaret, 43–4, 205
Allegro, John, 133
almah, 171
Almosino, Moses, 33
Alone of All Her Sex (Warner), 169

alternative traditions, 17
amon, 24, 25, 30, 65
Anat, Lady, 14, 95, 112–13, 114, 116, 125, 126, 127, 136, 171, 213
Anat Bethel, temple of, 126, 127
Anat-Jaho, 126
Anat-Jaho, temple of, 125–6
Anatolia, 63, 65
Ancient Near East, 12, 18, 60, 63, 66, 88, 96, 101–18, 123, 126, 129, 136, 149, 182, 216
Ancient World, goddesses in, 12, 14, 81
androcentric religious concepts, 6, 13, 17
androcracy, 198, 226
androgyny, 94, 167, 213

Anglican church, and ordination of women, 156–7
Anselm, 167
anti-Judaism, 145
antiquity, and Nature, 24
anti-semitism, 222, 223
'Antisemitism in Britain' (Long), 162
apaugasma (eternal light), 53, 54
Aphrodite, 67
'Aphrodite' (Orphic Hymn), 209
Apocrypha, 8, 10, 32, 37, 53, 202
Apocryphon of John, 88, 97, 213
Apsu, 104, 105
Apuleius, Lucius, 72, 81, 83, 210, 211
Aquinas, St Thomas, 155, 158, 220
Aranyi, 188

Archbishops'
   Commission on
   Women and the
   Ministry (1936),
   156
aretalogy, Isis', 84
Aristotle, 70
Arius, 206
Ark of the
   Covenant, 209
Ark of the Lord,
   127
Artemis, 75
Arthur, Rose, 87,
   93, 94, 96
asceticism, 169
Asertu, 215
Asham Bethel,
   temple of, 126,
   127
Asherah, 112–16,
   122, 215, 216;
   attributes, 16; as
   Creatress of the
   Gods, 215; and
   relationship with
   El, 112, 114, 215;
   and Garden of
   Eden stories, 7;
   and God, 15; in
   Hebrew bible,
   14, 217; and
   Jahweh, 128–9,
   136, 218; as Lady
   of the Sea, 112,
   215; and lions,
   210; love of,
   135–6; and
   sexuality, 16,
   134; and Tree of
   Knowledge of
   good and evil,
   134; and Tree of

Life, 7, 130, 131,
   134; and trees,
   130–31, 134, 136,
   218 see also
   Athirat, Lady
Asherah, the, 130,
   131, 217, 218
Asherata, 129
Asherim, 131
Ashtart, 215
Ashteroth, 14, 122,
   130, 135–6, 216
Asia Minor, 18, 70
Assyria, 18
Astarte, 115, 122,
   214, 216
Astarte, temple to,
   127
Astarte-Ishtar,
   122–4
Atargatis, 115–16
Athanassakis,
   Apostolos, 201,
   207
Athart, 115
Athena, 49
Athirat, Lady, 113–
   16, 214, 215 see
   also Asherah
Aubert, Jean-
   Marie, 157
Augustine, St, 154,
   155, 158–9, 185,
   186, 225
Authorised Version
   (AV), 9, 24, 218

Baal-Hadad, 112–
   16, 131, 182, 215,
   226
Babylon, 63; exile
   of Jews to, 65

Babylonia/
   Babylonians:
   goddesses in, 18;
   as a home of
   healing,
   astronomy and
   mathematics,
   109; and magical
   beliefs/practices,
   74; Paradise
   Garden of, 103;
   Sabbatu of, 124
Babylonian
   Creation Epic,
   104
Bacon, Francis,
   183, 192
baetyl/baetylus,
   126, 127, 176, 217
Bain Marie, 205
Balnia Mariae, 205
baptism of blood,
   75–6
Barbelo, 88–90, 93,
   104
barley, 125
Barnstone, Willis,
   221
Baruch, 99, 202
Begg, Ean, 171
Ben Sirach
   (Ecclesiasticus),
   32, 33, 99, 103
Berosus, 106
Bethel, 126, 127,
   176
Bethel, temple of,
   126
betulah, 171
Betz, Hans Dieter,
   71–2
bible, Hebrew, 8;
   and Apocrypha, 10;

Asherah in, 14; and Book of Wisdom of Solomon, 37; and denial of female divinity, 173; and goddesses, 7, 11, 14, 16, 119, 174; translated into Greek, 24; and Nature, 185; and people of Jewish faith, 9; 'purity' laws, 174; and Revised Standard Version, 9; and sexual rituals, 137; and Shekinah, 150; Wisdom in, 14, 21, 142, 202

Bible, The: androcentric bias, 6, 17; and Apocrypha, 10; in forefront of gender politics, 13; and goddesses, 12, 194; Good News (GNB), 10; King James (Authorised Version), 9; Oxford Annotated, 10; Protestant, 37; Revised Standard Version (RSV), 9; Revised Standard

Version Common, 10; Revised Version (RV), 10; Roman Catholic, 37; and Sophia, 8

Binah, 179

birth, and sexuality, 16; virgin, 166, 168–71, 173

birth control, 86

bisexuality, and Gnostics, 90

Black Virgin, 171

body, as defilement, 208

Bonaventure, St, 155–6

Bonnard, Pierre, 142, 143

Book of Breathings, 85

Book of Wisdom of Solomon, the (BWS): authorship, 38–9; and Hellenistic world, 37–8, 39, 50, 55; Hochma in, 77; and Hochma-Sophia, 199; and rational enquiry, 34; timing of, 60–61; and Wisdom, 6, 19, 24, 36, 37–60, 65, 69, 86, 89, 184, 194, 202; and Wisdom-Hochma-Sophia, 179

Books of the Law

see Torah, the

Borsippa, 109

boseth, 216

Boulding, Elise, 221

bread of the Presence, 128

breast milk, 172–3

'breath of life', 53, 82, 180

Briffault, Robert, 217

Brooten, Bernadette, 17

brotherhood groups, 198

Brown, Peter, 208

bull sacrifice, 75–6

Bultmann, Rudolph, 220

Burman, Rikkie, 224

Burney, Charles F, 145, 146

BWS *see* Book of Wisdom of Solomon, the

caduceus, 109

cake-making ritual, 120, 121, 124–5, 127, 136, 138

Camp, Claudia, 9, 17, 201

Canaanites, The (Gray), 112

Canaanites, 112, 128, 136, 171

canon law, 158

Cardea, 26

Cassuto, Umberto, 213

celibacy, 158, 171

chaos, 96, 104, 105
'chariot drawn by lions', 6, 16, 62, 64, 65–6
chariots of fire, 65
child bearing, 41, 123, 174
childlessness, 41
Chinese footbinding, 163
Chipko women, 181, 188–9
Christ, Carol P, 17, 162, 223, 224
Christian Fathers, 87, 153, 155, 168
Christianity: and anti-material world viewpoint, 99, 137; and appearance of the Book of Wisdom of Solomon, 60–61; and Augustinian theology, 225; birth and growth of, 61, 87; accounts of divinity and directions, 194; domination of male Christians over women, Nature and non-Christians, 139–40; exploitation of Nature, 185; and goddesses, 12, 16; and Isis, 82; claims to be founded on love,

140; normative, 17; Protestant, and New Testament, 9; and punishment of females, 99; condones slavery, 140; takes root, 137; and Trinity, 53; and Wisdom, 7, 139–64; sees women as source of sin/death, 174; women's sexuality held in contempt, 137
Christology, 54
Church, the: view of women, 155–8; and Wisdom, 16
Church Fathers, 45–6, 99, 138, 140, 145, 158
Clarke, Ernest G, 49, 50, 51, 207, 208
Clement of Alexandria, 153–4, 166
Code Napoleon, 157
Cohen, Daniel, 26
'Coil of Tiamat, The', 106
Collyridians, 124, 138
Colossians, 25, 145
Commandment(s): and BWS, 41; first, 21, 134; and misogyny, 173–4;

and Nature, 185; obeying, 31, 36
contraception, 86
Conzelmann, Hans, 220
Corinthians, 148
Corn King, 196, 197, 225–6
Cornford, Francis M, 211
cosmic harmony, 78–9
cosmic law, 22, 28, 31, 78
cosmic order, 24, 27, 82, 182, 191
cosmic sympathy, 72
cosmos: Aphrodite unites, 67; and goddesses, 101; and Nature, 24; and righteousness, 34; understanding and controlling, 71; and Wisdom, 26, 55, 98
Cost of Conscience movement, 162
covenant: and the Torah, 32; and Wisdom, 29
cow and suckling calf, 129
creation: androgynous, 94; and Barbelo, 90; and divine order, 85; and goddesses, 7, 18, 101; and Great

Mother, 76, 79; Hebrew stories, 110; and Isis, 6; and knowledge, 15–16; and Ma'at, 6; as a male preserve, 15–16; and mist, 53; renewal of, 54; sacredness of, 191; and science, 15–16; and Sephiroth, 177; and Sophia, 89; source of Adam's, 184; and Tiamat, 104, 105; and the Torah, 32; and Wisdom, 6, 11, 12, 15, 21–2, 23, 26, 27, 28, 30, 32, 40–41, 42, 54, 65, 79, 142; and woman, 184

Crete, 18, 63

crime, 59

crucifixion, 148, 164

Crudens' Concordance to the Old and New Testaments and the Apocrypha, 218

culture, and man, 154, 155, 162

Cybele, 64, 75

Cyme, 84

Cyprus, 63, 127

Da'at, 30

Daly, Mary, 106

dancing, frenzied, 77

dark(ness): and evil, 54, 208; and Ishtar, 125; and light, 69

David, 127

Davies, E Gould, 221

day, and night, 69

dead: Isis as Protector of, 84; Ma'at judges souls of, 85, 111; Mot, association with, 112

Dead Sea Scrolls, 38

Deane, William J, 50, 51, 204, 207, 208

death: and Anat, 113, 114; and birth, 197; and the earth, 101; and pregnancy, 197; and sexuality, 16; and sin of Adam and Eve, 184

deep, the, and Tiamat, 104, 105 see also sea

Delcor, Mathias, 217

Delos, 82

Delphi, 82

Demeter, 49, 207

Descartes, Rene, 14

Dever, William, 128, 129, 217

Dialogues (Socrates), 203

Dicacarchios, 70

'Did Jahweh have a consort?' (Meshel), 128

Dionysus, 64

Divine King, 196, 197

double-faced material, 12–13

dragon, Tiamat as, 104, 105

Driver, Godfrey R, 214

Dubiago, Sharon, 190

Dugbo, 214

Dunn, James, 147–8

Durdin-Robertson, Lawrence, 106, 210, 211

Dworkin, Andrea, 160, 221

dyad, God as a, 94

earth: creation of, 28, 29; exploitation of resources, 182, 185–6, 218–19; and goddesses, 11, 18, 19, 101, 102, 123, 181; and Great Mother, 76; and Greek science, 70; and heaven, 11, 28, 45, 60, 65, 79, 84; and Isis, 84; and Jesus, 185; and mist, 52, 53; Mother, 184, 189; and reproduction, 19; and soul, 181; veneration of,

193; Wisdom's journey to heaven from, 33
Eastern Church, 153, 165
Ebers Papyrus, 73
Ecclesiastes, 202
Ecclesiasticus (Sirach), 53, 103, 202, 203
eco-feminism, 187–92
ecological–feminist theory of Nature (Ruether), 187
ecological needs, 7
Egypt: and Bethel, 127; deities in, 63; goddesses of, 6, 18; iconography, 209; story of Jewish women in, 120–22; and science, 70; temples of, 126; Wisdom in, 81–100, 149; women's premier places in professions, 212
Eisler, Riane, 198
El, 112, 114, 215
El-kunirsa, 215
Elat, 114
Elephantine, 122, 125, 126
Eleusinian mysteries, 76
Eleusis, 82
Englesman, Joan C, 211
Enki, 110

'Enmerkar and the Lord of Aratta', 107
Ennoia, 87, 89
Enoch, Book of, 33–6, 99, 175, 202, 203
Enuma Elish, 104, 105, 214
Ephesians, 147
Ephesus, 75
Epic of Creation, 110, 214
Epic of Gilgamesh, 103
Epicureans, 71, 74
Epicurus, 71
Epinoia, Sophia of the, 97
Epiphanius, 145
Essenes, 39
Eudes, St Jean, 169
eukineton (mobile), 50
eunuchs, 41
Euthyphro, 203
Eve, 28, 90, 99, 154, 166, 168, 170, 184
evil: and darkness, 54; origin of, 97, 98, 137; and women, 160, 161, 162, 164, 167, 172, 174
Exodus, 21, 50, 59, 128
Exodus, the, 58, 59
Ezekiel, Book of, 65–6

Faith and Fratricide (Ruether), 139
Fall, the, 28, 90, 97,

134, 155, 164, 169, 170, 185, 191
Farrington, Benjamin, 70, 71
Father, 179; and feminine aspects, 165; Jesus' access to, 152
Fatima, 172
female oppression and persecution of, 137 see also women
female divine/divinity: accounts pointing to, 13; and Christianity, 16; and countering bible's androcentric bias, 6; effect of loss on position of women in society, 7; Goodenough's perception of, 45; hymn of praise to, 48; and Judaism, 16, 64, 173–5; and old world in transit, 61; all recognition perishes, 159, 164, 182; and 'singly born' 49; within certain places and objects, 7
Female Principle, 64, 69, 191, 209

'Female Principle in the Universe', 45

Feminine, the, and Book of Proverbs, 9

feminine principle, 188, 189, 190; death of the, 188

feminist theological criticism, 13–14

fertility: and goddesses, 19; of the land, 82

Fiorenza, Elisabeth Schussler, 17, 202

First Australians, 161

First Commandment, 21, 134

First World War, 222

Fisher, Elisabeth, 221

Fohrer, Georg, 210

forest, 188–9, 219

Fourth Gospel see John

Francis, St, 155–6

Frazer, James, 216

frenzies, 76, 77, 78, 211

From Apocalypse to Genesis (Primavesi), 191

Gadon, Elinor, 171

Gage, Matilda Joselyn, 139, 157–8, 219

Garden of Eden stories: and Asherah, 7; compared with Wisdom's creation, 28; and Epic of Gilgamesh, 103; and Tree of Knowledge of good and evil, 130, 134

Gasparro, Giulia Sfameni, 76

Genesis, 22, 28, 40, 53, 54, 55, 58, 94, 95, 104, 105, 127, 146, 168, 178, 184, 202, 208

genocide, 161

Georgi, Dieter, 39, 204

Gese, Harmut, 22, 23, 203

Gimbutas, Marija, 202

Gnosis: the nature and history of an ancient religion (Rudolph), 90

Gnostic Gospels, 81, 87

Gnostic texts, 6, 94, 96

Gnosticism/Gnosis, 65, 87, 88, 94, 99, 149, 212; Valentinian, 94, 96, 99

God: and apaugasma, 53; breath of, 53; and consort, 7; and creation, 11, 21–2, 23, 26, 27, 28, 32, 35, 42, 90; as a dyad, 94; and evil, 161; as female or with female aspect, 180; gender of, 5; Hochma's relationship with, 15, 22, 24, 30; image of, 177, 179, 184; immanent and transcendent, 186; masculine, 173, 179, 222; the Mother, 23, 138, 172, 222; and Nature, 186; omnipotence, 51; patriarchal unity of, 31; and Shekinah, 7, 150, 176–9; and Sophia, 8, 38, 40; as source of help and salvation, 59; as source of knowledge, 42; and spirit, 39, 40, 55, 177, 199, 208 see also Wisdom

'Goddess of life and wisdom' (Albright), 103

Goddess Shrew (Matriarchy Study Group), 180, 212

Goddess spirituality, 14

goddess(es): ancient, 194;

Black, 8;
classical, 14; and
cosmos, 101; and
creation, 7, 18,
101, 102; and
earth, 11, 18, 19,
101, 102, 123,
214; Egyptian,
81; and fertility
principles, 19;
Grandmother,
115; Greek, 18,
63; healing, 7,
102; Hebrew, 7,
11, 14, 16, 63, 65,
119–38; Hellenic,
6, 12, 16, 60, 63,
64, 79, 150;
hostility
towards, 6, 12;
of indigenous
peoples, 14;
inventiveness,
102; Israelite,
218; and lions,
66, 210;
longevity, 19;
maintaining, 102;
moon, 101, 102;
Mother, 63, 112,
117, 129, 171,
215; mother
creator, 24; and
Nature, 6, 11,
19, 65, 77, 101,
102, 107;
renewing, 102;
stars, 123; sun,
102, 114, 213; as
sustainers, 101;
as teachers, 6,
11, 101, 102;
undefeated, 12;

veneration for, 6,
101; and Virgin
Mary, 171;
Wisdom as, 9,
11, 18, 26, 78, 79,
181 see also under
individual names
of goddesses
Goddesses, Women
and Jezebel
(Ackroyd), 119
Golden Ass, The
(Apuleius), 72,
81, 211
Golden Bough, The
(Frazer), 216
Good News Bible
(GNB), 10, 24
Goodenough, E R,
45, 64, 69, 205,
209, 210
Goodison, Lucy,
213
Goodrick, Arthur
T S, 52, 208
Gratian of
Bologna, 167
Graves, Robert,
210
Gray, John, 112
Great Mother, 18,
64, 65, 66, 75–8,
79, 151 see also
Mother of the
Gods
Great Mother of
Phrygia, 18, 75
Greece/Greeks,
223; fire, 50, 52;
and goddesses,
18, 63; notion of
night, 54

Greek language,
Hebrew bible
translated into,
24
Greek
philosophers, 6,
50, 63, 70, 74
Greek science, 70–
71, 79
Greek-English
Lexicon (Liddell
and Scott), 24,
65
green revolution,
189
'green' thinking,
187
'greening of the
Earth, the', 193
Greens, 195
Griffin, Susan, 182,
190, 224
groves of trees,
130–31, 185, 217,
218
Gudea, 214
guilt, 28, 180
Gula (Gula-Bau),
108–9, 117
Gurney, Oliver,
215
gynandry, 94

Hadad, 112
hais, 125
halloth, 127–8
Hammurabi, 108,
132
Hanna Hanna, 115,
117
Harding, Esther,
197
Harper, G M, 209

Hayes, John H, 204
healer/healing: and
  Great Mother,
  76; and
  Hellenistic
  goddesses, 79;
  and Isis, 82; Lady
  of, 109; and
  Ninhursag, 110;
  temples of, 108;
  Wisdom as, 12
Healing the Wounds
  (Plant), 187, 190,
  191, 225
heaven: creation
  of, 28, 29, 67;
  divine female as
  Lady of, 100; and
  earth, 11, 28, 45,
  60, 65, 79, 84;
  Enoch journeys
  to, 33–4; and
  goddesses, 11,
  18; Inanna as
  Lady of, 110; and
  Isis, 84; manna
  from, 49; and
  mist, 52; Queen
  of, 18, 120, 121,
  122, 124–8, 136,
  138, 172;
  Wisdom's
  journey to, 33,
  175
Hebrew goddesses
  see goddesses,
  Hebrew
Hebrew religion *see*
  Jews/Judaism
Hebrew wisdom,
  14, 19, 37, 63, 81
Hebrews, and
  cake-making
  ritual, 120–21,
  127

Hebrews, Epistle
  of the, 54, 148
Heliopolis, 86
Hellenism, 37
Hellenistic world:
  and BWS, 37–8,
  39, 50; Egypt
  and Asia Minor
  become part of,
  70; goddesses in,
  6, 12, 16, 60, 63,
  64, 150; Greece
  as centre of, 63;
  and Isis, 81–2;
  Jews in, 66;
  magic in, 71–5;
  and Nature, 6,
  16, 19, 70, 182;
  and numerology,
  43; and Queen of
  Heaven, 136; and
  Wisdom, 6, 12,
  16, 35, 37, 63, 64,
  149
hen, mother, 144
Henry, Sandra, 43–
  4, 205
Heraclitus, 74, 75,
  211
Heschel, Susannah,
  224
Hestrin, Ruth, 210
heterosexuality,
  174
hierarchy, 145
hieros games, 133
'historical roots of
  our ecological
  crisis, The'
  (White), 185
Hittites, 115, 182,
  215
Hochma, 41, 119;

attributes, 16, 69,
  137; becomes an
  attribute of
  Jahweh, 137;
  converted into
  the Torah, 137;
  and creation, 22;
  described in
  contradictory
  terms, 26;
  disappears, 148–
  9, 173; disguised,
  175; as female
  figure of
  Wisdom, 8, 11,
  21, 24; and Jesus,
  151–2, 166; as
  male, 179; and
  Nature Goddess
  of Orphic
  Hymns, 64–5;
  and Paul, 145;
  relationship with
  God, 15, 22, 24,
  30; and
  Shekinah, 150;
  and Sophia, 38,
  76, 88, 148, 199;
  and 'Thunder'
  text, 96; as
  transcendental
  cosmic order, 24;
  and Virgin
  Mary, 172
holism, search for,
  14
Holocaust: Jewish,
  161; Roman, 121
Holy Ones, 132
Holy Spirit: and
  BWS, 39, 40;
  female identity
  of, 165; and God,

39, 40, 55, 177;
and Virgin
Mary, 170; and
Wisdom, 39, 40,
49, 139
Homer, 103, 117
Homoiousios and
Homoousious, 206
Hooke, Samuel H,
109, 214
humans: behaviour
of, 79–80; and
Great Mother,
76; immanent
presence of
Wisdom within,
52, 54; instructed
by goddesses,
102; and Isis, 84;
masculine
gender of in
Wisdom
literature, 21;
Mother of, 18;
and
reproduction, 19;
spark in, 42; and
Wisdom of God,
142
Hypatia, 205
Hypostasis of the
Archons, 96

Ialdebaoth
(Yaltabaoth), 96,
97–8
idolatry, 59
image worship,
134–6, 137
immaculate womb,
problem of, 172
Immanent Divine,
54, 190

immortality: and
bull sacrifice,
75–6; and Isis, 6,
82, 84; and
Nature Goddess,
77; and Osiris, 82
Inanna, Lady of
Heaven, 110–11,
117, 123, 216
Incarnation, 148
India, 63, 188
Innin, 123
Iris, 73
Isaiah, Book of, 171
Ishtar, 122, 124,
125, 132, 172,
210, 216
Ishtar gate,
Babylon, 66
Isis, 19, 56, 73, 95,
209; aretalogy,
84; as Creatrix,
81, 83, 84;
forgotten, 100;
as Great
Physician, 82;
holy, 49; and
John, 151, 152; as
Mistress of
Magic, 82; as
Mother of
Medicine, 86; as
the Mud of the
Nile, 83, 100;
and Nature, 83;
nature of, 6, 83;
and resurrection
of Osiris, 82–3;
and Wisdom, 67,
81, 82, 84, 150;
worship of, 171
Isis and Neith,
temple of (Sais,
Egypt), 95, 204

Islam, 173, 194
Israel, biblical: Ben
Sirach associates
Wisdom with,
32; God's
biblical
relationship
with, 128; and
portrayal of
goddesses and
wicked queens,
119–20; kings of,
33; marriage of
Jahweh with,
136; and
masseboth, 217;
and Shekinah,
176, 177;
character of
Wisdom in, 20;
Wisdom's
instrumentality
in, 59
Israelites, 49–50,
58, 177

Jacob, 32, 127
Jacobsen, Thorkild,
105–6, 107, 214
Jahweh (Yahweh):
and Asherah,
128–30, 136, 218;
and his people,
59; and Hochma,
13*f*; Lady Anat
twinned with,
126–7, 136; and
Queen of
Heaven, 125,
128; and
Wisdom, 9, 25,
26, 27
Jayne, Walter A,
210

Jeremiah, 120, 122, 124, 127
Jeremiah, Book of, 120–22, 125
Jerome, 158, 159, 169, 222
Jerusalem, 34, 120, 125, 126, 127
Jesus Christ: and access to the Father, 152; and *apaugasma*, 53, 54; attributes, 151–2; crucifixion, 148, 164; denial of any sexuality to him, 159; and the earth, 185; and feminine aspects, 165, 167; as first-born of all creation, 145–6, 147; and Hochma, 151–2, 166; and Isis, 82; Jews deny as Messiah, 223; as Light of the World, 208; masculinity of, 162, 163, 167, 179; Motherhood of, 222; 'O Amen' title, 25; as only begotten, 49; resurrection, 148, 153, 164, 171; and salvation, 152, 162, 163–4; Sophia of, 96; and the vine, 103; and

Wisdom, 7, 16, 29, 49, 139–48, 142, 152, 153, 163, 166; and witch crazes, 160, 162; as the Word, 149, 221
Jesus-Sophia, 140, 144, 152
Jewish Background of the Gnostic Sophia Myth, The (Macrae), 87
Jewish Encyclopaedia, 15
Jews/Judaism: accounts of divinity and direction, 194; and Alexandria, 37–8, 66; alternative form of Judaism, 209; of BWS, 39; deicide charge, 223; and denial of divine female, 173–5; and denial of Jesus as Messiah, 223; exile to Babylon, 65; and Gnosticism, 88; and goddesses, 7, 11, 16, 137; Goodenough's perception of female divine in, 45; and Holocaust, 161; and Isis, 82; and monotheism, 21; and Nag

Hammadi Library, 94–5; normative, 17; Orthodox, 222; return from exile, 132; sects, 39; seen as subordinate and inferior by Christians, 139–40; and Shekinah, 7, 53, 139, 150, 176–9; 'traditional', 41, 137; wise men of, 15; and Wisdom, 31, 35, 175
Jezebel, 119
Job, 11
Job, Book of, 11, 22, 23, 27, 202
John, 29, 45, 49, 53, 54, 141, 149–52, 208, 221; Prologue to, 49, 148–51, 222
Johnson, Aubrey, 214
Josiah, King, 131
Judaism *see* Jews/Judaism
Julian of Norwich, Dame, 221–2
Jung, Carl G, 74, 210
Justice, 69, 85, 110, 117
Justin, 158

Kabbalah, the, 177, 178

Kabbalah and its Symbolism, The (Scholem), 178
Kabbalists, 43, 65, 106, 177, 178
Kadesh (Qodsha), 132
Kalypso (nymph), 103, 117
kamanu, 124, 125
kana, 220
kawanim, 124, 125, 127
Kee, Howard Clark, 82, 85
Keret, 116
Khirbet el Qom, 129
King, Ursula, 225
King, Ynestra, 190
King James bible (Authorised Version), 9
Kings, 40, 131, 143, 218
Kition (Citium), Cyprus, 127
knowledge: and creation, 15–16, 29–30; and Wisdom, 42–3
Knox, Wilfred, 220
Kodesh, 224
Koester, Helmut, 71, 220
Kono people, 214
Korsak, Mary Phil, 203
Kramer (inquisitor), 160
Kramer, Samuel N, 214, 216
Kubaba, 75

Kuntillet Ajrud, 128

Laws of Hammurabi, 109
legends, and pagan faiths, 13
Leonard, Dr Graham, 156–7, 162
lepton (subtle), 49–50
Leviticus, 128
Liddell, Henry George, 24, 65
light, 42, 53–4, 69
Light of the World, 208
Light Stream, 64, 69
Lilith, 209
lions, 6, 16, 62, 64, 65, 66, 78, 132, 210
Loades, Ann, 167, 221
Logos, ('Word') 149, 150, 151, 166, 179, 222
Lost Gods (Allegro), 133
Lourdes, 172
Lucius, 72, 81, 83
Luke, 141

Ma'at, 209; and divine order, 85, 117; forgotten, 100; judges souls of the dead, 85–6, 111; and measuring, 85, 110, 111; nature of, 6; soul's Negative Confession to, 198–9; and Wisdom, 86, 150
McCabe, Joseph, 158
McCrickard, Janet, 213, 214
MacLaurin, E C B, 171
Macrae, G W, 87, 88
magic/magicians: and Greek philosophers, 6; Hellenistic, 71–5; and understanding of Nature, 79
Maier, Walter A, II, 215
maldevelopment, 188
Malleus Maleficarum, 160, 161, 162, 220–1
man/men/male: and androcracy, 198, 226; creation as, 15–16; and culture, 154, 155, 162; dominance by, 163, 198; formed, 53; in image of God, 154; infertility, 41; and Jewish tradition, 174; male Christians vent hostility on women, 169,

175; relationships with women, 7, 12; and spirit, 154, 162, 164; and Wisdom, 11; and women's intellect, 43; and the world, 14
mania, 76
manna, 49–50
Marduk, 104, 105, 106
Mariolatry, 171
Mariology, 169
Mark, 141, 143
marquette, 158
marriage, sacred, 132–3
Marshack, Alexander, 213
Martin, Luther, 72, 210
Martines, Lauro, 220
Mary, Virgin, Queen of Heaven, 7, 167–73; bears a Son, 166, 168, 170; and Collyridians, 124, 138; as model for mothers with sons in wars, 170, 222; set apart from Nature and from human nature, 171; virgin birth, 166, 168, 169, 170; and Wisdom, 16
masseboth, 217

Matriarchy Study Group, 180, 212
Matthew, 141, 144
matter, 137
me, 110, 111
megaliths, 217
Memphis, 122, 126
menstrual periods, 101, 124, 174, 180, 197, 213
Merchant, Carolyn, 183
Mercury, 109
merkavah, 65
Meshel, Ze'ev, 128, 129, 217
Mesopotamia, 103, 109, 132–3
Messina Colloquium, 212
Metamorphoses (Apuleius), 72
meteorite (*baetyl*), 126, 127
Meyerowitz, Eva, 214
Meyers, Carol, 202
midrash, 15
Migdol, 122
Miriam of Alexandria, 205
mirrors, 132
misogyny, 7, 145, 147, 155, 156, 158, 168, 169, 173, 182, 190, 195
'mist', 52–3
Monaghan, Patricia, 213
monogones (unique), 49, 51, 89, 150, 207
monotheism, 17;

aligned on male concepts, 61; and Anat-Jaho, 126–7; and Asherah as cultic symbol, 218; and Gese, 22; and Judaism, 21, 99; and masculine deity, 16; patriarchal, 60; saving, 35; separates God and humanity, 45; of totality, 54; and Wisdom, 31, 175
Moon, and female divinities, 101
Moses, 21, 32, 177, 205, 224
Mot, 112, 113
Mother Church, 139
Mother Earth, 184
Mother-Father, 89, 93, 95, 182
Mother Nature, 184
Mother of the Abyss, 96
Mother of the Gods, 6, 16, 62, 65, 66, 211
Mother of the Universe, 93
Mothers for Peace, 222
Mummu, 104, 105
Murray, Margaret, 213
mysticism, 186
mythology: Hittite,

215; and pagan
faiths, 13

Nag Hammadi, 87,
90, 93, 99
Nag Hammadi
Library, 94
*Nag Hammadi
Library in English,
The* (Robinson),
88, 212
Native Americans,
14, 161
'natural' cult
(1980s), 218–19
Nature: and Anat,
171; as artificer,
68, 69;
attributes, 69;
Christian
demonisation of,
159; control of,
99, 105; and
creation, 24, 68,
69, 77, 79;
gradual death of
rich world of,
192; divine status
denied, 7, 99;
domination of,
100, 139, 182,
184, 187; and
Enoch, 33–4; and
Epicureans, 71;
as eternal life,
64; exploitation,
137, 164, 182,
185, 187; as
female, 182, 183,
191; and God,
186; and
goddesses, 6, 11,
19, 65, 77, 101,

102, 182; and
Great Mother,
75, 76; and
Greek
philosophers, 6,
74; and
Hellenistic
magic, 73; and
Hellenistic
world, 6, 16, 19,
70; 'inferior' to
spiritual
dimension, 181;
interpretations
of term, 182–3;
and Isis, 83; laws
of, 31, 182;
containing male
and female
within herself,
68–9; male
power's
destruction of,
192, 226; and
misogyny, 190;
as 'mother of
all', 75; Orphic
Hymn to, 67–8,
69; as Prakriti,
189; and
salvation, 164;
Sophia as female
principle in, 64;
and Soviet
ideologists, 192;
and study of the
Torah, 35; and
Virgin Mary,
171; and
Wisdom, 6, 12,
15, 34, 35, 36, 42,
60, 64, 67, 68, 69,
71, 78, 175, 181,

182; and women,
154–5, 164, 182
Near East, 12, 124
Nebuchadnezzar,
108
Neith, temple of
Isis and (Sais,
Egypt), 95
Nepthys, 73
New English Bible
(NEB), 24
New Testament, 8;
and goddesses,
14; as gospel of
salvation, 185;
identification of
Wisdom with
Jesus Christ, 140;
and Protestant
Christianity, 9;
and Revised
Standard
Version, 9; and
Wisdom, 7, 142
Newton, Isaac, 14
night: and day, 69,
208; and light,
54; and Nature,
69
Nike, 206
Nin-din-dung, 108
Ninevah, Goddess
of, 116
Ningizzida, 109
Ninhursag, 110
Ninti, 110
Nisaba-Nidaba,
106–8, 118, 130
noeron (intelligent),
48
Noph, 122
numerology, 43,
206

numinous, 135, 177

Odyssey (Homer), 103
O'Faolain, Julia, 220
Old Europe, 202
Old Testament *see* bible, Hebrew
Olson, A, 220
Omoroka, 106
orgiastic rituals/ behaviour, 77, 80
original sin, 185
Orphic Hymn to Aphrodite, 62
Orphic Hymn to 'Rhea', 211
Orphic Hymns, 16, 19, 49, 62–70, 150, 201
Ortner, Sherry B, 154–5
Osiris, 73, 74, 82
Oxford Annotated Bible, 10

pagan faiths, 13
Pagels, Elaine, 87, 94, 185
Pallas Athene, 207
papyri, magical, 72, 73; Ebers, 73; Paris, 73
Paradise Garden, 103, 110
parthenogenesis, 169
parthenos, 171
Patai, Raphael, 217
Pater Familias, 147
Pathros, 120, 122
patriarchy, 11, 14,

16–17, 31, 43, 170, 187, 197, 198
Paul, 153; and identification of Wisdom with Jesus Christ, 140; and Isis, 82; and Wisdom, 144–9, 163
Paul, Epistles of, 141
Pelagius, 225
Pentateuch, 41, 58
Persephone, 49, 150, 151, 152, 207
Persian empire, 63
Pharisees, 39
Philo, 38, 39, 43, 46, 74, 99, 162, 206, 210, 221
Phoenicians, 127
physicians, Gula as Queen of, 108–9, 117
Pibechis, 73
Pirani, Alix, 204, 214, 225
pithoi, 128
Plant, Judith, 187, 190, 225
Plaskow, Judith, 17, 162, 224
Plato, 74, 203
Plessis, Joseph, 216
Plotinus, 72, 210
Plutarch, 19, 83
poison, 195
polymeros (manifold), 49
Post-Pauline tradition, 145
power-from-within, 51, 191

power-over, 51, 191
Prakriti, 189
pregnancy, and risk of death, 197
primary sources, 72
Primavesi, Anne, 191–2, 203, 225
Pritchard, James B, 215
Proserpine, 207
prostitution, sacred, 49, 95, 131–4
Protennoia, 87, 89, 92–3, 94
Protestant Christianity: and Authorised Version, 218; and New Testament, 9; views foundation of Western society and law, 147
Proverbs, Book of, 9, 20–29, 31, 35, 41, 42, 65, 67, 68, 89, 103, 131, 145, 147, 152, 178, 202
Psalms, 22, 134, 135, 202
Pseudepigrapha, 33
Ptah, 85
punishment, 31, 34, 35, 36, 59, 99, 160, 169, 175
'purity' laws, 174

Q, 141
Qodeshem, 95, 132, 215

Qodsha (Kadesh), 132, 215
Qodsu, 215
Queen of Heaven, 7, 18, 102
queen of light, 18
Queen of Sheba, 143
queen of the Darkness, 18
Queen of the Home, 174
Queen of the sky, 16
Queen of the South, 141, 143
queen of the underworld, 18
Quispel, Gilles, 94–5
Qumran groups, 38

Ra, 73
rabbinic literature, 8, 32
Rad, Gerhard von, 203
rain, 112, 113, 116
Raine, Kathleen, 202, 209
Ranke-Heinemann, Uta, 208
Ras Shamra texts, 111–12, 114, 115, 116, 126, 130, 214, 226
redemption, 75
Reed, Evelyn, 221
Reese, James M, 48, 49, 204, 207
Reider, Joseph, 48, 49, 50, 204, 205, 207

renewal, and sexuality, 16
repentance, 34
reproduction, and goddesses, 19
reshith, 145–6
resurrection, 148, 153, 159, 171
Revelation, 25, 95
Revised Standard Version (RSV), 9, 10, 20, 24, 40, 141, 145
Revised Version (RV), 10, 24
reward, 31, 35, 36, 175
Rhodes, 63
ribs, 110
righteousness, 31, 34, 35, 39, 40, 59
Ringgren, Helmer, 215
Robbins, Russell, 221
Robinson, James M, 88, 213, 220
Rohrlich-Leavitt, Ruby, 106
Roman Catholics: and Apocrypha, 10; views foundation of Western society and law, 147
Roman conquests, 63
Roman empire, and Isis, 82
Roman holocaust, 121
Roman law, 147
Romans, 39, 75

ruach (spirit of God), 55, 177, 208
Rudolph, Kurt, 90, 94
Ruether, Rosemary Radford, 17, 139, 152, 155, 159, 187–8, 191, 219, 220, 225

Sabbath, 124, 137
Sabbath bread, 138
Sabbatu, 124
Sadducees, 39
Sage, 42, 46, 50, 54, 56, 57, 58, 60, 184
Sais, Egypt, 95, 204
salvation, 75, 76, 77, 79, 83, 96, 98, 148, 152, 153, 162, 163–4, 185, 194
Samuel, 127
Sandars, N K, 106, 214
Sanday, Peggy, 220
Sandmel, Samuel, 209, 210
saviour, Isis as, 6
Scholem, Gershom, 178, 224
science: and creation, 15–16; Greek, 70–71
scientific method, 74
Scott, Diana, 68
Scott, Hilda, 192
Scott, Robert B Y, 24, 25–6, 65, 203

sea: Asherah as
    Lady of the, 112,
    214; Atargatis as
    Mistress of, 115–
    16; and
    goddesses, 102;
    as source of life,
    106 *see also* deep,
    the
seasons, cycle of,
    102, 117
Second World
    War, 161
sefer Torah, 175–6
Seleucus, 70
self-hatred, 170
Sephiroth, 177–8,
    179
Septuagint, 10, 24
seven pillars of
    Wisdom, 25
sexual intercourse:
    and cycle of life,
    197; and Jewish
    tradition, 174;
    and pleasure for
    women, 168–9,
    170; and Torah,
    176
sexuality: and
    Asherah, 16, 134;
    in Christianity,
    137; and evil,
    167; and holy
    women, 49, 95,
    131–4; in
    Judaism 137; and
    lotus blossom,
    132; and *Malleus
    Maleficarum*, 160;
    and Nature, 137;
    sexual
    celebration, 123;

and Wisdom, 31,
    women's, 167,
    172, 174, 185
Shakan, 176
Shapash, 114
Shataqat, 116
Shekinah, 7, 53,
    139, 150, 176–9,
    186, 208, 209, 224
Shiva, Vandana,
    181, 188–9, 225
Showerman, Grant,
    82–3
Siduri Sabatu, 103–
    4, 117
Sima, 126
sin/sinners, 28, 31,
    35, 40, 59, 76, 77,
    134, 148, 154,
    155, 170, 174,
    180, 184, 185
Sirach, 34
sky, God makes
    firm the, 67
slave trade, 161
slavery, 140, 197
Smith, Mark, 218
Smith, W R, 217
snakes, 132
socialist principles,
    192
Socrates, 203
Socratic problems,
    23
Solomon, King,
    129, 131, 143, 217
Sophia: all
    powerful, 51;
    ambivalence in,
    7, 149; and
    bisexuality, 90;
    Christian
    worship of, 140,

144, 220; and
    creation, 89, 95;
    downfall of, 38,
    93, 96, 173; and
    Eastern Church,
    153; of the
    Epinoia, 97; as
    female principle
    in Nature, 64;
    and Gnosticism,
    87–8; as God
    Herself, 38, 40;
    as a harlot, 149;
    and Hebrew
    Wisdom, 81; and
    Hochma, 38, 76,
    88, 148, 199; and
    Ialdebaoth, 96,
    97–8; of Jesus,
    96; and John,
    151; laudation
    of, 56; and light
    stream, 45; and
    Logos, 179; loss
    of universality,
    152; as part of
    Jesus, 146–7;
    perceptions of,
    96–7; powers of,
    38; and
    'Thunder' text,
    96; and Wisdom,
    7, 8, 11, 86, 87,
    98
soul, and nature,
    181
South American
    Indians, 14, 161
Soviet Union, 192
Spiral Dance, the
    (Starhawk), 197
spirit: and God, 39,
    40, 55, 177, 199,

208; and man,
154; and
Wisdom, 40–43,
98, 152
Sprenger
(inquisitor), 160
Starhawk, 51, 190–
91, 197, 207–8
*Staying Alive:
women, ecology
and development*
(Shiva), 181,
188–9
Stoics, 48, 49, 74,
204
Stone, Merlin, 213
stones, 217
Storm God, 215
storms, 112
Suarez, Francisco,
168, 169–70
submission, 170,
173
Sumer, 106, 216,
223
Sumeria, goddesses
in, 18, 107
sun, as female, 102
Supreme Spirit, 88,
89
sustainer/
sustenance: and
Hellenic
goddesses, 79;
and humans, 77;
Isis as, 81; and
the *me*, 111; and
Nature Goddess,
77; Wisdom as,
6, 12, 30, 36, 98
suttee, 163
Syene, 126

synagogues, 175,
176
synchronicity, 210
Synoptic Gospels,
141, 142
synthetic fibres,
218–19
Syria, 112

Tablets of Destiny,
105, 106
Tahpanhes, 122
Taitz, Emily, 43–4,
205
Talmud, 32
Taurobolium, 75–6
Taylor, Thomas,
201, 207, 211
teacher(s):
goddesses as, 6,
11, 79; Wisdom
as, 6, 12; woman
as religious, 39
Tebunah, 30
technites (fashioner),
24, 56, 65, 150
Tehom, 105
Teilhard de
Chardin, Pierre,
186, 225
Tell Taanach, 129
Teubal, Savina, 17
Terra Mater, 189,
191
Tertullian, 154
theodily, 161
Theodotus, 94
Theotokos, 170
Therapeutae, 38–9,
60
Thomas, D
Winton, 214
Thrace, 63

Thunder, 93, 94, 95
'Thunder Perfect
Mind', 90–92, 96
Tiamat, 96, 104–6,
111
To Nature (Orphic
Hymn), 67–8
*To the Mother of the
Gods* (Orphic
Hymn), 62, 65,
209
Torah, the: and
creation, 32; and
'eternal now'
concept, 32–3;
Hochma
converted into,
137; mystical
appreciation of,
35; study of, 33;
and Wisdom, 16,
31–3, 36, 99, 162,
175, 176; as
Word of God, 33
Tree of Knowledge
of good and evil,
130, 134
Tree of Life: and
Asherah, 7, 130,
131; and
Kabbalists, 177;
and Shekinah,
179; and
Wisdom, 7, 26,
31, 103
trees: and Asherah,
130–31, 134, 136,
218; and Chipko
women, 188; and
groves, 218
Trinity: and
Anselm, 167;
Mother as

second person in, 222; nature of, 46; Wisdom as Third Person in, 139, 153; workings of, 53

Turkey, 63, 65

underworld: and goddesses, 18; and Inanna, 110–11, 216; and Ma'at, 111, 117; queen of, 18

universalism, left-wing, 222

universe: and Greek philosophers, 74–5; nature of, 34; Wisdom loses position as origin of, 36

Uriel, 34

Urjahu, 129

Uruk, 109

Valentinians, 94, 96, 99

Venus, 122, 123, 126

Vermaseren, Maarten J, 18, 19, 202

vine, 103

virgin birth, 166, 168–71, 173

Virgin Mary see Mary, Virgin

virginity, 155, 167–73

'Vision of Gudea', 107

Warner, Marina, 169, 220, 222

West Africa, 214

White, Lynn, Jnr, 185

Whiting, Pat, 86

'wild men' groups, 198

Wiltshire, 47

wings, 55, 208–9

Winston, David, 49, 50, 51, 206, 207

Wisdom: as active agent in ordering the world, 12; adjectives describing, 46–51, 69, 206; as alter ego of God, 6, 40, 60, 177; in Ancient Near East, 101–18; as architect, 24, 25, 26, 30, 36, 42, 46, 150, 163; as artificer, 24, 25, 65, 69; attitudes change towards, 6, 35; as attribute of God, 11, 20, 142; and Barbelo, 90; becomes absorbed into Jesus Christ, 49, 139, 140, 148; becomes possession of greedy men, 6; 'beside God', 6, 21, 23, 28, 36, 67;

as binding/uniting force, 25–6, 27; as breath of God, 53; and BWS, 6, 19, 24, 36–60, 65, 69, 86, 89, 98, 150, 152, 184, 190; and Christianity, 7, 139–64; conventional view of, 21; and creation, 6, 11, 12, 15, 21–2, 23, 26, 27, 28, 30, 32, 35, 36, 40–41, 42, 54, 55, 65, 69, 76, 78, 79, 98, 142, 163, 181, 204; disappears, 6, 12, 36, 59–60, 159; downfall of, 12, 98; drawing strength from, 199; in Egypt, 81–100; Enoch's account of, 33–6; in error, 98; as exemplar of women's full potential, 8; as friend, 195, 200; gives birth to herself, 24, 27; as God Herself, 36, 40; as God's companion, 6, 30, 136; as God's mentor, 11, 15, 31; as God's mother, 15; goddesses, 9, 11, 18, 26, 78, 79,

181; and Great Mother, 76; as guardian or trustee, 27; as healer, 12; Hebrew, 14, 19, 37, 63; and Hellenistic goddesses, 6, 12, 16, 63, 64; hidden, 11, 17, 60; identical with God, 204; identification with God, 42, 43, 45–6; immanence, 52, 54; independent of God, 26, 36; as intellect, 43; interrelation with God, 55; and Isis, 82; and Jahweh, 25, 26, 27; and Jesus, 7, 16, 29, 49, 139, 140–48, 152, 153, 163, 166; journeyings, 32, 33; and knowledge, 12, 42, 43, 46, 55, 56, 179; lamp of, 195, 199; and light, 42, 53–4, 69, 150, 151, 178; as little child, 11, 24, 25, 26; and Logos, 150–51, 221; as master workman, 24, 25, 26, 30, 56; as mediator/

intermediary (bridge between creator and created), 12, 22, 27, 28, 29, 36, 40, 42, 45, 60, 65, 79, 163, 181, 221; as mother of world and humanity, 15, 46, 60; and Nature, 6, 12, 15, 35, 36, 42, 60, 64, 67, 68, 69, 71, 78, 175, 182; and patriarchal tradition, 11, 16–17; plans for renewal, 12; praised, 35, 60; and radiance, 42–6, 69; relationship with Sage, 56–8; as repository of all knowledge, 12; seven pillars of, 25; sexual intercourse with, 31; and Shekinah, 53, 150, 177, 178, 179; and spark in humans, 42, 45; and spirit, 39–43, 98, 152; as a spiritual principle, 22; as sustainer, 6, 12, 30, 36, 98; as teacher, 6, 12, 28, 30, 42–3, 55, 56, 67, 98, 163, 181; and the

Torah, 16, 31–3, 36, 99, 162, 175, 176; as a transcendental force, 22, 23; and the Tree of Life, 7, 26, 31, 103, 131, 134; and Trinity, 139, 153; as an uncreated law, 26; understanding of, 195; universality of, 29–31, 36, 56; and Virgin Mary, 16, 172; and wise men of Judaism, 15; and the world, 27–8; and world order, 22, 23

Wisdom literature, 21

witch crazes, 7, 158, 159–62

Witch Museum, Jersey, 160–61

Witt, R E, 82

Wolkstein, Diane, 216

women: and advent of death into the world, 154; barren, 41; and the body principle, 155; and carnality, 154, 157, 158, 159; Christian demonisation of, 159; and Church Fathers, 138, 153;

defilement of, 53; divine status denied, 7; domination, 139–40, 158, 162, 198; and eco-system, 189–90; and evil, 160, 161, 162, 164, 167, 172, 174; exclusion from divinity, 14, 154; exploitation 164; and the Fall, 134, 155, 164; full potential and Wisdom, 8; and God as male, 179–8; and image of God, 154; inferiority for, 7; intellectual status, 43–4; in Jewish tradition, 164–5; male power's destruction, 191–2; and nature, 154–5, 159, 182; oppression of, 157, 182; ordination of, 156–7, 162; persecution of, 163; and pleasure in sexual activity, 168–9, 170; position in society and loss of female divinity, 7; relationship with the world, 7;

relationships with men, 7, 12; as religious teachers in early Jewish sects, 39; St Augustine on, 154, 155; self-hatred, 170; sexuality of, 167, 172, 174, 185; and Shekinah, 176, 177, 178; and sin, 154, 155, 158, 159, 174; and study of the Torah, 33; subordination, 139–40, 155, 167, 198; in Therapeutae, 38–9; virginal, 155; and wise women–midwife, 212; and witch craze, 7

Women, Church and State (Gage), 157
Women's Liberation Movement, 212
Women's Mysteries (Harding), 197
world, the: in circular motion, 69; Nature creates, 24, 68, 69; and Wisdom, 27–8, 182; women's realtionship with, 7
world order, 22, 23

Yaho *see* Jahweh
Yugoslavia, 222

Zevit, Z, 128, 129, 217